pressing on

MUSIC IN AMERICAN LIFE

A list of books in the series appears at the end of this book.

THE RONI STONEMAN STORY

pressing on

Roni Stoneman

AS TOLD TO *Ellen Wright*

UNIVERSITY OF ILLINOIS PRESS

URBANA AND CHICAGO

Library of Congress Cataloging-in-Publication Data

Stoneman, Roni.

Pressing on : the Roni Stoneman story /

Roni Stoneman ; as told to Ellen Wright.

p. cm. — (Music in American life)

Includes index.

ISBN-13: 978-0-252-03191-5 (cloth : alk. paper)

ISBN-10: 0-252-03191-1 (cloth : alk. paper)

ISBN-13: 978-0-252-07434-9 (pbk. : alk. paper)

ISBN-10: 0-252-07434-3 (pbk. : alk. paper)

1. Stoneman, Roni.

2. Banjoists—United States—Biography.

I. Wright, Ellen, 1942–

II. Title.

ML419.S797A3   2007

787.8'81642092—dc22 [B]   2006030906

This book is dedicated to

Eugene Allen Cox, Rebecca Cox Benton, Barbara Ellen Cox,

Robert Alan Cox, Georgia Hattie Hemrick,

Anne Faber, Jennifer Wright, Emily Wright, and John Wright

CONTENTS

Illustrations follow pages 64 and 150

ACKNOWLEDGMENTS

This book is Roni Stoneman's view of her life. It is an oral history, written from seventy-five hours of taped interviews. (For more on this process, see the afterword.) We have dispensed with the usual accompaniments to historical documents, footnotes and editorial comments, because the essence of this narrative is its psychological truth. This is the way one woman, who led a particularly intriguing life, experienced it. We have, however, made every effort to ensure that the text is historically accurate. If there are inaccuracies, we sincerely regret them. We have also made every effort, while still being true to the events that occurred, to avoid hurting people. If we have inadvertently erred in that regard, again we are sorry. While this narrative gains in intensity by limiting itself to one woman's experiences, it loses, of course, as far as a wider perspective is concerned. We hope that this account will stimulate other writers to fill in the blanks and present their viewpoints of the pivotal moments of country music and TV entertainment chronicled here. For a fuller ac-count of all the Stonemans, readers should consult Ivan M. Tribe's *The Stonemans: An Appalachian Family and the Music That Shaped Their Lives;* for a general history of bluegrass, Neil Rosenberg's *Bluegrass: A His-tory;* for the sociological background, John Wright's *Ralph Stanley and the World of Traditional Bluegrass Music;* for the role of women in bluegrass, Murphy Henry's forthcoming book on the subject (all available from the University of Illinois Press) and for more on *Hee Haw,* Marc Eliot and Sam Lovullo's *Life in the Kornfield* (Boulevard Books).

We owe great debts to many people. To the scholars who have helped us: Ivan Tribe, without whose meticulously researched book ours would have been several years longer in the making; Norm Cohen, Judy Mc-Culloh, Murphy Henry, and John Wright, who read the manuscript and made knowledgeable and helpful suggestions; and Leon Kagarise, who captured the Stonemans in the fifties, sixties, and seventies in a series of wonderful photographs. To other helpful readers who also made superb editorial comments, Jeanne Lockridge, Carole Smith, Emily Wright, Jennifer Wright, and our agent, Victoria Pryor. To the women who transcribed the tapes and often gave valuable advice: Beverly Zeldin-Palmer, Lea Pinsky, Katie Sharkey, and Amber Day. To those who helped with the photographs: Dick Bangham, Paul Lane, Joe Lee of Pete's Pluckins, Mike Seeger, and Cookie Snyder. To Roni's children, Eugene Allen Cox, Rebecca Cox Benton, Barbara Ellen Cox, Robert Alan Cox, and Georgia Hattie Hemrick, and her sisters and brother-in-law Donna Stoneman, Patsy Stoneman Murphy, and John Murphy, who provided photographs and made themselves available for extensive interviews. To others who helped us in numerous ways: Johnny Bellar, Noka Noble Blanco, Alexandra Bellow Calderone, Jimmy Case, Ginny and George Chestnut, George Edelin, Anne Faber, Gus Friedlander, Stuart Geisbert, Robert Gundlach, Henry Head, Sam Lovullo, Marcia Minor, Joanna and Mark Pinsky, Portia, Melrose Smith, Peggy Stanley, and Gerry Szymanski.

And special thanks to Virginia Leigh Bolden, for making Roni laugh. And to John Wright, for his extraordinary support at every stage of this project.

PREFACE

This is what usually happens: There I'll be, up on stage at some state fair or bluegrass festival or club in Nashville. I'll be having a great old time, picking my banjo and telling stories about life in the mountains, really feeling the love that comes from the audience, and loving them back. I finish and go to sit behind the record table. Or I wander over to a concession stand to get a funnel cake. And then comes the part I like just as much, maybe more, than performing. People walk up to me and we start to talking. I'll be asking them about themselves, where they're from, that kind of thing, trying to find out about their lives.

But they'll be wanting to talk about my life. They'll reminisce about the years (almost twenty of them!) when they watched me play Ida Lee Nagger, the "Ironing Board Lady," on *Hee Haw*. "You were just like us," they'll say. I look at them and grin. They don't have rags in their hair or a big gap in their teeth. They're not wearing a sloppy pink bathrobe. But I know what they mean. Ida Lee was a hillbilly icon, and there was something about her being so feisty and battling life that really connected with people. She made them proud of their hillbilly roots. "You had her just right," they'll continue. "How'd you know?" And then, after we discuss that for awhile, will come a question like: "Ummm . . . Minnie Pearl and Lulu and Archie—they weren't that funny in real life, were they?" Or maybe some young woman banjo player will walk up and say: "People keep calling you 'the First Lady of Banjo.' Were you really the first girl out there playing bluegrass banjo? How'd you learn? How'd all those men musicians treat you?" Or a fan of country music will ask,

"You performed with Johnny Cash and June Carter, didn't you? And Loretta Lynn? And Faron Young? That's so cool! Was Faron as crazy as I keep hearing?" Or somebody who's into the history of country music will wonder, "What was it like growing up in such a famous family? Is it true there were really thirteen of you kids all playing music?" There will be a pause and then in a lowered voice, "I can still remember the first time I heard Scott on that fiddle. Never was anybody like him! What a tragedy!"

So we'll be talking, and I'll be answering the questions, and then right in the middle I'll have to dash off to drive to the next show, or someone will interrupt us, and we never get to finish. It's really frustrating. But for me the worst is when people come up and don't talk. Or when some of them don't talk. There'll be a woman, and I can tell just by looking at her, by the way she looks at me, and doesn't look at me, that she's being beaten, that she's scared of talking on account of her husband standing next to her. And I'll want to tell her, I know how it is. I know because I was there. I've had a broken neck, I've been punched in the face and worn heavy makeup to cover the finger marks. I'll be wanting to get her aside, to talk it over with her, and to see if I can help her get out of it. I'll want to ponder with her about why so many of us mountain women get into those situations.

But it seems like there's never a way or enough time. So I thought I'd write this book. It'd be like having a nice conversation with you all, and I'd be able to answer those questions about what it was like to grow up a poor mountain girl (yes, there *were* all those children—in a one-room house without water or a real roof), what it was like to work on *Hee Haw* with all those great comedians (yes, they *were* that funny), how I knew how to play Ida Lee (I *was* Ida Lee), and what it was like to be a woman banjo player in a man's world (whewww!). And I'll be able to tell you about some of the heartache in my life, the things that most people don't know about—like that I was married five times, was beaten down physically and mentally. And that I was the sole support of my five kids, once did laundry by hand at one dollar a basket while performing music six hours a night six nights a week and caring for three babies, and at another time was turned down for jobs as a hotel maid (this was *after Hee Haw!*). But it won't be all Gloom, Despair, and

Agony On Me, like in that skit on *Hee Haw*. I also want to tell you some funny stories—about famous entertainers, about Nashville in its heyday in the sixties (again, whewww!!!), and about what it's like to be a country musician on the road (whewww!!!! whewww!!!).

Now, of course I'm hoping that these things also will be interesting to people that I haven't had a chance to talk with yet. In other words, I hope, friends and neighbors, that when we meet some time down the road, after a show or maybe on a street in Nashville, we can just sort of pick up where I left off. I can imagine some conversation where one of you brings up a story from the book, and I say, "Yep, it's true, it's true. It was just like I wrote. Faron really was that crazy—and that wonderful! Your uncle grew up with him? No kidding! And he also borrowed money from him? My God, tell me about it!" Or one of you says, "I've still got a bottle of those hair curlers too! Hard to throw them out, isn't it?" and we get off on a nostalgia trip, joking about them. Or another one of you says, "I also had a passel of kids and no education and a husband who wouldn't help." And we stand there getting to know each other, talking about how it was and what we did.

I'm really looking forward to it. So, as I've often said to myself, "Let's get to going!"

pressing on

ONE

Family

I think it would be nice to begin with the story of how Daddy and Mommy met. None of us kids knew about that until one day in the sixties when we were on the road—the Stoneman family band going from place to place, as we did, to play show after show. We were riding along, and, well, I was bored. I said, "Daddy, how'd you meet Momma?" I can remember it like it was yesterday.

"I heard her give her first cry, that's how."

"You did what?"

"I heard her give her first cry."

"How was that?" I said. "You all weren't related, were you?"

"No! Don't you ever say that! That's against the laws of God, no!"

"Then how did you hear her give her first cry?"

"Well, you know my Daddy, Elisha Stoneman, was a mountain preacher around the Galax area. And any time a woman that was with child . . ." (Daddy never used the word "pregnant." He would say "in a family way" or "a woman that was with child.") "Whenever a woman that was with child was having trouble giving birth, they would call the minister. They had the midwife but they always called the preacher and the doctor if the situation was desperate. Well, my father set forth 'cause Bill Frost's wife, Pattie Frost, was having a bad time. I was about eight or nine years old, and I got on the back of the horse with your Grandpa Elisha. It was a crisp fall night and I was cold, and we rode all the way across the mountain 'til we got to a cabin. The cabin had just two rooms, with the kitchen off from it. This was the usual way. The kitchen would be off from the other rooms because of the heat in the summertime, and in case of fire. So I walked up on the rock porch with Grandpa Elisha, and a man met him at the door that was real nervous. It was Bill Frost. Off to the right you could hear a couple of women in the room with Pattie Frost. Well, your Grandpa Elisha was taken into that room and I stayed in the sitting room. I sat down, cross-legged, Indian style, in front of the fireplace, and was warming myself, and rubbing my hands. I heard a lot of praying going on—hellfire and brimstone, really getting down into it. Then I heard a baby give a loud cry, and soon they brought it out wrapped in a blanket and gave it to me, and told me to pray with all the people in that sitting room for it to have a long life. So I held that baby and prayed. And the baby turned out to be the woman I would later marry, your mother!"

"Gosh!"

So that was how my parents met. It was in 1900.

Now to my grandparents. The one grandparent who was not there in that cabin was Daddy's mother, Rebecca. She had died, which is maybe why he was so cold that night, not having the proper clothing. Daddy said she was a very quiet, very strict southern lady. He remembered her being terribly sick and then dying of what they called childbed fever. Grandpa Elisha remarried, but he and this wife finally ended up in a parting of the ways, so Daddy never really had the warmth of a mother in his young life.

Grandpa Elisha was a serious man. He did not believe in fiddle playing or banjo picking. He thought the fiddle was of the devil because it made you want to dance and sing and "frolic." Grandpa Elisha didn't believe in "frolicking." I think he was not a very easy person to get along with. Starched—that's the word for people like that. They don't want this, and they don't want that. He thought everyone had to go along with the church or you would die and go to hell for it.

My mother's parents were totally different. Bill Frost, the other man in the cabin, my other grandpa, not only believed in frolicking, he was a ringleader, being one of the finest old Virginia fiddle players around. He told me he played for lots of the frolicking in the cabins in the Galax area. They'd roll back the rug and everybody would dance, and he and a couple of his buddies would pick and sing all night. He said the men were not allowed to drink in front of the ladies, but they would usually have hard cider or something stashed away in the springhouse. So there would be a lot of trips out to the springhouse before the evening was over. The whole idea was to pretend they were not partaking—though when their eyes got red and they got to reeling a little bit, well, it's hard to believe the ladies were as dumb as the men thought they were.

Grandpa Frost and his buddies would also play music in the churches. Most everybody thought that was okay, to play your fiddle or your banjo in the church meeting for the gospel hymns.

Grandpa Frost was not only a great musician, he was a great story-teller. And I adored him. When I was little and my parents and us kids had gone to live up in Maryland, Momma used to send me back to the mountains in Galax for three months in the summer. Grandma got in the habit of going to bed around dark, and then me and Grandpa would go out on the front porch, and Grandpa would tell stories. He specialized in scary ones.

One night he said, "See right over yonder, that little clearing? Well, once there was a cabin there, and a man lived in it with his wife and three little girls. But he got messing with some woman and he wanted to leave his wife. So he set the house afire, and he locked that door where they couldn't get out! He killed his wife and three little girls!"

I shivered.

"When I was a young man," Grandpa continued, "I'd go courting at night over the mountain. Now if I wanted to make a shortcut coming back, I'd have to pass through that clearing, but all the people said it was haunted, and that at night you could hear the screams and cries of that woman and those little girls.

"People refused to go near the place. And my momma kept saying, 'Bill Frost, you come up through that clearing again, them haints is gonna get you!' Well, I didn't pay much attention to her, your great-grand-mother. So, on one particular night I had just come over the hill with my horse down into that clearing. It was a full moon night, so bright you could see everything, and the nighttime mountain sounds—those hills were alive with sound.

"I looked over to the hearth of that old burnt-out cabin, and there was this white thing sitting there!

"Here I am on my horse, with this oil lamp shining on this spooky white thing! I rode closer. 'Who is it?' I said. Nobody answered. 'By God, who is it?' I cried. And I was about ready to shoot. But I got off of my horse and walked over and by the barrel of my gun lifted the sheet right up. And there was my momma's face! I almost shot my mother! She was trying to scare me! She waited for me, all that time, by herself down in that terrible place with all those wailing haints!"

That night when I went to bed I smothered myself with blankets.

Grandma Pattie Frost wasn't always telling stories. But when she said something . . . well, we knew it counted. One time Grandma said a really strange thing to me. I was about eight or nine years old. All of a sudden she looked at me real funny, right in the eyes, and she said, "A man who will have children and will not support and take care of his little ones, he's not a good person. He's not favored in the eyes of God."

It was as if she saw my whole future.

On to the younger generation, Daddy and Mommy. I think Daddy's childhood was pretty harsh, no mother and riding around the moun-tains with Elisha. But after Daddy married Hattie Frost, Momma, things started looking up. One day when he was walking by a store, he heard a record of a friend of his singing, Henry Whitter. Daddy thought he could do better. So Momma encouraged him and encouraged him, and he went up to New York and he convinced those record people to try him. And that led to him doing lots of recording sessions in New York, sometimes with Momma, and sometimes with other people. They mostly sang the old traditional mountain songs, but they occasionally sang current ones, such as the one about the *Titanic* (which it seems Daddy wrote part of, or at least arranged in the way that became famous): *Oh it was sad, it was sad / It was sad when that great ship went down / Husbands and wives, little children lost their lives / It was sad when that great ship went down.* That song was a big hit in 1925—people said it sold a million copies. In these recording sessions Daddy would play guitar, and there would be other traditional instruments—banjo, mandolin, fiddle, autoharp—and a lot of great harmony singing. The first "records" they made were really wax cylinders. Then after the wax cylinders came those old 78s. Daddy recorded with a number of different companies, including Edison's. I still have a few checks with Edison's name on them.

New York was of course a big challenge for a mountain preacher's son. Daddy would often tell about the time when they were almost arrested. He took his band into a big New York bank, and they were carrying their instruments with them. Then suddenly it sounded like there was a loud air raid and policemen ran in from all sides. They thought they were going to rob the bank because robbers used to keep machine guns in fiddle cases. My poor innocent Daddy was protesting, "No, no! They're just instruments! We're just hillbillies from the Blue Ridge Mountains!"

Maybe it was experiences like that that made Daddy decide it would be good if the record companies came down to Virginia! Anyway he was the one who arranged the famous Bristol Sessions. In 1927 he got Ralph Peer from the record company to come to Bristol to record the local musicians. They put ads in the paper announcing the auditions and mentioning all the money Ernest V. Stoneman was making by recording his songs. So lots of country musicians showed up, including the Carter Family and Jimmie Rodgers. Many people say the Bristol Sessions were where country music was born because those musicians went on to be superstars in the thirties and forties. And then in the sixties the Carter family songs were picked up again in the folk revival, songs like "Wildwood Flower" and "Keep on the Sunny Side." All that is true. But it's also true that Daddy and Momma recorded more songs at the Bristol Sessions than anybody else. At the recent celebration of the seventy-fifth anniversary of the Bristol Sessions, the town named a road Stoneman Family Drive.

Later we'd always tease Daddy when he'd play those old records, because all the songs were sad. I'd fall on the floor and pretend I was dying. And he'd say, "Dadblame it, if you don't get up and quit acting like that, I'm gonna knock you plumb across the room! You can laugh all you want to. I made more money than any of you'll ever make!" We would also tease him about his guitar-playing style, which was very simple. His strum was boom chick boom chick boom chick chick chick. Played with two finger picks and a thumb pick. The thumb is the leader. When he played the autoharp, it was basically the same thing—three picks and the motion came from the wrist.

Anyway, Daddy was right. He did make a lot of money, was one of the richest men in the area. Then the Depression hit, and people couldn't afford to buy records. Since he was a kind man, he had signed on to a lot of loans for his neighbors in Galax. So the family went from high cotton to sheer poorism. I call it poorism because anybody can be poverty-stricken, that's nothing. The kind of poor my family was was way beyond that. At one point in 1932 the sheriff got in the car with Daddy, about to repossess it, the one thing my parents had left, until Daddy outwitted him. Daddy said that he'd give it over as soon as he could stop, just behind the fence up ahead. But the fence, as he knew, was the county line, so the sheriff had no lawful right in the other county. Daddy got to keep the car and continue on his way.

Which was a good thing because my mother and older brothers and sisters (I hadn't been born yet) were also in the car. Daddy was moving the family up to the Washington area to live. There he was hoping he could get jobs with the government or with churches doing carpenter work. And he did. He was a very busy man, at times doing four jobs at once. But none of them paid much, and sometimes there was no work at all, so the family remained pooristic. He would also be trying to earn more by playing music in the evenings. There were a lot of other people from around Galax who had gone up to the Washington area to find work, and they of course liked his kind of music.

Daddy was very clever, and he came up with several musical inventions. One was a box that he put the autoharp on so it sounded much louder—the box worked like a resonator. Another was a special pick. The normal picks would just fly off with the kind of playing he was doing.

What he designed was a pick that went up the finger. I was part of that invention. I used to bring him things to see, like old toys I had found. And one time I said, "Look at this toy, Daddy. It's got a wire in it." He said, "Wait a minute, let me see that." He took his pinchers out and he studied the wire and looked at his finger. And then he made a pick with a spiral. I remember watching him, a little kid standing by his chair, proud that I was able to bring him something that he liked and needed. The pick's now in the Country Music Hall of Fame.

Anytime when he wasn't working or playing music, he was reading. He especially liked geography. He used to say you can't go wrong with geography books: "Land's gonna stay that way unless an earthquake comes." Turned out he was right. Later he won twenty thousand dollars on one of those quiz shows, *The Big Surprise,* answering questions on geography.

I've saved my mother for last, the newborn baby that cried so loud in the cabin. People never gave her enough credit. It was always my father getting all the glory. Which is great. I'm really proud of him. I've always felt I was a very rich woman, and I was a very rich little girl, because I had a father like him. But my mother, Hattie Ivana Frost, also deserves a lot of credit. She played banjo, the old-time mountain style, brilliantly. She could tune the banjo eight different ways. Grandpa Jones on *Hee Haw* brought that up to me, and I went home and asked Momma about it. "Yeah," she said, "he once told me he wished he could tune the banjo as many ways as I could." And she was the fiddle player on many of Daddy's records. The reason I get so upset about Momma not getting credit is because I do not understand it. This is how they wrote up the Bristol Sessions in the paper—"And a young matron played the fiddle with Ernest Stoneman"!

Aside from being a great musician, Momma was very beautiful and very sweet. When she was a young girl, she was engaged several times. But she wasn't just a gallivant. She was a true lady. She was very fashionable, took care of herself, had her face fixed all the time and her hat to match her purse, and her purse to match her shoes. Even when we got very poor, she took care to look the best she could.

And she was very strict about manners. For instance, ladies should never sit with their legs apart. You always have to put your knees together when you cross your legs—you have to touch your other ankle. Momma made sure I learned that well. One day I'd been playing horseshoes with the boys. And I came in and I went "Well, I beat them!" and I sat down so my ankle was crossing on top of my other knee, the way a man sits. Momma reached over and grabbed me: "Don't you ever do that again!" That night I got the worst whupping I ever had, cried for about twenty-five minutes.

Another lesson from Momma: "Don't ever stoop over. You gotta kneel. You bend with your knees and then pull yourself up. It's not ladylike to do it the other way." This turned out to be a very useful habit to get into since I would often be on the stage wearing my short dresses and have to pick up a banjo or a guitar lying on the ground. In fact all of Momma's etiquette advice turned out to be important. When I would be playing honky-tonks and horrible environments, acting like a lady made it safer.

What I'm saying is that Momma was a proud southern belle. She learned all this from her mom, Granny Frost, and from Aunt Phinney, Granny's sister. These were Virginia women, but they were not from the deep deep hills. Even though they went through hard times, they always tried. Grandpa worked in the mines and in the furniture factory, and sometimes he only made a dollar a day, but when Momma was about eight, he bought her a porcelain doll.

Before the Depression, as I said, Momma had a good life being married to Daddy. My older sister Grace remembered having pretty little silk dresses and nice shoes. In the thirties, when the Depression hit, you can imagine how it must have been for Momma—to go from high cotton into stark naked nothing.

According to family lore, Momma bore twenty-three babies. Some were born dead, but fifteen lived, and thirteen survived into adulthood. And our house in Maryland had only one room. We didn't have anything but beds and homemade chairs and children. But Momma kept on trying. I remember her painting the old floor. It was a worn-out linoleum, and she painted it with gray enamel—gray, because that was the only color she could get—and then she drew flowers on it, little daisies, trying to make it look like it was bought that way. The walls were made of boards and studs. Me and Momma rolled up papers and took a stick and shoved the paper in to keep the wind and the snow out. Then we tried to wallpaper that. Momma said, "We're gonna wallpaper this place so it looks better and the kids don't get splinters." Some people who had some old wallpaper laying around had given it to us. I mixed up the wallpaper paste with my hand, and we put the paper on those old rough boards (you'd have to go around the studs). I also helped her paint a porch, pink because somebody gave us pink paint. It looked like Pepto-Bismol.

And she made a garden. We had nothing but red clay around the house, so we would get dirt from the woods. She'd get wheelbarrows and buckets of that dirt, and she'd start planting. She had flowers in the yard, and two dogwood trees, and flowers in tin containers on the porch. When things would bloom, she was so proud of them. The flowers came from neighbors—she would go for a walk and the neighbors would give her little sprigs.

Tears come to my eyes thinking about all this, about how hard she worked, about her hands. She would say, "I can't even put my stockings on, my nails are so jagged." She had work hands from doing the scrubbing and taking care of us all. There was so much to do. She'd say she could put her foot on a cradle and push it and hold another kid on her hip and still make the gravy.

Momma had Grandpa Frost's sense of humor. My opinion, if you don't have a sense of humor, you are in deep trouble. You've got to take the hard times with a smile as well as a tear. Momma had that specialty—she would often take something sad and come up with something humorous. It's another thing she taught me.

She'd tell funny stories on herself. One story had to do with back in the early days when they were up in New York recording. (Those trips made a big impression on my parents!) As she told it, she was dressed in silk, and was wearing a long fur-trimmed coat and a beautiful hat: "And I said, 'Ernest, I just got to have a dip of snuff.' But there was no store anywhere around to get me a box of Tuberose snuff. So Ernest finally found out from a cab driver that you could get snuff in Hell's Kitchen. But the cab driver was scared and would only go a little ways into Hell's Kitchen. Then we had to get out and walk to the store where this Irishman was at." She paused. "Can you imagine, walking in Hell's

Kitchen?" And all of us kids, our eyes got real big, because you could just imagine Hell and it having a kitchen. She went on: "I was holding onto Ernest's arm so hard. And then a man came up behind us and hit me right in the middle of my back with a stick! It liked to have killed me, but I got my snuff."

The way she took snuff was like everything she did, elegant. She would be dressed up, prissy, and she would take a little bit of snuff and put it at her lip, and hold it so gently, and dab her handkerchief at her mouth.

Momma hated whining, and she had a particular hatred for whiney songs. I'd go up to her and say, "Momma, I got a great song, I got a great song." And she'd say, "Well, sing it, child, jes' so long as it's not mournful. Lord a mercy, I swear if I hear another mournful song, I do believe I'm going to faint!" "No, Momma, it's not mournful." And I'd start singing that song about a little girl who was out playing on a field when a snake bit her and she died: *I hear the screaming of a little girl far away / Daddy come kill this awful dreadful snake.* And Momma'd chase me, run after me through the house and all over the yard.

Momma was just real spirited. She would, say, be walking in her garden, and everything might be going well for her (and believe it or not, sometimes things did) and she'd be singing, and she'd turn around, and give me that sideways look, and she'd just take her hand and swish the skirt of the old worn-out cotton dress she was wearing. She was a sensuous woman. Though she never talked of sex or used the word sex, she was beautiful and she had a lot of sexuality and she knew it.

Momma held her own with Daddy. Of course she loved my father and my father loved my mom, but I often heard him yell and I heard her yell right back. There's a story about that that they both told me. It took place in 1929, the Crash. Momma didn't know about it, didn't know that the bottom had dropped out of everything, so she was hanging up some new lace curtains and three or four of the people she had working for her were helping. And Daddy came in. He had heard about the Crash back up at the store. All the people were running around frantic. He walked in the door, and she was up on a ladder hanging the curtains and saying, "Ah, now that looks good." Daddy went over and jerked them down on the floor. "We can't afford them!" Well, she ran and got the gun they had in the house, and she aimed at him. She went click, click, click, clicked it three times, trying to get it to go off. Now, I think Momma knew the gun wasn't loaded since there were children around, but she was making a point. She was letting him know he wasn't going to treat her like that.

Momma was very religious. Daddy was too. He was hardworking and believed in living the righteous way. He didn't preach to us all the time about God and Jesus. He lived it. But Mommy—I'd see Mommy pray, wring her hands and pray all night long for her children to come home safe. She would pray so hard that she had calluses on her knees. I used to say, "Momma, you have nun's knees."

Well, I sort of ran over the business of there being all of us children, but of course that was a big part of Momma's life. I remember once asking Daddy about that.

"Daddy," I said, "I got to thinking how many brothers and sisters I have. How come you all had so many children?"

"It was Hattie's fault."

"Um . . . what do you mean it was Mommy's fault?"

"Well, I tried to help her not have children."

"What did you do?"

"Well, during the Depression they used to have a birth control center set up downtown in Washington. One day I went down and stood in line all day with nothing but a piece of chewing gum in my mouth. The women were getting diaphragms. I waited and waited and it came my turn to come up where the nurse was. 'My wife needs a diaphragm,' I said. And she said, 'Mr. Stoneman, you have to go home and bring her down here so we can fit her.' So I went home and told your mother. She started screaming, 'Lord have mercy, you're trying to kill me! You're trying to send my soul to Hell, that's what you want to do!' And she went on raving and staving, saying that the Bible says be fruitful and multiply and it was against the rules of God for her to be fitted for a diaphragm and how dare I go and waste a whole day standing in line for her to be killed because she knew that God would do something horrible to her if she prevented having children when she could have them."

When I think back on my childhood, one of the few major problems I have with Momma was her favoritism to her boys. At the time I just accepted it, and now I think that that favoritism goes along with being a southern mountain woman. Anyway she treated the boys special. The girls did the housework. We even carried the water from the well in heavy buckets. The boys would always get out of doing it—"Aw, Ma, we'll do it after awhile." "Well, somebody better go get some water here, 'cause we're running out." So we girls would have to go. Then we'd have to do the washing, and washing blue jeans on a scrub board is not easy. The boys would just sit there and play music.

A lot of men made sarcastic comments on all those children: "Weelll, what did your father do for spare time?" Nasty cracks. But my opinion, that's the only time my parents had of their own. And maybe that was the only way they knew to show love. I don't remember them hardly ever holding hands or touching each other or kissing. No romancing. Remember that my daddy didn't have a mother. And if you've been around children, you know how a woman is needed in a boy's life, to teach him how to show love in little ways to a woman.

I think that my parents really loved each other and that making love, being intimate, was very important to them. Momma once said to me, "Lord a mercy, Ernest would come in from New York, or wherever he was playing, and next thing you know, I was in the family way again."

As I said, I was a very rich little girl because of my parents. When I think of the examples they set for me—the courage, spirit, persistence, creativity, morality—well, I'm very grateful.

TWO

A Classy Person: Aunt Jack

Granny Frost had three children, my mother Hattie, her sister Irma Lee, who for some reason we called Aunt Jack, and Aunt Jack's twin, Bolen. Aunt Jack was a classy lady. She was childless. And we were always impressed with her because she didn't have kids. Instead she had lots of things.

She was beautiful like Mommy and she dressed in elegant dresses and hats. She was neat and tidy. Even when hard times set upon her, she would sew every button just right. She had the Frost sense of humor, and she was independent acting, a liberated woman. Of course I didn't know the word then—they hadn't invented it—but she had an extra energy. I always thought, "Boy, she can do things on her own! Boy, is she smart!"

Aunt Jack was also a fine musician, played the mandolin and guitar with Mom and Dad in the twenties when they made those recordings.

"Did you play real good, Aunt Jack?" I'd ask her. "Naw," she'd say, "I just faked it. I'd just run my fingers up and down, and they'd think I was playing good."

Her husband Smitty was born in New York and he worked as a writer for a New York newspaper though they lived in Washington, D.C. I would stay with them sometimes. She would be trying to help me by taking me out of that one-room shack and teaching me about the city. Well, one thing she taught me was that there was a city—a place where the roads go straight, not winding around! And she taught me about such delicacies as having bananas in cereal.

She died a tragic death. One day when we kids came home, Momma said that Aunt Jack had gone to the hospital. An ambulance had come and gotten her because she was burned up in a kitchen fire. Right away we went tearing over to the hospital.

The doctors made us stay in the front area of the hall. They wouldn't let my mother in the room.

But I broke away and ran right down the hall, looking in at the people, trying to find Aunt Jack. And there in this one room was—looked like a lobster, this woman. I wasn't sure if it was her, this thing sitting up in the bed. She was pure red. There were blisters on her hands sticking up, and her fingernails had been burnt off. Horrible, God, it was horrible!

"Hi, Roni," she said.

"Aunt Jack, is that you?"

"Yes, it's me."

"Oh, Aunt Jack!"

She stared at me.

"It's a hot time, Roni," she said. "It's a hot time in the old town to-night."

The next day she was dead. Her lungs had been burnt too. That's what killed her, bless her heart. She was a wonderful, wonderful lady.

THREE

My Childhood

My brothers and sisters: Eddie was born in 1920, Grace in 1921, John in 1923, Patsy in 1925, Billy in 1926, Nita in 1927 (Nita died when she was five), Jack in 1929, Gene and Dean in 1930, Scotty in 1932, Donna in 1934, Jimmy and Rita in 1937 (Rita died when she was a baby), me in 1938 (May 5), and finally Van in 1940. So I was the second to youngest. My birth certificate said "seventeenth Stoneman, female." It was a while before they got around to naming me. And then it was Veronica Loretta, after two sisters of Aunt Jack's husband Smitty.

When I was growing up, we were living in that one-room shack in Carmody Hills, Maryland, Prince George's County. It was not known as a very desirable area. The people from the hills, trying to get work, they would find the place out. Most of them were from Virginia, West Virginia, and Kentucky.

In that one room there would be twelve or fourteen of us, depending on which of the older kids had left home. Under the big room was a small dirt dug out basement where Daddy slept. I talked about Momma's trying to fix the place up, but it was a pretty sorry situation. Poorism, we were ate up with poorism. There was no roof, just a canvas tent. We had one little wood stove in the middle of the floor. That's what we used for heat in the wintertime, and Maryland can get pretty cotton-pickin' cold. Daddy bought that piece of land and built the house with whatever he could get. When he would do work for churches, they would give him the lumber from an old church they were tearing down.

The front door was always left open in the summer, and there were no screens in the windows, so the flies went in and out. No closets. We'd have four or five kids to a bed. Momma would sometimes use straw tick mattresses. That was for the bed wetters—the urine would go right through the straw.

We didn't have a bathroom or running water. We had a well. To wash up, we used a wardrobe that we set catty-cornered. Me and Donna would get behind it. We had a washcloth and a washbasin for our face and our hands and arms, and the upper part of our body. And then for the lower part, we had a pan and a rag, and different water.

There was one dresser, sitting over in the corner. The boys would put a pan of water on it and shave, and sometimes we'd all get to running around, or fighting, and we'd knock the pan over. On the wall was a razor strap my brothers nailed there so that Daddy couldn't grab it too easily.

Light bulbs hung down on wires, three or four bulbs, like you'd see in a cheap poolroom. I'd look up and gaze at all the colors from the light bulbs, a kaleidoscope of colors.

We didn't have much food. Eggs because Momma had chickens, and canned vegetables and fruit we'd bring back from the summers in Galax. Beans, lots of beans, and cornbread. And Momma'd make a kind of cake and pour icing over it—similar to Moravian sugar cake. We didn't eat a lot of meat but sometimes we'd have boiled ham, or a little liver or fried steak. And mackerel. Daddy'd take the mackerel out of the can, leave it in hunks, and then fry it in cornmeal. We had it for breakfast a lot because Daddy said it was good for your eyes.

A little like people today, we never ate dinner at the same time. My brothers would come in at four, five in the morning, and take some of the leftover pinto beans or biscuits and gravy. One night we'd all gone to bed, and set aside the gravy in a pan for whoever happened to straggle in. Mommy wasn't there because she was taking care of Granny, who was sick.

Well, my brother Dean came in and he got the gravy and put it on some biscuits. Then he cried out, "Hot damn! What the heck is this? It tastes like old wallpaper paste!" And Daddy yelled from downstairs, "I made the gravy. It's not wallpaper paste." I went and looked. Daddy had got the flour out of a paper sack, and it had the red on it that marked Momma's wallpaper flour. So we kids started laughing and making fun of Dean, chanting, "Dean came in and ate wallpaper paste. Dean came in and ate wallpaper paste!" And he said, "What the hell are you talking about? You ate it too." "But it was warm when we ate it!" we said. "Makes all the difference in the world!"

I always looked like a ragamuffin. We couldn't afford store-bought clothes, so Momma would make flour sack dresses. The school we Carmody Hills kids went to was over in Seat Pleasant, where there were people with more money, so sometimes a teacher would get together a bunch of clothes and send them down to the Stoneman children, the poorest of the Carmody Hills kids. The clothes were from the other children in the school, and that was bad because they would recognize your dress. Someone would say, "Hey, she's got my dress on. My mother gave away my dress and I didn't want her to." You'd stand there, and a bunch of her girlfriends would come over, and then you had to fight for your life. One fight that sticks in my mind was about a beautiful yellow dress. That was worth fighting over. Sometimes you wore one of the boys' shirts or a boy's pair of shoes. And then you had to fight the boys.

I was always embarrassed about my clothes. I remember one particular day when I was wearing my brother's britches. I didn't have a belt, so I took a stick and put it in a belt loop and twisted it and then turned it down into my waistline. The stick worked—though you'd have to be careful all day so you didn't get gouged in the ribs. But when I stood up to read in class, it looked like I had a big knot sticking out—even though I was trying to hide it with my blouse, and putting my left arm over it. And a kid, his name was Walter, called out, "Lookat that hillbilly Stoneman. Got a stick in her britches!"

Of course medicine and doctors were out of the question. We didn't have the money. So in an emergency we'd go to the charity hospital. Jimmy was born there the year before I was. And they somehow put him in a pile of clothes, threw him down the laundry chute. He was lost for awhile. We would make fun of him for it later, but he always took it seriously.

When it was my turn to be born, Momma was having a terrible time, so they had to take me with forceps. And Momma said that's why my eye was crooked—the forceps gouged at my eye, and then injured my neck.

The eye tormented me for much of my life. The name they have for it is wall-eyed. It means when *you* look straight ahead, the *eye* looks toward the wall. My neck, well, a few years later, I developed a big growth, as big as your fist. I couldn't turn my head, and I was violently ill—fever, nausea, on death's door. They took me to a hospital run by the Catholic Charities. The doctors there saved my life. Afterwards my mother always wore Catholic medals, and I still wear my Catholic medal. I can't go anywhere without it. If I lost it, I'd be . . . just lost.

Well, when they first took me to the hospital to be operated on, they gave me antibiotics. It was in the early forties when the antibiotics, penicillin, had just come in. Two or three times a day I was getting a shot in the butt. I was so full of holes that Momma counted them when I came home.

I remember the doctors telling Momma that I needed blood. I had O positive, Daddy did too, and he lay down and gave me blood, the blood going straight from his arm to mine. Later I was dating a man named Dr. Henry Head, and I told him this story. He said, "Well, my father invented that machine, Dr. Jerome Head." I think that's such an amazing coincidence.

There was one other medical crisis when I was little. Mommy had been away with Granny in Galax. She came in the door, and I was over in the corner, in the bed. Right away she could tell I was very sick. She helped me open my mouth and my throat was white, coated, my tonsils practically together. And I had been having hallucinations from fever. Daddy hadn't noticed. He was busy practicing with the boys with a new amplifier nailed on the wall over my bed. Momma said, "Lord Gosh,

Ernest, she's got diphtheria." They took me to a hospital in Washington. The doctors quarantined you in those days, and I was in a room just by myself for a long time, seemed like forever. Daddy would come over to see me after work, but Momma couldn't come because there was so many kids at home to take care of. Well, I guess as I got better I wanted some attention. Anyway, at one point I remember standing up in this crib-like bed, holding onto the sides, serenading one of the doctors. At the top of my lungs I was singing, *Ain't gonna marry a doctor / I'll tell you the reason whyyyy / He goes around the country makin' people die / Chewing chawing gum, chewing chawing gum.* That poor doctor!

Well, again they had been sticking needles in my butt. And when I finally got to go home, Momma put black salve on it. She used it all the time, that black iodized salve. It came in a little jar, and when you bumped your head, when you got hit with a rock, she would always grab for it. If you got burned, she used butter or Cloverine salve. There were lots of home remedies like that.

We didn't have money for dentists. Once my jaw tooth was abscessed real bad, so Daddy got the old tooth pullers from his little case of tooth puller stuff. He'd been working on a house, and my jaw was way out by the time he got around to it. The tooth had four roots, two abscesses on different roots.

I had another dental problem, a large gap in my front teeth. But that was not something Daddy could take care of, and I only learned years later that a proper dentist could have done something about it if we had had the money. Turned out it was a good thing we didn't—that gap in my teeth later became a trademark when I was on *Hee Haw.*

Because there was no money, we had practically no store-bought toys, but I did get one when I got home from the quarantine. Before that, I had had a doll that Momma had made me out of a big old lumberjack sock. She put button eyes in it, and she sewed a mouth. I was born for babies. It's in my blood. I would sit and stare at that doll and rock it all day long. Children who don't have a lot, they can imagine—their dreams are so real, their imagination so big. It seems as if God says, "Well, this is something I'm gonna give this child, this gift." I would imagine the prettiest face on that little rag doll, just an old rag that Momma had stuffed with cotton balls.

I took it up to the house of my girlfriend, Mildred. Now, Mildred had a nice new doll she got for Christmas. She suddenly said, "Here, let me feel your doll," and she grabbed it. "This doesn't weigh much. It doesn't even feel like a real baby." I went home and I said, "Momma, she said my doll doesn't feel like a real baby." "She said that, huh?" "Yeah. But I love my doll, Ma."

And then after I came out of the hospital, Momma went and became a nurses' aide for awhile in a hospital in Washington, and with the money she earned, she bought me a snowsuit and a doll. The snowsuit was wine-colored, made of wool, a coat and leggings to match. The doll opened and closed her eyes and went "waa waa." I carried this doll around everywhere.

We didn't get lots of toys for Christmas. The first Christmas I remember was when I was about six. I can recall Daddy saying, "Hattie, I got to go up to the store and get the children something for Christmas." He came home with oranges and nuts. I remember him giving them around—he took my little hand with his very big one and said, "Hold your hand out," and I got an orange and some nuts, walnuts and chinquapins. "This is the best I can do," he said.

That was the year Scott went out to get a Christmas tree. He suddenly said, "I'll get the best darn Christmas tree that ever was made! We're gonna have the prettiest tree in the world." He went out, him and his buddies, and they came back dragging a holly tree with red berries all over it. My mother saw it and immediately started praying—she thought we were going to be jailed. It was so tall it touched the canvas roof. And we kids were so happy. My mother said, "It's the most gorgeous thing I ever saw. Now children, don't fall into it. All those needles—you're gonna get hurt. Lord have mercy, don't step on them." Because we were barefooted. It was a beauty. We all just stood around and looked at that tree.

Since we kids didn't have toys, we invented things to do, "diversions." There was the time Scott and one of my other brothers had me lie down and gave me "chicken pox" by dripping candle wax on me. When Momma finally came home, I said, "Momma, it burns!" "Well, I guess so!" she said and went for the butter. My brothers were responsible for another adventure—when I fell in the outhouse. And this is a story I sometimes tell when I'm performing, because a lot of people in my audiences remember all too clearly the days of the outhouses. Well, one day, when I was about eight years old, I had to go to the outhouse. I passed Jimmy playing in the yard, and I warned him not to come near the outhouse—because sometimes my brothers would get sticks and beat on it. I went inside and there in the corner was a mud-dauber's nest. Well, I climbed on the two-by-four, and all of a sudden some of my other brothers threw a piece of lumber on top of the roof. The mud-dauber nest fell. This big mud-dauber started buzzing around and every time he'd make a dive at me, I'd go "Whoooop!" and I'd lean backwards. About the third dive he made at me, I fell, head over heels into, well, let's call it the "Pits of Hell." I did land feet first, thank God. I started hollering "Help! Help!" Jimmy finally came and looked into the hole. "Whaaat's the matter, Ronnnni?" (he always talked real slow). What did he think was the matter?!!!! Finally Jimmy ran and told Momma. "Lord God!" she said. When she looked down and saw me, she started praying. She prayed and she prayed. I thought, If she don't finish praying and get me out of here, I'm gonna die! But I knew better than to tell her to quit praying. She finally pulled me out and all of the neighbors came and formed a bucket brigade. But even after they washed me down with that trusty old lye soap that Grandma made, I still had an ungodly smell on me. When I started to go to bed that night, six feet kicked me out: "Momma, the outhouse kid ain't sleeping with us." I slept on a pallet of straw on the floor for the next three months.

It's amazing any of us survived. Momma would try to get us doing nonviolent creative things. For instance, when it was raining, she'd put a scarf on her head and go out with a dishpan and dig up red clay and bring it in the house. She'd have all of us young children sit at the table, and she would give us clay to make things. And one time Jimmy, he looked at this red clay and didn't know what to do with it. Had a big hunk of clay about as big as his fist, all rolled out. And there was a railroad spike laying around that Daddy had brought in to show us kids what the spikes looked like that the men used to lay crossties. So Jimmy stuck it in this hunk of clay. I'm sitting there making a snake. "This is a snake! Lookat it!" I said, and I'm concentrating, trying hard to make its fangs. Well, Jimmy walked up behind me and took that ball of clay and hit me right on the top of my head. I let out a scream. The blood flew. Jimmy claimed to the end of his life that he didn't do it to be mean. "I had to find something to do with what I made!" he would say.

Even Donna, sweet gentle Donna, got in on the mayhem. Donna was left to take care of Jimmy, Van, and me an awful lot. Well, one day Momma had to go to the store. She had to walk six, seven miles up to the grocery store to get anything she needed. And that morning we had had pancakes, and all the leftover batter and other garbage was put in this great big bowl on the table. Now Momma always said, "If I'm ever not here, and a storm comes up, don't you all stay in this house. You go over to Eddie and Katherine's." (My oldest brother and his wife lived right across the creek.)

Momma was terribly afraid of storms. She was taught to be, I guess, up in the mountains. She swore she once got knocked off a porch by lightning. When it stormed, the old canvas covering that we had instead of a real roof would go "Whompy, whompy, whompy" because the wind would get up underneath where Daddy had tied the canvas down with a cord. Momma would get us all in the corner and she would pray—"Oh, dear God in Jesus' name, take care of us, take care of my little children." Then she'd start talking in a tongue, saying things you couldn't understand. It would just flow out of her. She wasn't trying to impress anybody—that's why I know it exists, talking in tongues. I think some folks try to impress people with that, but I know my mom didn't. The whole scene was like baby chickens coming up under the mother hen, and she putting her wings out, protecting them. We never had a tree fall, and we saw them sway almost to the ground.

So this one time when Momma went shopping, a storm came up.

Donna said, "We got to go to Katherine's."

And I was being a brat.

"No, I don't want to go! I wanna stay here! It ain't raining yet!"

"We got to go. If I don't take you and Van and Jimmy to Katherine's, I'm gonna get a beating! C'mon, Katherine'll give us stuff to eat."

"No, I ain't gonna go! I wanna eat here."

So we got into a real fight, and it ended up with delicate, fragile Donna sitting on top of me, holding me down with her knees, and cramming that old pancake batter and garbage into my mouth.

"Eat here? Okay, I'll make you eat here!"

Now it sounds as if I'm the victim in all of this stuff, but just like in this story, I was a brat too. I was always hyper and dirty and getting into things. I can remember times when I was specially aggravating, would be running around the house, rooting into things, zip, zip, zip, worse than a two-year-old. When we got into trouble, I was generally the one whupped. My brothers were too big, all except Van, who was spoiled because he was the youngest, and Jimmy, who never got whupped because he was an epileptic. That's why he talked so slow—the epilepsy. My mother would say, "We got to take Jimmy to John Hopkins again, see what kind of medicine we can get for him. Poor little thang sleeps all the time." So we all understood. And even when he should have been whupped, he wasn't. Donna, in spite of the pancake batter incident, was pretty much always good and demure.

The whuppings, well, I better explain them. They were no big deal. Everybody out there in those days got lots of whuppings. In our house Momma was generally in charge of them. She'd get a switch from the yard, sometimes get three or four of them and tie them together at the bottom, where she could get a good grip on them. And she would make you dance. It would whistle—tchoo, tchoo. Switching would be like you were running through a briar patch. Sometimes blood would come out of your legs and run down, but it was nothing like child abuse.

Because we didn't have toys, it was really special later on when we got a television set. We used to watch the comedians. Daddy loved Judy Canova, and I remember looking at her with her pony tails and thinking, I want to be like Judy Canova. And Imogene Coca was wonderful, the way she could create the fun within herself. She just spoke out, Hey, here I am and you're going to laugh 'cause by golly I ain't leaving here 'til you do.

We also loved Carol Burnett. Her "husband" would come in and say, "Where is he? Where is he?" accusing her of having another man. She'd be mopping the floor and she looked like death, she's dressed awful, had these old shoes on. And she says, "Who?" And he says, "Where is he? Where'd he go?" And then he picked her up and she just let her arms go limp. Years afterwards I saw Carol Burnett in California when we were doing a television show and I went over to where she was doing her show. And while she was off camera, she would be either reading or doodling. She gave me about five pages of her doodling—she was really a great artist, she could draw anything. But what impressed me was that she was real quiet between takes, she wasn't always "on." And then she'd go right back into the character she had been playing.

The TV was very blurry, so when it really mattered, we would go to a friend's to watch. And that's what we did when I was a teenager and Daddy was on the *The Big Surprise* quiz show. He kept winning week after week, until he finally missed a question. We were proud, but we were so dumb and poor that we didn't really get that excited. I think I was more excited about him being in New York. I said, "Look, he's up there in New York with all them tall buildings!" Well, with the money he won, he bought clothes for us to wear and a new dining-room table, and a ring for Momma, to replace the one he had to sell when the Depression hit.

I don't know how my parents did it, manage to raise us all. Daddy was good at psychology. He would say when people asked him about all his kids, "I had a lot of young'uns and every one of them is different. Every one of them has different thoughts and different needs." Mommy never had time to give us the one-on-one attention that kids today get. She didn't say, when I was running around, "Hey c'mere. Sit down on my lap. I love you." Never. But she loved me. If she was washing dandelion greens or fixing beans with a pan in her lap, I'd come up and lay my head on the side. She'd move the pan and let me lay my head right there, and she'd put my hair behind my ears and pet me and caress me and say, "Poor little Roni, poor little Roni."

FOUR

Music

More than the invented games, more than the television, the main thing we had instead of toys was music. Like most of the people from around Galax, Daddy would make his own instruments. And here's one of those times him being good at psychology came in. He wanted us kids to learn to play, so he'd put an instrument on the bed and warn us, "Now, I'm not finished with that one yet. I don't want you picking it up when I'm at work. And it better not be out of tune when I get home." Well, soon as he got out of sight over the hill, we'd make a dive for that instrument. Scott would usually get there first. Then I'd cry and holler and eventually it would be my turn. And everybody'd be playing with it all day long. Then when we'd see Daddy coming, we'd yell, "Get it in tune, here comes Daddy! Is it in tune? Okay, put it on the bed!" And we'd all run away from the bed.

It worked a little like the Suzuki method, where the younger children imitate the older ones. The Stonemans practiced it before the Japanese named it. A group of kids, instruments laying at our disposal, and we thought, well, if my brother can play it, I can too.

Most of my older brothers could play several instruments, but those of us that ended up doing the most with the music started specializing. Patsy played the autoharp, Donna the mandolin, I went for the banjo, Van the guitar, Scott the fiddle, and Jimmy the bass or what we called the whomper. (It looked like a cross between a bass and a banjo, but was played and sounded like a bass.) No one told us which instruments would be ours, we just figured it out. It was as if the instruments chose us. And because of Daddy's warning, we learned really well how to tune instruments! To this day I can't tune by electric tuners.

Although Scott was expert at all the instruments and was my main teacher for the banjo, and Donna's for the mandolin, the fiddle had chosen him in a really special way. Every summer, as I said, I would go back to Galax for three months. Usually me and Van and Mommy, and sometimes some of the other kids. It was great being there—we'd eat the big purple grapes on the vine, go down to the spring and fill buckets of water and put them on the front porch, and go out to the granary to get the corn.

One time Scott was there too. He came to help take care of Grandpa, who had fallen off a hay wagon and broken his neck. Well, Grandpa was propped up in a little bed, and Scott took one of his fiddles and was just squawking on it—he was about eleven. Grandpa looked over. "Son, you've got it," he said. "You have a mighty fine bow wrist."

In the next couple of days, Grandpa started getting out of bed. "C'mon," he said to Scott, "let's walk up to Granny Holler. I want to teach you something." I went with them. I was always beside Grandpa—he couldn't hardly shake me if he tried. I was like a parasite, like Spanish moss. I was only about six, but I remember how I watched Grandpa to see if he was walking okay as we went up the hill, Scott helping him and me holding his other hand. We sat down on a big flat rock. Grandpa said, "Now I want you to be real quiet. Just listen." We listened to the mountain sounds. "There's the mockingbird over there," said Grandpa to Scott. "Can you hear him? He's mocking the whippoorwill. Now that's the way you play it on the fiddle. That's how you learn the mockingbird song. You come up here and listen to the birds." Scott would later be famous for the way he played the mockingbird song.

Scott played the fiddle all day long. Once when I was really young, I asked him about that, why before breakfast, before anything, he'd pick up his fiddle. He said, "Well, that's the only way you're going to learn anything, Roni." And it would be the last thing he did at night. Sometimes he'd get to teasing Mommy. We'd be in the house, it'd be dark, and we'd be playing marbles on the floor, again because we didn't have too much to play with. About that time you'd hear the sound of a car honking, honk, honk, honk. Momma'd say, "Lord God, who's out there tooting that horn?" I'd say, "I don't know." She'd get up and look and say, "Ain't no car out there." And she'd come back. Next thing you know—honk, honk, honk. Momma'd say, "Lord God, Ernest, who in the name of God is that?" And we'd go back and look and hear honk, honk, honk. Scott would be under the window with the fiddle, making car horn sounds. That honking sound became part of the "Lee Highway Blues." Other times he would make a cat fight. It sounded so real Momma would cry, "Lord God, my cats are getting killed out there!" and she'd run out in the yard, saying, "Here kitty, kitty, kitty!" Of course sometimes I think Mommy would catch on, but she would pretend like she didn't.

Jimmy had perfect pitch. Mr. Vaultsides (at least that's how we said his name) was the music teacher, and he was an Italian fellow and so handsome. Now, when I was in my second year in the sixth grade (it's embarrassing to say, but true), I was in love with him. I remember sitting there and swooning over this man. And all my girlfriends did too—"Oh, he's so cute." He'd just smile and go about his business.

Mr. Vaultsides was bound and determined to teach me how to write music notes. He would draw a big S and then those black dots with flags on them flittered out through the lines. But I never could get it all straight because I wasn't hearing it. He would teach us over and over, bless his heart. He would draw more pictures with flags. And I tried, I really did, but I never got those flags right. There could have been flags all over Texas, I still wouldn't have gotten it. I always made straight Fs in music.

On one particular day I had brought a bass fiddle string, a gut string, from home. I tied a piece of wood at the end and made a circle of the string around a part of the desk. And while Mr. Vaultsides was playing the piano, I'd pull on the string. Bam Bom. You pull it in different ways, and of course it'll make different sounds.

"Mr. Vaultsides, Veronica is making noise with that stupid string," said the kid sitting in front of me.

"It's only this," I said, holding up the string, "and I almost had your same key."

"Veronica, you're disturbing the class. You're going to have to stay after school."

Now, because I would always walk my brother Jimmy home and take care of him, he had to come to the music room and wait with me. They had to let him because he was an epileptic and we had to walk such a long way. I'd protect him. If any boys jumped on him or teased him, I'd fight them. I was like that Norman Rockwell painting, "Hang Tough"—little kid staring out, raggy with a black eye, socks hanging down. My sister Donna gave me that painting. She said, "That's just like you, Roni, that's just like you."

So I'm sitting there after school, and Jimmy comes in. Now he was always taking pills, the medicine for his seizures that they gave him at Johns Hopkins Hospital. It made him slow moving and sleepy.

"Hiiiii, Rooniiii," he said that afternoon when he came in.

"I have to stay after school," I said.

"I'llll staaay heere and waiiit for ya." And then he sat down beside me and dozed off.

Mr. Vaultsides started playing the piano—da da da de dea. He was really giving it what-for and making those concerto sounds, prissy piano licks. I don't know if they call them licks, but we did.

"Mr. Vauultsides," says Jimmy, suddenly.

"What is it?"

"Yooou're in B flaat."

"What did you say?"

Jimmy hummed and held his hand to his ear.

"Yoou were plaaying in B flat."

"Do you play the piano?"

"Nooo."

"Well, how did you know I was playing in B flat?"

"I can tell annny key you're plaaying in," said Jimmy.

"You can?"

"Yeppp. I caann do thaat." And Jimmy put his hand on his right knee and looked down at the floor, like he often did: "Yeppp. I caann do thaat."

"Well, let's hear you name this," said Mr. Vaultsides. And he played in all kinds of keys, and Jimmy went "Hmmmmm" and told him every key, minors and everything.

"Well, you're watching me play. You know how to play," said Mr. Vaultsides.

"Nooo, I donn't. Daddy can't maake a piano. But as loong as I caann hear it, I caann tell."

I'm sitting there wondering what's going on here, what's the big deal, because we always took Jimmy for granted. Everybody did stuff like that at our house.

But Mr. Vaultsides came up and he grabbed him by the shoulders and he said, "Can you really do that?"

"Yeaaahh."

"All right, I'm going to sit you back here in the chalk closet, and then we'll see if you can do it."

So he put him out in the closet.

Mr. Vaultsides started playing all kinds of weird music, fancy. And Jimmy called out every one of the keys and chords. Mr. Vaultsides then opened the closet door, and Jimmy came out and said, "Caann we gooo nowww?"

Mr. Vaultsides was trembling. "Do you know how many professors of music can't do that?"

When we played the instruments, we'd experiment with them the way Daddy did when he made them, and the way I was doing with that bass string. I remember Billy once putting a light bulb in his banjo head with a battery. And he said, "Come here, Roni, look at this. Listen how loud it sounds." He went doodle doodle doodle doo. "And the light makes the head dried and tight, so it doesn't get out of tune because of the humidity or heat. And it looks all lit up on the stage."

Soon people from all around knew about the family, and parents would sometimes just drop off their kids in front of the house with their instruments. Zeke Dawson, for example, who later got real good on the fiddle and played with Loretta Lynn. His father and mother taught music at some big institution there in Washington, and they at first didn't like Zeke playing country music. But Momma and Daddy talked them into saying it was okay.

In the spring or summertime if you walked out the front door, turned to your left, went up the hill, and then looked back, you would see little groups of my brothers and their friends in different places, all playing music—and lots of neighbors who came by to listen.

All this surrounding us kids with music eventually paid off. And in fact the first time it paid off in a big way was when I was very young, before I could really play the banjo, in 1947. I remember this so clearly. I was standing right beside Momma by the table, and there was some beans on the stove, and some cornbread Momma had made. Daddy came in and he sat down at the chair right at the head of the table, and he said, "Hattie, there's gonna be a contest at Constitution Hall. The winner gets twenty-six weeks on Connie B. Gay's TV show. I want to get in that contest." Momma said, "Well, Ernest, go ask the boys if they would pick with you." Eddie was "the boys," I guess, along with the rest of them.

After awhile Daddy came back, didn't look too happy.

"What's the matter, Ernest?" said Mommy.

"Well, Hattie, they don't want to play with me."

"And why not?"

"Because they got electrical instruments now, and they say I play too old-timey for them."

Momma, as I said, had a lot of spark in her.

"Well, I'll tell you what, Ernest," she said. "How long before the contest?"

"Oh, 'bout three months, I guess."

"Well, that gives you time to start making instruments for the little ones. We'll take the little ones, and we'll just beat 'em, Ernest Stoneman! We'll beat 'em! Just get my fiddle fixed up and I'll go and fiddle for you."

And I remember saying, "Wow! Do I get to go?"

So every night or so Daddy would carve out the neck of a new instrument. On Saturday, we'd go downtown and get things like a skin for a banjo head or cheap brackets from the hardware store. Daddy would even make the clamps for the instruments. And glue—he had sheets of glue that were thin as paper, yellow, and he'd put them in a can and heat them on our oil stove. To make the instrument extra solid, he would use a drill and set a wooden peg up into the neck.

So when the time for the contest came, we all got in our old rumble-seat truck. We rode around on seats made of toolboxes, and the lids of the boxes would bounce when we went over a bump. Well, I can't count how many times we got our fingers mashed. And Daddy'd say, "Dadblame it, don't you know to watch your fingers? You're gonna need them for picking. Now, dadblame it, watch them fingers!"

Off we went to the contest. And when we opened up the doors at Constitution Hall, it was nothing but shiny marble floors. I had never seen such a hallway—the house wasn't hardly that big. And I went flying, like the Gravy Train dog, sliding, then running straight back, and then sliding down the hall again. Momma said, "Lord God, in the name of Jesus, come back here! Where in the world are my young'uns going? Roni!" Down the hall on my left there was a dressing room. A guy was putting on fake eyebrows and a moustache and taking white stuff from a jar to make the eyebrows and the moustache whiter. I went up to his dressing table and I stared him right in the face, wondering why is he doing that? Then I noticed his boots came way up, and I thought, "They're too big for him, so he's like us." Because we always had those hand-me-down shoes.

Momma said, "Lord have mercy, in the name of Jesus, quit bothering that poor old man." It was of course Grandpa Jones, who later became one of the stars of *Hee Haw*. He was actually a young man then, but he was making himself look old. He said, "She's not bothering me." And Momma said, "Well, I have to get my fiddle." Grandpa said, "I'll watch out for her, you just go get your fiddle." So here comes Daddy, hobbling because of his arthritis, and he got his guitar, and all the kids got the instruments that he had made, and they started tuning. But I didn't have to because I was just going to be singing, so I kept staring at Grandpa. "Would you like to have a hot dog?" he said. Well, I had never had a hot dog. We had beans and cornbread and vegetables, never had hot dogs.

"Yup," I said. "Do you want a Coke?" "Yeah." And I went walking with him to the concession stand.

I can still see this in my dreams and in my thoughts. I'm walking along beside Grandpa Jones, and he was okay with me because he was like us. Though this time I was more prissy than usual since I had on my first pair of patent leather slippers—my brother Billy, in the service in the Pacific, had sent Momma money to buy me and Donna shoes. She had sewn our little dresses out of feed sacks that had a little flowery pattern. And I'm walking along proud in my feed sack dress and looking at my shoes, and every once in a while I'd look over at Grandpa's boots. I can just *feel* myself there, and feel the joy I had of being with that man. So we got to the concession stand. He said, "She wants a hot dog." And then he turned to me, "Do you want mustard?" What did I know about mustard? "Yup!" I said. So then I was walking back, carrying my mustardy hot dog and my Coke, and I'm spilling my Coke as I go. "Oops, you got it on your foot," he said. We both stopped, and I put my Coke down on the floor and took my napkin and wiped off my new shoes.

My older brothers went on stage first, playing their electric stuff. I'm standing out in the wings, just watching, and I thought, Well, they didn't do as good as that other bunch did. There were about three hundred bands in that contest, at least it seemed like that to me. It was a big prize. You'd get all those weeks on Connie B. Gay's show. If we won, it would mean Daddy would be able to buy the materials to put a real roof on the house to replace the canvas tarpaulin.

And then it was our turn—"Ladies and Gentlemen, the Stoneman Family." Daddy had us sitting down in a U because there were only two microphones. We were going to sing "Somebody's Waiting for Me," and Daddy had lectured us children: "When you sing, open your mouth and sing as clear and loud as you can." So that's what we all did. And Momma, well, after watching my older brothers, she was mad, she was ready for bear! She was bringing that fiddle bow down, dom, dom, dom, and Daddy was playing his guitar as hard as he could. Some man out in the audience yelled, "Swing her, Ma, swing her!" Then the people were screaming for us. Connie B. Gay went out and announced, "The winners are—the Stoneman Family!" Well, we were asked to perform again, and we tore the house down. My older brothers were peeking around the stage. Momma said, "Come on," so they came out and joined us. I thought, That ain't fair, and I stayed in front. I wouldn't let anybody get in front of me.

We got the twenty-six weeks of appearing on the show. We'd do songs like "Hand Me Down My Walking Cane" and "Golden Slippers." This was before we had a TV, and in fact some little girl told Donna she had seen her on TV, and Donna didn't know what she was talking about. Daddy had to take us down to the store to see one!

The money we earned did buy us a real roof. Daddy got lumber for it, new lumber. And then he put a ceiling underneath. He used tin instead of wallboard, tin squares. I used to lie in bed and count them.

FIVE

Learning the Banjo

I described how Grandpa Frost helped Scott with the fiddle, but he also was the one that taught Momma to play the banjo in all those tunings. Like the other mountain banjo players, Grandpa used to make his banjos with the animals he would kill. He would get the hairs off the skin and stretch it on the drum of the banjo to make the head. Daddy, when he made instruments, would just go to the store and buy a skin head. Nowadays of course people use plastic.

My Grandpa Frost is maybe why I ended up being a banjo player. When I was about seven, he told me a story about a young lady who came to Virginia in a wagon train and played banjo. The girl's family was going through the mountains, and they stopped at the campgrounds at Galax, which is where Grandpa saw her. The girl was sitting on the back of a wagon, barefooted, swinging her feet, playing old songs like "Cumberland Gap," and he was struck on her because of how good she played.

As he bragged on her, he took them blue-gray eyes and he just stared at me.

I said to myself, I'm gonna play the banjo and make him proud of me.

But Scott was the one who became my main teacher on the banjo. And he was determined I was not going to play the old-fashioned clawhammer style of Grandpa, Momma, and the wagon train girl. He was going to have me play the new three-finger style that Earl Scruggs was making so popular. The sound was sharper, more ringing, more driving—bing bing bing. You played with picks, and it was very hard to learn.

Often when I would start practicing, Momma would say, "Roni, we got to have the dishes done," "Roni, Roni, you got to sweep the floor." I'd say, "Mommy, I never get to practice. I gotta practice, Mom, I gotta learn." She'd say, "Well, daggone it, honey, you gotta learn how to sweep the floor too." I would sneak out in the back, in the woods. The banjo was pretty heavy, so I'd practice on a tree stump. I'd just stretch my legs out apart, put the banjo on the stump, and reach around it and pick and pick.

Scott would come out. "Did you get it right yet?" I'd say, "I will, Scott, if you just . . ." "Now, don't stop, and don't make it sound like a gallop." A gallop is using your forefinger and your middle finger at the same time and not separating them. You're blurring it. "Each string has a personality," Scott used to say. "Each string's got its own sound and that means it's got its own personality and its own character. It has to sound so you hear it. And keep the strings ringing at all times, even if you have to go boom, ching, boom, ching. Take your index finger and hit the second string and then take the thumb and your middle finger and pull the strings, bong, ching, bong, ching. Keep them strings a-ringing."

He made Donna on the mandolin and me on the banjo really strong players. He would get mad and scream right in our faces, "Don't play like a girl! I don't want you ever playing like a girl! Just because you're a girl ain't no sign that you don't have ten fingers. You have two hands like a man, you've got a brain like a man, you've got strength in your arms. Press down on those strings. You can play like a man." He was really obsessed with that.

He'd say to me, "I want you to practice 'Foggy Mountain Breakdown' until you hate its guts, as if it had innards." He made me practice the rolls. He said, "If you learn the way Earl Scruggs does 'Foggy Mountain Breakdown,' you'll have all the rolls you need to know. It's got every roll in the world. Same with 'Dear Old Dixie.'" He'd show me how to slow down records to hear the rolls.

There was a neighbor kid, Jimmy Goran, lived up the street. And he saw me all the time walking around going one-two-three, one-two-three, practicing my rolls. He'd say, "Here comes that retarded, knock-kneed little hillbilly playing that stupid banjo." But I was really interested in getting those rolls going smoothly, and I didn't care what he said. I *was* knock-kneed. He was right about that. I guess because I was so skinny, my knees automatically knocked together. The insides of my knees were bruised and so were my ankles.

As a teacher, Scott didn't have any mercy. "You're sounding like a girl. Make them notes clear. Mash those strings." And he'd press my fingers down. Now, when you're learning, it's so frustrating. I'd say, "All right, don't teach me anymore, Scott." Then I'd go downstairs in the basement and get on my knees and cry—and then practice some more. Why I wanted to play so bad, I do not know. Probably because of my grandfather's story of the banjo-playing girl. And maybe also because of what I said about always being the one punished when we kids were acting up. I asked Momma one day, "How come I'm the one who always gets whupped?" "Well," she said, "if you played an instrument and your Daddy had to take you out to play with him, maybe he wouldn't whup you so much." But I can't say for sure that those reasons are the whole explanation. They certainly don't say why I wanted so bad to play like Scott wanted me to play. I don't know, other than I loved him so much.

When you got it, he was like a pep rally. He would make you feel you could do anything. You could set the world on fire, no matter how many great musicians there were out there. You were going to get in that contest tomorrow, and he was going to play the guitar behind you, and you were going to win.

I remember preparing before one of those contests. Now my banjo head was pretty dirty on the front from me dragging it around, so in the morning before Daddy went to work, I said, "Daddy, can I turn this head around? It's awful dirty." "No, you can't. You just can't do it." But when he left for work, I got to looking at that thing and I thought, I can take all these brackets off and I can push that head inside out. And I did it. Daddy had taught me how to put the head on. You had to wet it and then pull it down a little bit and let it dry, then wet it and pull it down and let it dry, and so on.

One of Scott's buddies was Bill Emerson. He was from a very wealthy successful family—his father owned some car dealerships. One day I was practicing my old banjo, and Bill walked in with Scott. He pointed at me.

"You can't play three-finger picking style," he said.

"I can too!"

"Naw, you ain't gonna learn it."

"What makes you say I ain't?"

"'Cause you're a girl."

"So what? I can play, and I can play faster than you."

"No, you can't either!"

And I walked over to him with my little homemade banjo—him standing so tall with his brand new banjo—and I kicked him as hard as I could in the shin.

Momma got after me: "Roni, you stop doing that. You're a young lady and you're not supposed to be fighting."

"I'll kick him in the other leg, Ma, if he don't quit telling me I can't play!"

Scott was smiling, enjoying the whole thing.

Years later when Bill Emerson was performing with a fine band, the Country Gentlemen, I went to see him play—he was really a great player. He also became a leader of the navy bluegrass band in Washington. And much later when I was in Buckeystown, Maryland, and they were giving me an award for all my years of banjo work, the presenter was . . . Bill Emerson. He said, "I am very very proud to present this to Roni Stoneman. I am overjoyed." And a tear came to his eye. "I told ya!" I said, and I grinned.

Our idol was Earl Scruggs, the genius of the three-finger picking style. One day, Scott came to me and he said, "Roni, guess what! Lester Flatt and Earl Scruggs are gonna be over at Glen Echo Park." It was kind of an amusement park. Oh, my God, I thought. Not my hero!!

So we go over there and I walk by the dressing room. The door was open and Scruggs was sitting in there, a quiet man, holding but not playing his banjo. I had on my little old feed sack dress, and I just stood there in the doorway staring at him. I was probably about ten but because I was so little and thin I must have looked about seven.

"Do you like banjo music?" he asked finally.

"Yep."

"That's good."

I twisted the hem of my dress around. "I play banjer too."

"You do?"

"Yes, I do. I play banjer."

"Do you play clawhammer?"

"No, I play three-finger, like you."

"You play three-finger style?"

"Yeah. You know how I learned it?"

"No."

"Well, I have a record player. And I put your records on and slow them down. Then I tune my banjo down to the sound, and I get your rolls like that."

"You mean you slowed . . ."

"Yeah, I got your rolls to 'Foggy Mountain Breakdown' just right."

"You have my rolls?"

"Yeah, you know like your rolls, down your fingers . . ."

"Yeah, I know what you mean."

And then I said, "I don't do nothing fancy. I just play like you."

He must have been trying really hard not to burst out laughing. "I'm so glad. Well, sometime you'll have to pick for me."

"Yeah, I will, I will." And my eyes were as big as watermelons.

There on his lap was a Gibson Mastertone. I went, Oh my gosh, a Mastertone. I was in love with the Mastertone and with his banjo picking. And that was the "world's famous" Earl Scruggs.

My banjo playing was getting better. I remember one night, really morning, it was about 2:30, Scott came in with five of his buddies. He started shaking me awake.

"Roni, get out of bed, get out of bed! We gotta go to Balt'mer."

"To Balt'mer? What for, Scott?"

"There's some bands up there that undercut me. They told the man they'd play for twenty dollars cheaper. We gonna get up there and show them a lesson."

"What we gonna show them, Scott?"

"C'mon, get up!" he said. "Let's go. We gotta go!"

So we drove all the way to "Balt'mer." The place we went to was a joint, a huge honky-tonk. I had never seen so many sailors and soldiers in one congregation of people! There was nothing but military everywhere.

A bluegrass band was playing loud, and Scott says, "I want you to go in first, and pretend like you don't know me." Now, at that time I was still very young, probably about twelve, and, again, much younger looking, about nine, a pitiful underfed waif wearing old bibbed overalls, socks held up by rubber bands, and raggedy loafers. Scott said, "I want you to go up there and ask the guy, 'Can I play your banjo?' Then you get up there, and you play 'Foggy Mountain Breakdown' and you play 'Cripple Creek,' then you go into 'Dear Old Dixie,' and then you play 'Foggy Mountain Breakdown' again."

So I went up to the bandstand.

"C'n I play your banjer?" I said to the banjo player.

"No!"

"Just one little song on your banjer? Or his banjer?"

"No."

Then Scott walked in and stood at the back.

"Let the little girl play!" he shouted.

And the sailors started yelling, "Let the little girl play one of your banjos!" "Let her play!" "She's not gonna hurt your banjo."

"You scared the little girl's gonna play better than you?" someone called out.

And everyone laughed. Then the manager, or maybe he was the owner, came over.

"Let her play," he said. "Let her play your banjo."

So the guy had no choice.

"Thank you for letting me use your banjer," I said.

"What's your name, little girl?"

"My name's Roni."

"And what are you gonna play for us, Roni?"

"'Foggy Mountain Breakdown.'"

Well I lit into "Foggy Mountain Breakdown," played it as fast as I had been trained to by Scott. And it was fast. I almost outran the band. Here I am, twelve years old, the only girl in the world at that time that could play three-finger picking style banjo (not bragging but that's the truth). Scott's in the back and he's grinning. The sailors and soldiers screamed and screamed. Then I played "Cripple Creek," then "Dear Old Dixie," then repeated "Foggy Mountain Breakdown," just like Scott had told me. They didn't want to let me off the stage. They were still screaming. And when I put down the banjo, they picked me up and threw me in the air, like a football hero. They passed me on over their heads, yelling, "Yea, yea, yea!" all the way the length of the hall. I was scared out of my mind.

The band just stood around on the stage. They couldn't play. Scott went up to the bandleader and said, "I told you, you son of a bitch, I was gonna get back at you." Scott was hired back that night.

In the next few years, as Donna and I got to be better musicians, Scott would often take us with him to play music, his two sisters. We would get up against these big men. We'd just stand there, and Scott would say, "Play." He had trained us and by golly he was gonna show us off.

There are lots of different ways of playing three-finger picking style banjo. People tell me that I have a distinctive sound. I did invent something. I had been practicing about two years, and I was just playing around with my right hand and I found I could do a roll twice and still keep the timing. Scott said, "What it is is a double roll." And I said, "That's what I thought too." Years later Gus Friedlander of Chicago's Old Town School of Folk Music told me that I was doing triplets over a two/four beat—for those of you who understand that kind of language! The double roll was something I just felt in my soul, and I'd stick it in where I wanted to. I think what makes a special sound also is the way you accent the notes. A professor of music once said to me, "You play differently from everybody else. You punctuate every note."

There are lots of banjo players I really admire. Don Reno of Don Reno and Red Smiley. They were from around our area, and they played in places we played, so I got to watch them from the stage as a young girl.

And Raymond Fairchild. Now, he's a showman on the banjo. When he plays "Johnson's Mule," he's playing behind the bridge of the banjo, and it sounds exactly like a mule braying. And nobody else in the world can do it. He goes mmmmm boom chick boom chick, and his face is just so solemn and he never looks down at his fingers. He can do all that chromatic stuff too, the flashy style where you play a lot of individual notes. But he doesn't do too much of it. Too much chromatic and you lose the feeling of the banjo. You might as well play a guitar or a zither. Raymond Fairchild does just the right amount.

And Ralph Stanley, the master of mountain music—of course I really admired him. It wasn't just that the singing was lonesome, Ralph's banjo playing was too. Anybody can sing a lonesome old mountain song if you're from the hills—*Oh faaair and tender laaaadies*. But to have the lonesome sound that Ralph Stanley has in his playing, that comes from the inner soul. There's nobody in the banjo world that plays as lonesome as he does. When I play, I play fast, and the faster I get, the happier I am. I'm fast moving, and it just comes out that way. Scott was the same way. He was hyper and he was the fastest fiddle player in the world. But Ralph, he's slow moving. He studies everything. He walks like he's studying each step. And he plays that way too, though he can play fast if he wants to. He's from hard times, and the sound of the hills is in his sad heart and it comes out in his banjo. He's very popular now. Sad feelings are coming back into our music. Every time the economy gets down, acoustical music comes alive, or as Momma would say, comes to the front.

Well, back to my becoming a banjo player. In the late fifties, when I was still a teenager, I became the first woman ever recorded playing three-finger style. That was because Mike Seeger came into our area collecting music. When I first met him, I kept staring at him, and I said to myself, Now, he's different. What's making him look different? It was his clothes—he was wearing brown corduroy pants and old tennis shoes, or sometimes sandals. I had never seen a grown man dressed like that. He had a recorder, and he recorded my parents for one album on southern mountain music and then me for another album on banjo Scruggs style. He also recorded many other people, and this was really a great thing. If he hadn't done that, there would have been a lot of old-time musicians

without any kind of recognition. It was sure a big deal for me. After that
record came out in 1957, with me playing "Lonesome Road Blues," the
only woman on the record, I became known as the First Lady of Banjo,
and that's what people call me today.

But it took awhile for that to get around, and for some time after, I
was still using homemade banjos. The first banjo Daddy made for me
had a tiny neck. The second one he made when I was older was bigger,
but it still wasn't great—it was never all that kosher when it came to
being in tune. And I needed a good banjo because I was getting jobs
and playing with Scott more. One day Scott said, "There's gonna be a
contest at Sunset Park and the prize is a Vega banjo." I said, "Okay, I'm
gonna go up there and get that banjo." "Well," said Scott, "S——" (I'm
not going to use his real name) "is gonna be in that contest, and he's
gonna bring his clumerage of people, all them people he drags with
him from New York." He called it a clumerage, and years later when I
used that word, someone corrected me—"'entourage,' it's 'entourage.'"
And I said, "Well, I like clumerage better, even if Scott made the word
up, because it also means a-clamoring—those people just a-clubbering
and a-clamoring around!" Anyway, Scott said, "S is just reading the
music. But he's got his clumerage of people and they'll gather around
the stage and applaud real hard so that he'll win the contest. It doesn't
make him any better. That's what you ought to do, get a whole bunch
of people around to clumerage the stage. If you find a tree where there
might be mikes hanging near, just get near the tree and gather your own
clumerage."

So I went up there and I got in the contest, though I didn't notice any
other girls. It came down to two banjo players, me and S. And before the
final showdown, I was playing out under a tree. There's a picture of me.
I was wearing a gold-colored shirtwaist dress and I had a scarf around
my neck. I had a real long neck, which my brothers used to say was a
stovepipe neck. Donna said, "Wear a scarf. That'll hide it." So I often
did—and my neck looked like a stovepipe with a scarf! In the picture
you can see that there were a lot of people all standing around watching
me—my "clumerage"—but I was oblivious to them.

Then I went back up there on the stage and was really working hard, really giving S a run for his money. There were ten judges. They called both S and me into this room off at the back of the stage.

"Roni, we can't give this contest to you," said one of the judges. "The crowd is yelling for you, but we can't give you this banjo."

"Why?"

"Because you're a girl. And if we give it to you, they'll tear this park apart."

"But you said they was yelling for me."

"Well, there's some people out there don't want a girl."

S was standing behind me. And the judge said, "We gotta give it to him, Roni. We can't let you win."

The emcee said, "Ladies and Gentlemen, the winner of the banjo is . . ." And he called out S's name, and S walked out, with all of his buddies cheering for him.

I saw him carry the banjo off. I just stood there and watched that banjo go.

SIX

Education

I wasn't the most "scholaristic" child in the world. I just didn't take to school for a lot of reasons. First of all, and maybe most important, there was my eye. I couldn't see the blackboard because my eye was crooked. And when I would read, sometimes the lines would blur into a big straight line and make me sick to my stomach.

Then there was the clothes thing. I talked about having to fight if I was wearing some other kid's clothes, but shoes were also a big problem. I remember one time in particular. Now, the teacher'd have us sitting in a circle like a horseshoe. That day I had Daddy's socks on, held up with rubber bands, and I was wearing my brother's shoes, tied around my ankle a couple of times to hold them up. Most of the other little girls were wearing patent leather slippers, with little lace around their socks. I'm putting my feet way up under the chair trying to hide my shoes while listening to the teacher read Dick and Jane. Crash! I fell off my chair.

The teacher said, "Veronica, get out of this classroom, now! Go sit in the hall!" So I sat out in the hall, all day long—for three days. The kids would come by and laugh.

Another problem was that even when I wasn't trying to hide my shoes I couldn't sit still. I would wiggle. I'd take my right leg, cross it over my left, and then I'd shake my leg. "Mrs. Pate, Veronica is kicking my desk again!" I would feel miserable. I kept watching the clock to see 3:30 come around, turning this way and that. My back ached. My shoulders ached. I'd raise my hand to go to the bathroom just to get exercise.

I remember well the teacher who sent me out in the hall. She shook me one time, real hard, and screamed as loud as she could—she'd scream right in your ear.

Now another thing that was hard about school for me was that I didn't get why they were teaching the stuff they were teaching. Why wouldn't they teach me what I wanted to learn? Why did they keep telling me about the coffee beans in Colombia or Brazil when I wanted to learn about the United States? So I would ask, "How come I can't learn about Virginia, or maybe Tennessee?" And the teacher would say, "Veronica, sit down. If you had a brain, you'd be dangerous."

Same thing with reading. I wasn't interested in Dick and Jane. Or even Spot. "See Spot and Jane. Mother is in the kitchen cooking." And I thought, "No kidding, there she is in the kitchen!" That was so dumb to me. So the teacher came down and told Daddy that I couldn't read very well. But Daddy never fussed at me for not learning well in school. What he did was to give me songs to copy down for him, and I learned to read through that. The songs were from a book called *Cox's Folk-Songs of the South.* I took it to school, and I was sitting there in the back of the room reading it: *Oh John Hardy was a wild and reckless man / He cared not what he done / He killed two men in the Swanee camp / Because he was too nervy for to run / Hot damn! Too damn nervy for to run.* And I was reading where the song originated from and who wrote it. The teacher came over and took the book from me because it wasn't Dick and Jane.

But some of the things about school were good. The teachers had a hard time with me, and some of them were great, very understanding. For instance my third-grade teacher had a spelling list, and she would walk around the room saying the words and we'd have to spell them.

I remember one time she had on the list "country" and "cousins" and "mountains." She walked up to my desk and stopped. "Veronica," she said, "has lots of country cousins." I thought, She's talking about me, isn't that wonderful? "Veronica's country cousins live in the mountains." I thought it was so kind of her to use me for the words because I was getting attention in school for the first time in a nice way. I learned to spell those words really quick.

She also corrected my pronunciation. For example we came to the word "chimley." I was having a hard time spelling it. She said, "How do you say that word?" "Chimley." "Veronica, it's chimney." I went, Okay, though it didn't sound right to write chimney when it was chimley all my life. And "pitcher." I would say "pitcher" for "picture." "No, that's different," she said, "that's 'pic-ture.'" I remember laughing at the time. It seemed so odd. Now, of course, when I'm writing a letter or something, I am really grateful. And basic things like "two," "to," and "too." It's so good to know those things—like "no" and "know"! Boy, that third-grade teacher was important in my life.

But altogether schooling was not my forte. It just wasn't. It's too bad because I don't consider myself slow. In fact I think of myself as sometimes too fast thinking. I forget what I'm saying because my mind's going too fast, like fast-forward on a video—zooooooom. Even in those school days I would feel that I was thinking faster than any kid in the class. But I guess a lot of people do that if they're hyper.

Anyway, when I got to be sixteen years old, and I could quit school, I walked all the way to Carmody Hills, it was several miles, and back, just to get the written statement that my mother said I could quit. The principal said, "We can't let you go, Veronica, unless your mother signs this." "Okay," I said, "I'll be right back." And I was so glad. Isn't that awful? (By the way, that long walk to school was another problem. In the wintertime I would be frozen half to death.)

To end on a more positive note, schooling wasn't for me, but learning is. I'm not educated, far from it. But I find everything interesting. I spend a lot of time reading and I love going into bookstores and libraries.

I wasn't a bad child. I had things to see and things to say. On one of my report cards, the teacher wrote "Veronica has ideas, but not our kind of ideas." That was the best report card I ever brought home. And Momma was proud of me.

SEVEN

Sex Education

My sex education wasn't any better than my other education. I was about fourteen or fifteen years old when I "became a lady." I remember getting really angry that day, and my back hurting, and I'm sitting in the school desk, wiggling around even worse than usual.

After school I was pitching horseshoes, and I suddenly said, "God, I got to go to the outhouse." I went to the outhouse and I found something was radically wrong. Oh, Lord, I was dying! So I took off running. I jumped a creek, I jumped over a ditch, hurrying to get to Mommy, who was working in the yard.

"Mommy, I'm dying! Oh God, Mommy, I'm dying!"

"What is it child? What is it?"

"I'm bleeding down there."

And Momma took me in her arms and said, "Poor little thang." She cried and she said, "You're not dying, honey, you're not dying. Let me see what we can do to help you."

She never told me what it was. That's how things were then. Usually the mothers didn't sit you down and tell you. Donna told me. Mommy just said, "Well, we have to fix that up," and she started making me a little pad from some rags that she pinned in my panties. Then she had Daddy go get me a belt and some Kotex pads. But I didn't know how to use them, and I kept pulling them . . . 'Scuse me, you men out there, I have to get into some technical details here. You women know how long the tabs on the old Kotex pads used to be? Well, I had pulled those tabs all the way up to the ends. You can imagine how taut it was, and how it hurt. I was miserable.

So Momma said, "Well, honey, this means you're a woman now." And I thought, I don't want to be a woman, sew me up! I knew better than to tell her that, but I was thinking if this is being a woman, I don't like it. I didn't like being a girl anyway. I had always wanted to have the freedom boys and men had. For instance when I was younger I had wanted to be a hobo. But being a hobo was definitely not in Momma's plan for me—"Lord have mercy, child, you can't be a hobo! Girls don't be hobos."

I got over that. But my period—every month the pain. My back would kill me. Now Momma didn't drink, but she'd keep whiskey in a medicine bottle. She would say, "You fight fire with fire." And she would give me a spoonful of whiskey, with sugar in it so I could get it down. Then she'd put a hot water bottle on my tummy. Mommy didn't tell me much about sex, but she was always sympathetic about female problems.

When she did talk about sex, what she told me wasn't always helpful.

Take her explanation of homosexuality. I was up at the house, about eight or nine years old, I guess. The boys had been playing music, and then they started talking about queers. "What's a queer?" I asked. And they wouldn't tell me: "Get out of here, Roni. Get out!" So, I see Momma's down in the yard digging in the ground, making her garden. (She spent a lot of time on that yard.)

"Ma, the boys are up at the house talking about queers. What's a queer?"

"Lord God, honey! Well . . . I . . . I couldn't tell you no such a thing as that. I never will be able to . . . I just can't tell you."

"You ain't gonna tell me?"

"Lord have mercy, honey, I . . ."

"Well, I'm going up the hill and ask Sweet William."

Sweet William was an old guy who had been in World War I. He was shellshocked, so every time he heard an airplane, he'd fling his arms around. Daddy told us kids that Sweet William was a hero and he better not ever see us teasing him, and we should help him when we could. He had the prettiest garden, snapdragons, bleeding hearts, but mostly sweet Williams, and he would give Mommy little pinches of flowers. All us kids would go by and talk to him. He was very kind.

"You come back here." Momma grabbed hold of my dress. "Don't go ask that poor old man about that. Well, I reckon I'll have to tell you, but don't you tell a living soul I told you this."

"Oh, I won't, Ma. I swear I won't."

"Well, honey, it's . . . terrible. It's a man that . . . that's got balls in his jaws."

That's all she knew, I guess. Maybe somebody told her that and she was just repeating it. Anyway, I went around thinking it was like golf balls. People would give us things, like a clock, and we'd take them apart. With the clock you could make a whole bunch of spinning things. Well, one time someone gave us golf balls. And I said, "Scott how come they keep on bouncing when they're so hard?" He said, "I don't know. Let's check it out." So he got the butcher knife and he cut one in half. And there were thousands of rubber bands wrapped around inside, thousands.

So golf balls in his jaws. That's a horrible thing, I thought, but I was satisfied with the explanation. All right, years later, we're in Nashville, playing a show with someone who had jowls real bad. Daddy was doing "The Little Log Cabin in the Lane." I remember that song because I remember how easy it was to pick with him. Which meant that I could stare at this jowly guy while I was playing. And I thought, Now that's a real queer—he's got balls in his jaws.

That was all my mother knew, the best she could come up with. It was confusing anyway, because mountain people like my grandpa would say, "Well, that man's mighty 'quar.'" And "quar" meant different, a little strange, quirky. So how in the world were we supposed to know that queer wasn't being queer in just a quirky way? Like going around with balls in his jaws.

I really didn't know the basics about sex until I was married. And even then I didn't know that you got pregnant from semen. In those days you prided yourself on not doing anything before you were married. I kissed a lot, but nobody felt me up and down. Mommy said, "Boys will do naughty things to you if you let them, and you're not supposed to let them."

But it was Scott who really trained me. One day it was storming out, so we were at Eddie and Katherine's house. Scott took me over to the kitchen sink and said, "This is what love is to a boy who's telling you, 'I love you, I love you, and if you let me do so and so, everything is going to be okay because we'll get married.' This is what love is to that boy, Roni." And he grasped my chin tight in his hand, looked me straight in the eyes, and said, "I'm telling you the truth, Roni, you listen to me!" Then he reached for the spigot and he turned it on full blast and then turned it off. "That's what love is to them kind of men!" he said.

If it wasn't for Scott, I would have ended up in a lot of trouble.

EIGHT

First Love

My first love, it was really just a crush, was Chuck Davis. He was from the Washington, D.C., area, but because he was running with a bad crowd, his mom and dad brought him into Maryland. Two sisters, him, and his mom and dad. It was a nice house, two or three bedrooms, even though it was right next door to us hillbillies.

One day, I was about twelve, I was looking through the fence and he was playing horseshoes. He had rubber horseshoes, two were black and two red. At first I didn't know they were rubber. But I thought, They're funny horseshoes. I walked up to the fence. "How're you doin'?" I asked. "Okay." And he looked down at the horseshoes. Blond-headed, blue-eyed guy, real cute, about fifteen. He threw the horseshoes to the peg a few times. Kept missing. I was used to playing horseshoes with my brothers—we played with iron ones, of course, and you played for your life and you had to be good.

Five, ten minutes went by.

"I can play with ya if you want somebody to play with ya," I said finally.

"Ya know how?"

"Yuh."

"How ya gonna get here?"

"Wall, I c'n climb over."

So I rattled over that fence, and I got my skirt caught as I went. Of course it was already half torn around the hem because it was always being caught on a horseshoe peg.

But in spite of the rubber horseshoes, Chuck turned out to be real cool. One day a year or two later, we were out in the field playing football. And I wanted to show the boys I was pretty good and make Chuck notice me. So when one of the big boys kicked the football, I went running for it and I caught it against my chest.

I've got to stop and explain about my chest. I was flat. My God, I looked like the inside of an ice cream scoop. I had no breasts at all, none, zero, zilch. Well, Donna came up to me when I had gotten to performing a little, and she dragged me into Lerner's and she bought me a bra with pads in it. In those days they called them falsies. I just kind of tucked them into my bra, not knowing how to attach them.

Okay, so I caught this football. Bap, right in my chest. And one of my falsies fell out onto the ground, was lying there in that field. Everybody started laughing. But Chuck picked it up and slipped it in one of my skirt pockets. "Here, sweetheart," he said. "Go home and put it back where it belongs." And I looked at him with my crooked eye. A sexy little Dolly Parton teenybopper I was not.

NINE

My Brothers and Sisters

Now as I was getting on in my teenage years, growing up, so of course were my brothers and sisters. I wasn't that close to my much older brothers, John, Billy, and Jack. Or to Eddie, the oldest—he seemed to be always bossing everybody—though later I was grateful to him because he would stick up for me. I *was* close to his wife. Katherine wasn't beautiful in face, but she had one of the most beautiful souls that God ever created. Katherine became my second mother, although, unlike Momma, she'd always hum out of tune. It would get to us children—"Momma, Katherine's over at the house vacuuming, and she's humming out of tune." "Lord a Mercy, poor little thang." Katherine's vacuum cleaner was fascinating to me. I'd never seen one before. I would put it up to my face—chooooooooooo, against my cheek or my mouth. And to this day I am hung up on vacuum cleaners.

Dean and Gene were twins. Gene and I didn't get along at all—from my view he was real hateful to me for no reason. But Dean was real kind. Now when he was a young man, he would drink and make a point of embarrassing me, especially when some guy I would be trying to impress was around. For instance, when I was a young teenager, I had this boyfriend, Roger. Now Roger was the cat's pajamas. He had a green car with silver trim on it and dual pipes—boom, boom, boom. He'd pull up to take me out somewhere, which was exciting. I was thinking, That's a boyfriend and his car. Wow, I'm a girlfriend! I wouldn't let Roger come in my house because my brothers would be drinking and try to borrow money from him or sic the dogs on him. "No, don't come in," I said. "Just let your pipes go, and then I'll come out."

So this one particular evening, I'd done all the housework, got all the dinner dishes done, and I heard Roger's car going bambabam. At that time Dean was working for Beamon Pontiac, and a car had fallen on his foot, just crushed it. Now, he also had an eye that had been injured years before in a slingshot accident.

So there's Dean at the bottom of the hill, bad eye, his foot in a cast, on crutches, and drunk. And we were parked up there by the driveway.

"Please let's go, let's go!" I'm saying hysterically to Roger.

And Dean's staggering up that hill.

"We gotta go!" I'm practically grabbing the steering wheel.

"No, no, this man wants to say something," says Roger.

So Dean comes up to the window and he knocks on it, and Roger rolls his window down, and I'm thinking, Oh God, oh God.

And I was right.

"#*&****#&####********#####," says Dean.

That's why when I dated I always tried to do better than what we had at home!

But Dean turned out to be one of my favorite brothers. When I was living in a place with no heat, he went and bought me an old tin stove for eight dollars, though he didn't have hardly any money. And he and his wife, Fay, took care of my children when I had to be on the road, although they had children of their own to look after.

I was also not very close to my two oldest sisters. They were very helpful at times, and I'm grateful to them for that. But they got married and moved out of the house when I was pretty young. The main thing, though, was that we never did see eye to eye personality-wise. I was younger and hyper and they didn't understand me. Grace was always criticizing my appearance. She used to come to our house and look in our ears. We'd climb a tree to get away from her.

And Patsy always distrusted my judgment. Here's an example from about 1964. Patsy by then had been through three marriages. The first was just a young girl's fling, the second, a guy who ran a farm in Mississippi and told her to get out when he found she had breast cancer. The third ended tragically after just a year, when her husband Don Dixon died in a truck accident. She took it very hard. She would cry all the time and play music at 2:00, 3:00 in the morning and then go to the gravesite for the rest of the night. Now it's okay to mourn, but that seemed weird to me and I thought she needed help. So I said to her, "I'm bringing around a guy by the name of Jack Murphy, and he's from a well-to-do family, and he's smart, and he's funny, and I think you'll like him." And Grace said, "Don't bring your hoodlum friends around here!" And Patsy agreed. In other words, if I had friends, they were hoodlums. I don't know where my sisters got that. But I brought him around anyway. Patsy ended up marrying him and they had a great marriage until his death this past year. Although Patsy and I didn't always see things the same way, I really love and admire her. She was a mainstay in the family band after Daddy died, playing the autoharp. And now she goes around to music festivals and conferences talking about our family—she's been absolutely wonderful in the way she's promoted our music and kept it in the public eye.

The kids in the family I was closest to were the kids around my age, the ones I ended up performing a lot with—Van, Jimmy, Donna, and Scott.

Van was born just after me, the baby of the family. He was selfish, spoiled, lazy. That's not just me talking. That was the common family opinion. If there was anything to do besides playing music, Van wouldn't do it. But he was a fine musician. He was a terrific singer and one of the best guitar players you ever heard in your life.

He was also great at emceeing, although sometimes he wasn't as attentive to the audience as he should have been. I remember once in the sixties we were playing a charity, the Florence Crittenton Home for

Unwed Mothers. It was supposed to be a very good organization for young single girls who unfortunately got "in the family way."

Now, in general when we played for organizations, we would get asked back, year after year. And Van would always say, "Well, hope to see you again next year!" sort of hinting that the audience should tell the management to hire us again. And then he would rip into our final song. So he started to say that, and I'm beating him on the arm, trying to stop him in midsentence. He's going "Wha . . ? What?" "Van, you can't say that." "Why not?" And he said it anyway. He said "Hope to see you again next year"—to a bunch of young girls in an unwed mothers' home!

I've already talked about how close I was to Jimmy, and about some of the things that happened when we were young kids. Jimmy later developed a slapping technique on the bass that everybody in the bluegrass world tried to imitate. He would really whap on that bass, and he could get a special tone. The sound came partly from the way the instrument was remade. Daddy would take off the strings and the bridge and whittle the neck down on one side. It's going to be harder to play that way, and make blisters on you a thousand times over, but Jimmy would put tape on them and he'd get that sound.

The most brilliant musician of my siblings was of course Scott. We all knew that Scott was the best fiddler that we had ever heard. And he just got better and better as he got older. Sometimes he was playing so frantically the sweat would be pouring down around where the chin rest was, around the tailpiece, and the fiddle would come apart. I've seen him many times try to use strings and rubber bands to hold it together. And I've helped him hold it when he reglued it so he could perform for the rest of the night.

We all played the way Scott told us to. The banjo had a special drive. And he taught Donna a double lick on that mandolin. He also taught me how to talk on the stage. Scott could work an audience until everybody loved him. He was all over that stage. He'd play a real fast song and then he'd say, "I told you I was good. I'm great!" I ended up using that line "I told you I was good" a lot. Scott was the one taught me stage presence and how to communicate energy.

Scott didn't have a special fiddle. He would lose his fiddles, or he'd sell them, or somebody would steal one. People were always stealing Scott's fiddle. It was like a magic thing. If you were playing Scott Stoneman's fiddle, surely you were going to play like him. He put so much of his soul into his playing, surely that fiddle had something of him in it.

And once his fans went so far as to steal *him*. It was a kidnapping, a real kidnapping, by motorcycle riders. They heard him at some place and they really liked him and they wanted him to keep playing for them. He said, "Oh, I gotta go home. I gotta go now, boys." So they kidnapped him and they put him in this barn down in Georgia. They would feed him and take care of him and then have him play for them. I remember him coming in, when he eventually got loose, saying, "Roni, Roni, I swear to God it was awful. I had to dig a hole underneath a board and crawl out at night like a dog would. They kept having me play for them." He looked like a wild man. I said, "Well, that should have suited you fine, Scott. You're always playing all night anyway." But it really bothered him bad. The whole thing seems unbelievable but later there was a story of another musician getting kidnapped, Jerry Foster, a great songwriter. He and his band were in some beer joint singing and playing, and then he left to ride a motorcycle with some guy, and the guy kidnapped him for a few days. Jerry Foster himself told me that story. So it could have been the same bunch that took off Scott. That was just their way! And of course you couldn't go to the police. Who's going to believe some pickers who say that they were kidnapped to play music?

Scott was sweet with his wives. He eventually had four of them. The sweetness, well I remember he got a present for Cecile, his first wife, a nice little dress, and a blouse with ruffles on it. And he wrapped it up the best he knew how, and he'd just sit and stare at the package. He was like a little child, so happy.

I don't want to give the impression that Scott was some noble artist filled with all sorts of virtues. He had his faults like all of us. There was his drinking. That was the main thing. And then he was a conniver type, always sweet-talking you. He'd call me "Aunt Roni" when he wanted something. He did that to all of us. It wouldn't be "Jimmy, I need to use your bass." It would be, "Uncle Jim, honey, why don't you let me use your bass for awhile?" (The "aunt" and "uncle" was referring to all the nieces and nephews from the older married kids.) Scott was always conning us. He'd whup the sweet talk on you, asking for something that you would never allow, but then you'd end up letting him do it.

Scott also could be really irresponsible. Sometimes when we were playing, and he was between wives, he would want to be drinking and picking up girls. So he'd get people up on the stage to play instead of him, and these people often couldn't play for nothing. Scott would say, "Daddy, I swear this man can play better'n I can." And Daddy'd say, "Well, dadblame it, the last time you got somebody up here he couldn't play anything." And Scott would say, "But this one's different." And I knew he was going to be worse.

There was one incident that just about sums up Scott's character. I talked about how I won the banjo contest at Sunset Park but lost the banjo. Well the next year Scott says, "I'm going to go up there and get that banjo for you, Roni." And he did. He went up there and won, even though the banjo wasn't his primary instrument. So he came back with that Vega banjo. And I hugged this banjo, my first new banjo. I loved it. Then one day I went out shopping and when I came back, the banjo was gone. Scott had sold it for liquor. I cried and cried, but somehow I didn't hate him. You could never stay mad at Scott. "I'll get you another one, Aunt Roni, I'll get you another one next year."

Now to my wonderful sister Donna, my wonderful wonderful sister Donna. Donna's four years older than me. She's got, like me, the Frost sense of humor, though her humor and mine are different. Mine is more brash and in-your-face, one-of-the-boys kind of humor. Donna's is more subtle. She's like a subtle southern lady—she'll just look at you in the eyes, and she'll have that twinkle.

Donna is a brilliant musician. She was married at fifteen, to Bob Bean, who later became our family band's business manager. They lived with her in-laws, and I would see her upstairs in that little room that they fixed up for Bobby and Donna, sitting on that tiny secondhand couch, learning her mandolin, practicing what Scott taught her. Then she started also listening to Bill Monroe records. She worked and worked and created her own sound.

Donna is the most true-blue professional, female or male, I ever saw. She was always on the stage when she had to be, always dressed attractively, and she always did her music perfect, always gave 100 percent of herself, down to the bone marrow. When she did fair dates, she would be playing in the heat, with the sun baking down on her, and she would work so hard, dancing as she played, that later when she removed her blouse, it would have a white ring around the bottom from the salt. She was never nasty on the stage. She's always been a perfect sweet young lady. She came out of all that muck, all those honky-tonks and nightclubs we had to play, shining like a penny. I've seen that poor little thing finish playing some nightclub all night long, the smoke positively dripping off of her clothes from cigarettes. And she never never did anything wrong—she never drank, she never smoked, she never partaked of anything bad. There ain't many like that.

It was even more amazing because Donna was really beautiful. She was very concerned about her appearance. She'd get up an hour or two early so she could fix her face, blow-dry her hair.

She was a little stuck on herself, but that was natural because everybody was always saying how pretty she was. She was Daddy's little sweetheart. That's the way it is in a southern family—the pretty girl gets all the attention and always gets bragged on. Actually everybody in the world was in love with little dancing Donna. It wasn't her fault. She was just trying to be helpful to the family band, trying to sell the product. It didn't matter in our family who got the applause, as long as it was got.

And then, this was much later, she was betrayed. Her husband cheated on her. Cheating Donna was like taking candy from a baby, reaching down into a carriage and taking candy. Because she was so innocent and she didn't expect that kind of thing. And it was even worse because Bob Bean not only cheated her, he messed up the finances of the whole family in his job as the band's business manager. She never married again, she just turned to God. That was her way of coping. I'm glad that Donna's life has turned out the way it has. I'm sad that she had a man in her life that made her feel such sorrow. But in our family, a Christian southern family, if you've got Jesus Christ in your heart, you're the richest person in the world.

But I'm getting ahead of myself. People are always asking me about my relationship with Donna. I recall once when I was sitting in a plane with the radio show host Ralph Emery. We were going to a show that he was going to emcee. And he said, "Roni, your sister Donna is so beautiful. I know you're jealous over her. You must just hate her!" I maybe don't have the words exactly right there, but that was the gist of it. And I went, "Huh?" Because I was never jealous of her, never. She never gave me reason to be, for one thing. She always tried to help me look better. She put false eyelashes on me, she gave me lots of her things, clothes, a shoebox full of makeup. She would even buy me new things. And also I felt sorry for her because she was trapped in a way, always having to look beautiful. I had more freedom in my life and in the way I could behave.

But mostly I just loved Donna and felt honored that God had allowed me to have a sister like her that was so beautiful and so talented. I only wish she had more recognition for the things she's done in the music world. Even now she doesn't realize how good she was and still is. Johnny Carson once had on his show Jethro Burns, the great mandolinist, and he said to him, "Well, you must be the best mandolinist in the country!" "No," said Jethro, "Donna Stoneman is."

Donna and Scott were alike in their music, they were so good. It's hard to put into words what made them great when we never did really think about the music that way. It was probably partly that they played extra notes. A guy from Iowa once wrote to Patsy and me and said that he had been trying to decipher Scotty's version of "Ol' Joe Clark" and it took him twenty-eight hours! But there was something else besides the extra notes. I think it had to do with what I was talking about before, the accent, how they punctuated the notes. We all in the family knew how to do that, and I really don't know how we knew, we just knew. It's when you play with your heart and soul.

Recently I saw a program about jazz on the history channel. And you see these wonderful African American people and they were living in such poor conditions. My opinion? You gotta have something good come out of that. So they developed jazz. And I think it was the same thing with the Stonemans. We had hard times, a lot of children, bad circumstances. It was rough. But if you're that pooristic, you have to overcome it in some way. You use whatever talent you've got.

TEN

The Performing Stonemans

I keep mentioning about the family all performing together, so I want to focus for a little on how that went and how we worked with each other. At first when we were young, we'd be going out with Daddy, playing around the Washington area (after I had learned the banjo well enough to avoid those whuppings!). We were called Pop Stoneman and the Little Pebbles. There were other Stoneman family bands, and later we Pebbles would be in different groupings, because practically everyone played at least one instrument, and the makeup of the bands would change depending on who was available. But in any family band, it was the same. We were professionals. We'd keep rehearsing a song over and over until we got it right. Scott was our main guide, as I said, but if someone else was doing the lead singing and wanted the song done a certain way, we would try to do what that person wanted. Nobody was ever arrogant or on anybody's case or anything.

We were careful about the setlist and on that subject we always listened to Scott. To this day I go by his advice. You start off with a fast song to get the audience's attention. Then Scott would say, "And now, ladies and gentlemen, we're gonna play you a half-fast song" (and everybody would laugh), and he'd continue, "not too fast, not too slow, just half fast." Then we'd do a slow song, then a fast one again. And I'd dance around or do some comedy so the audience didn't get bored. After a few more songs, we'd end on a very fast song to rouse everybody up.

We were also real careful about how it all looked to an audience. We didn't use the word choreography, but we were always moving around. At first we'd be all lined up. But then if Scott went forward to take a solo break, I would step in and cover up the spot he left. Or Donna'd move over sometimes. And while Donna would take her break, I'd move to where Donna had been. And Scott would move back to where I had been. We were careful not to leave a hole.

Now when we were little, we had a chance to go to the Juilliard School. I can see it clearly in my mind. We were at home sitting at the table eating when four people came in, all dressed up. They were school authorities, intimidating. My parents were nervous, and my mother stood up because there wasn't room for everybody at the table.

"Mr. Stoneman," said one of the school authorities, "we've noticed that your boys aren't doing real well in school" (the understatement of the year!) "and that instead of playing ball, they sit around making up songs in recess. And we had them tested and know that they are musically talented." ("Tested"?—they'd been performing for years.) "The school district of D.C. is willing to pay for Scott and five of the other children to go up to New York and study music at the Juilliard School."

Daddy was quiet for a moment.

Then he said, "Well, that's real nice. I heard that that's a mighty fine school." He turned to us.

"Kids, that's a mighty fine school. The decision is up to you. Do you want to go?"

Nobody said anything. Then we all looked at Scott. He leaned his chair back so it was teetering on two legs.

"No, Pop," he said, "we want to stay here and play music with you and help you support us."

And that was the end of that.

We sometimes would play shows for wealthy people around the Washington area. And it was surprising to me that many of them didn't have any manners. They didn't regard other people's feelings.

For instance, when I was very young, maybe about nine, we performed at the Virginia Hunt Club for a debutantes' ball. (We didn't know what in the cat's hair a debutantes' ball was.) Donna and I were wearing little cotton dresses Momma had made for us in a calico-like material, and the boys had on shirts, bibbed overalls, straw hats, and red handkerchiefs around their necks.

I remember me and Jimmy getting off the stage. We were not supposed to mix with these people, but we didn't know that. So we went down to where they had the food. And Jimmy said, "Roni, there's some Jell-O on this table." It was a long table and there was this big thing of Jell-O-looking stuff. Jimmy said, "Get you a bowl, Roni." So I got a great big bowl, and we thought, Ah, now we're gonna have Jell-O. We only had Jell-O at school. We didn't have it at home because, well, God, was my mother going to make a barrelful? So we dug into it—and it was horrible tasting. We're spitting it out—pfft, pfft. "That is superb caviar," I heard a lady say.

Then Daddy came looking for us. When we got back up on the stage and were playing, it was clear the boys in the audience were flirting with Donna. They were staring at her and going, "Mmmm, ain't she cute? Ain't she cute?" Momma had made a bow to go with Donna's dress, for her to wear on the back of her head. Long beautiful blond hair and a big wide bow that stuck out on each side of her head. She was so dainty and talented and so just Godawful beautiful! The boys were crazy about her.

Well this made the clodhopper debutantes jealous, and they started nudging each other and making fun of Donna. Donna wasn't noticing them, she was busy playing her instrument, but I saw them. Daddy backed off from the mike for a moment and I walked right up to it. "I saw you girls makin' fun of my sister Donna," I said. "Well, we all die and doo doo!" The girls gasped. The boys were laughing their heads off.

There was another time a few years later that sticks in my mind. We were performing in a place in Virginia where they had steeplechases and fox hunts and such, and the audience was all dressed in those puffy leg things. The room was beautiful wood and had windows with stained glass in them. We were over in the corner playing, playing music for the people to drink by. And they *were* drinking. A guy with one of them outfits on was jumping around, and all of a sudden he fell into us, right into Daddy and all of us kids. The man's friends helped him up, laughing. But they didn't say anything to us. They had no manners about us. They treated us like we were nothing.

This kind of thing often happens to musicians. There's a story told to me by one of the boys who played with Brenda Lee. She was playing at a country club in Ohio. They were going to take Brenda Lee, the star, in the front door but her band around the back. Brenda Lee said, "No, I'm going with the band." She just lifted her dress and splashed through a big old mudhole and went right with the band. Her band loved her.

So there were problems with some of the fancy places my father took us to. But for the most part we were playing in honky-tonks, beer joints, and those were a lot worse. My father did not drink. My mother did not drink. But I heard her say to my dad many times, doing what I called Momma's "statement-making," she'd say, "Ernest Stoneman, every one of your boys is going to turn out to be drunks. 'Cause you're dragging them in such horrible places." And my daddy'd say, "Well, dadblame it, Hattie, I'm trying to keep them out of trouble! If they stay here, they'll get in trouble!" "Well, you got a point there, Ernest. But you gotta find a better place to play." And she'd point her finger right at him. I know Daddy went to his grave thinking about that, feeling guilty about taking us to those places.

Daddy couldn't shelter us. But he would try to teach us. He would say things like, "Remember, Roni, don't ever start drinking. Now, if you start off just having a beer a night, that's not a bad thing, one beer. But if you play every single night, you're gonna end up drinking more and soon it'll be a case a week." I knew he was right.

No matter what kind of place we were playing at, we tried to play the best we could. And that was Daddy's advice too. He said, "No matter how awful the honky-tonk is, you gotta pretend it's the most finest place in the world. Put it in your mind that you're playing a beautiful theater and people are there to listen. 'Cause you never know who's gonna be in there. Always play like somebody's coming in that can get you a TV show or a job with a recording company." And that's what we did.

Grandpa and Grandma Frost. He was a great fiddler and also a great story-teller. He specialized in ghost tales. Grandma specialized in mysterious mountain sayings. (From the collection of Donna Stoneman)

Momma and Daddy. Momma was always ladylike. See how her legs are crossed so elegantly? That was one of the lessons she tried to teach me. I was a hard case. (From the collection of Roni Stoneman)

One of Daddy's early bands, the Dixie Mountaineers. From left to right are Uncle Bolen Frost, Momma, Daddy, Aunt Jack, and Walter Mooney. Aunt Jack said she didn't really play good but just ran her fingers up and down the strings, and nobody knew the difference. She was too modest. The band was recorded at the famous Bristol Sessions of 1927. (From the collection of Patsy Stoneman Murphy)

Some of Daddy's checks from the Edison Company. That was really a lot of money in those days. Momma had silk dresses with purses and shoes to match. (From the collection of Donna Stoneman)

Opposite page top: All of us Stonemans, around 1942 or '43, at the train station in D.C. Back row (left to right)—Billy, Eddie, Grace, John, Patsy. Middle row—Momma, Jack, Gene, Dean, and Scotty. Front row—me, Jimmy, Donna, and Daddy holding Van. (From the collection of Donna Stoneman)

Opposite page bottom: Here we all are (except for Patsy, who was living in Mississippi), in front of our rumble seat truck. Top (left to right) me and Van. Standing, Scott, Momma, Daddy, Grace, Dean, Gene, and Eddie. Sitting, John, Billy, Donna, Jimmy, and Jack. (From the collection of Patsy Stoneman Murphy)

My gorgeous sister Donna with her prized F-5 mandolin. This was about 1955. She would have been around twenty. (From the collection of Donna Stoneman)

Opposite page: Playing on the front porch in Carmody Hills. From left to right, Billy, Momma, me, Daddy, Jimmy, Donna, and Scott. The front lawn would sometimes be packed with people who came to listen. (From the collection of Patsy Stoneman Murphy)

My wedding picture, taken at the local honky-tonk we went to after the ceremony. I was seventeen. The "pearls" are pop-it beads, the flower is paper. I wasn't smiling because I didn't want to show the gap in my teeth. Turned out there wouldn't be a lot to smile about in the next few years. (From the collection of Donna Stoneman)

Before the finals of the banjo contest at Sunset Park, I took Scott's advice and went under a tree and gathered a "clumerage" of fans. The scarf was Donna's advice—to hide my stovepipe neck. I won the contest, but they wouldn't say so and give me the prize, the storebought banjo I needed, because "you're a girl." (Courtesy of Leon Kagarise)

Opposite page: Here I am performing in a banjo contest at Sunset Park. On the guitar is Tony Lake. He taught me about love and table manners. Unfortunately, I couldn't marry him because (1) I was married, and (2) he was from the other—the good—side of the tracks. I got into the finals of the contest. (Courtesy of Leon Kagarise)

Gene and I quickly had four kids. We also had really hard times, with me being the main support of the family, and sometimes both of us being out on the road. The kids were deliriously happy when we finally got a house on the GI Bill and settled down near Nashville, with "real neighbors." Here I am with Eugene, Barbara, Bobby, Becky, and a neighbor. (From the collection of Eugene and Angela Cox)

Donna was famous not only for her mandolin playing but also for her wonderful dancing. The pickup on the mandolin was so she wouldn't have to stay close to the mike. People called her "Little Dancing Donna." (Courtesy of Leon Kagarise)

Grandpa Jones signing autographs at Sunset Park. Here you can see the whitening he used on his eyebrows that I noticed the first time I met him, when I was just a little girl. (Courtesy of Leon Kagarise)

My brother Scotty was the finest country fiddler ever and a great showman. He played so fast and furious, the sweat would be pouring down his face. It would make the fiddle come apart down by the tailpiece. (Courtesy of Leon Kagarise)

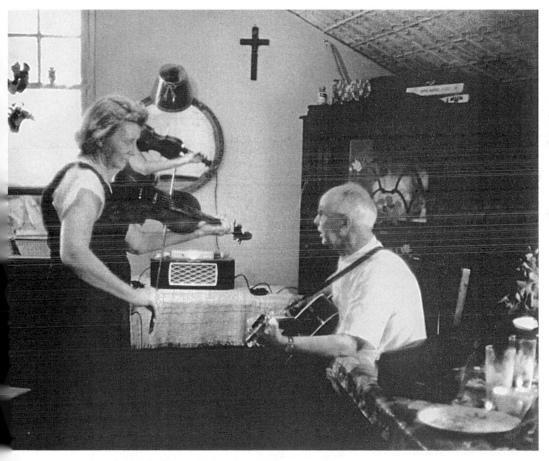

My mother and father in Carmody Hills in 1962. Look at the ceiling. For years when I was very young, we had no real roof, only a canvas tarpaulin. Then Daddy finally got enough money to make a real roof that had tin squares. I used to lie in bed and count them. (Photo by Mike Seeger)

This was the standard lineup for our TV program. From left to right, me, Van, Pop, Jimmy, Donna, and Jerry Monday. Jerry worked with us for several years. This photo shows our stage personalities, Donna sweet and demure, me joking around, and Pop doing his best to deal with us all. (From the collection of Eugene and Angela Cox)

ELEVEN

First Marriage

Now to my marriage, my first marriage, and my little babies. When I met Gene Cox, I was sixteen and playing with the family band at a club called Armstrong's. A guy named Aubrey used to come to hear us a lot, and one day I went over to his table and started talking to him.

"I have a brother that plays the banjo," he said. "He's in the navy."

"In the navy?"

"And he's got a new Gibson."

"A Gibson Mastertone?!"

"Yeah."

My God, I thought, I never saw one in person, except on the stage and that one Scruggs had.

"When is he getting out of the navy?"

"'Bout five months."

"Would you bring him down here . . . with his Gibson Master-tone?"

"Yeah, I'll bring him down."

So Aubrey Cox would come into the bar every so often, and I'd go over to talk to him.

"Your brother's not out of the navy yet, is he?"

"No."

"I can't wait to see that Gibson Mastertone. Do you think he'll let me look at it?"

"Yeah, sure."

One Sunday here comes Aubrey with this guy. I walked over.

"This is my brother Gene, just got out of the navy," Aubrey said.

"Oh, are you the one with the Gibson Mastertone?"

"Yeah, I've got one."

"Where is it at?"

"In my car. In the trunk."

A Gibson Mastertone in the trunk!

"Could you get it out? I'd like to see it: We got time. Daddy's taking a break now."

He went and got it and laid it on top of the table. I looked at it and then just ran my hand over it.

"Can I play it?"

"Yeah, you can play it."

"You can stand right here and watch while I play it."

I got to play it for the whole next set. And then I said to Gene, "Come on down to Carmody Hills, and bring your banjo."

I'm thinking, Wow, he's been in the navy, and he's got a car and he's got a Gibson Mastertone. But it wasn't just those things. Gene was young, very nice-looking, beautiful smile, and he had a way about him that was just wonderful. So he came down, in his 1949 Ford.

"Well, I haven't heard you play at all," I said. "Sit down in that chair there, and let me hear you play." He sat down in one of those homemade chairs and he played. And it was Godawful! I thought, Oh, no, it's terrible. But I can't tell him that. Gosh, I like this feller. Gosh, he's cute. But his roll isn't right. He don't know how to play. And he's got a Gibson Mastertone! My mind was going ninety miles an hour.

"How long you been playing?" I finally asked.

"'Bout a year. I don't play the finger roll exactly like you."

"I know. But I can teach you that."

"Yeah? I'd like to learn the way you do it."

So I started, one, two, three, one, two, three. Whenever he came court-ing, he'd bring his banjo. And we'd sit out in front of the house in his 1949 Ford, and I'd go one, two, three, one, two, three. He'd almost be getting it, and I'd say, "No, no, you're galloping again. Make it smooth—one, two three, one, two, three."

I thought he was my answer to all sad things. We were never going to have an unhappy moment. He was a good man, a kind man, never been in jail, and very important, never been a drunk. He wasn't like the people in the honky-tonks or the men in Carmody Hills or my brothers, always drinking.

Daddy liked Gene a lot, maybe because he played music. But I wasn't sure about Momma. So one day I began to talk to her about him. She was washing dishes. "Momma, I want to get married to him." She didn't say anything for awhile, but I could tell she was upset. I thought she was disappointed because I was so young. "Momma, he's from Virginia like us," I said. He was from Front Royal, around where Patsy Cline grew up. "He's a good man," I continued, "and he doesn't drink." She got real exasperated and she turned around and said, "Honey, you don't have to get a drunk to get a shitass!" I was amazed. She never used words like that. And in fact she said it so properly that it didn't even sound dirty—"shitais."

I didn't know exactly what she meant. And I still don't know, whether it was just because of my age or whether she was concerned because Gene didn't have a whole lot of spark or personality, and she guessed what was coming. Anyway, she turned back to her dishpan, and I went and got married. The wedding was in 1956, April 27. I was just shy of eighteen. Donna lent me her dress—it had a beige background with pink roses on it—and I had a little hat. I wore a necklace of plastic beads, those pop-it ones, which were kind of a beigy white, like pearls. Patsy had fixed my hair and put makeup on my face, rouge on my cheeks. After the wed-ding, we went to the Ozarks Bar and Grill, a D.C. honky-tonk. There was a flower lady walking around and she was also taking pictures. I still have the picture that she took. In that picture my eye is straight. One day when I was putting on my lipstick, my eyes felt funny. When I looked up in the mirror, I realized that my eyes were straight. I thought, Hey I can tell if my eyes are straight by the way they feel. I started practicing. So in my wedding picture my eyes are perfectly straight—although I'm not smiling because I didn't want anybody to see the space in my teeth. Gene had his arm around me, and I was just sitting there, looking like a little innocent child, first day of junior high school.

When we got married, I let him be the banjo player, and I dropped back and started playing the bass fiddle. He's the man, let him play the banjo is what I was thinking. If you could say I was thinking. In those days that's the kind of thing you would do—the June Cleaver time. I was letting him take the lead with the music because I didn't want to hurt his feelings. So he was the one that would go out playing with Daddy. And that was actually all right because I had been married only three months and there I was . . . yep, in the family way.

In fact Gene was playing with Daddy when I went into labor with Eugene. My water broke. I didn't know exactly what had happened, that's how dumb I was. I talked earlier about not knowing much about sex, but the story of my first marriage will really drive the point home—with a sledgehammer! Anyway my girlfriend said, "Oh, my God, your water broke." So I called the place the band was playing—"Gene, I'm ready to go and have the baby. My water broke." And he said, "Can you wait 'til I'm finished playing 'Foggy Mountain Breakdown'?" I laugh about that now, though at the time I was pretty mad. It turned out I could have waited, for that and a lot of other songs. I had a bad time having Eugene, spent thirty-eight hours in labor. No one was with me. The doctors would come in, and the nuns (it was a Catholic hospital), but they weren't helping. The doctor told me he couldn't give me anything because it was meant for the woman to have pain. I remember saying, "Please, just take your fist and knock me out." I was in a haze, a pain-ridden haze. I weighed practically nothing, not one hundred pounds. Eugene, when he eventually got born, weighed eight pounds and he was twenty-three inches long.

The next day my breasts started hardening up really bad. I didn't understand that because nobody told me it was going to happen. Now earlier, six months into the pregnancy, I'd wake up at night and there'd be yellow caking stuff on my arm, where my breasts had laid against my arm. I asked the doctor if that was okay. Oh, yeah, he said, that's fine. But he never actually explained it. Nobody talked to you about your body in those days. Something that God created and was natural and normal—they wouldn't talk about it! The doctor was a female specialist, but he was a very coldhearted human being who would get mad at you because you didn't know anything. Like it was your fault! But I was just a typical mountain girl, and we knew nothing. It's almost tearing to think of—we were just females that could produce children, and the men did us any way they wanted to. I'm proud of the women of today. I'm proud of them knowing so much.

So there I am in the hospital after having Eugene, and I told the nurse, "I'm hurting real bad." They brought a breast pump. They took my milk and gave it to somebody else's baby, and put mine on Similac. The result was my baby had colic for six months. It was meant that I should give my baby my milk. Because even though my breasts had never been big before, they had gotten really big. But no one talked much about nursing in those days. No one told me.

Eugene cried constantly from the colic. And then I got the Asian flu, and he got it. Now the old-timers' way of thinking is that if you nurse your baby, it won't get sick. The baby will have immunities. But of course I wasn't nursing Eugene.

We had an apartment, my first tiny apartment—with running water!—in a place called Gregory Estates. The singer Jimmy Dean lived right over the street from us. We paid sixty-eight dollars a month. Then Gene stopped working. Besides playing banjo with my father occasionally, Gene had a job at a factory. But after Eugene was about seven days old, his father never went back to work, even though they were going to make him a manager. I found out about the whole thing when three women showed up at my door.

"Come on in," I said to them. I remember they sat on my brand new couch. It was plastic, turquoise with little sparkles, and I was so proud of it. I also had a little blond coffee table. The legs screwed up into it. I now know it was really cheap looking, but to me then it was gold.

The women said, "Gene, why didn't you come back to work?" He said, "Well." One woman said, "The boss said he's gonna hire you to be over all of us, and we like you 'cause you're easy to get along with."

"No," he said, "I'm not coming back." She said, "Gene, you got a new baby here and a wife. You gotta come back to work." He never did. He would not work. Gene Cox never gave me child support in all the time of my children's lives. This is hard to understand. I never could comprehend why he wouldn't work. It was like a disease with him. Could be he caught it from his father and the other men in the family. They also didn't work—they would just lay around in bed all day—and Gene told me that when he was in the navy, in submarine training, he stayed in the box doing nothing longer than anybody else. Perfectly happy like that. So maybe I should have foreseen it.

Then three months later, I was pregnant again. It's probably hard to believe, but I didn't know how I got pregnant or how to protect myself. Gene should have told me. He was twenty-six years old when I married him. Why didn't he teach me something? I wasn't the one calling on him at night. I wasn't the one saying, "Knock, knock, can I come in here? Hey, wake up!" I was just trying to get along, trying to be a proper wife and mother. I had diapers up and down the clothesline, hung double or three times. I washed them out by hand, and then I ironed them. I thought that would make me a good mother, and make my baby real pretty and clean. Poor Eugene! I didn't realize I was making the diapers harder, rougher. I was doing everything I knew how to do.

Soon we had no money, were thrown out of the apartment. I didn't have a job, didn't know how to work, didn't know nothing. So I went to live with Gene's mother for awhile. Then she told me to get out, that she could support her son, but not me and the child. She said that my family had more than she did, but in fact they didn't—they were still living in that small house, though Daddy had built another room onto it. But I didn't want to stay with Gene's family anyway because Gene's father had TB.

I wrote to Patsy, who was married to her second husband and living in Mississippi, and she said I could come down there. Gene put me on a Greyhound bus. He didn't seem bothered by my going, if anything glad to get rid of the responsibility of us. I had a terrible time on the trip. Eugene was six months old and colicky and crying all the time and I was pregnant.

When I finally got to Patsy's town, it was the middle of the night and dark as could be. Patsy wasn't there. She later said the bus company hadn't given her the right time. I walked into a room that was like a poolroom. Filled with black people, real beautiful people. There was a cab parked out in front. I hadn't been around any kind of racial divisions much before, so I just walked right into the middle of the room, holding the baby. And I said, "Does anyone know where High Hopes Farm is, or how I can get there?" I guess it was a black nightclub. People were in there laughing, carrying on, music was going, everybody was playing pool and dancing. But all of a sudden there was a hush. I said, "There's a cab out front." A big man stood up. He had a tank top on, and the muscles rippled all over his chest. He'd been working in the fields, I guess. And he said, "I'll take you, little miss." And he took me in this cab. Here I was driving down these lonesome roads out in the middle of nowhere with this stranger. It was scary. But he was a fine man to do that for me.

Patsy treated me well. She didn't have any children, although later she adopted three girls. I was throwing up every morning, then taking care of Eugene. But her husband Horace Cain was not so nice. (He was the one who later kicked her out when she got sick.) I was there two days, and he looked at me and said, "When you're here two days, you're no longer a guest, you're a field hand." I thought, A field hand? What does a field hand do? He went on, "When the baby's asleep, you get out there and start pulling the corn." They needed corn to feed the hogs. So I went out to pull corn. I started pulling and I pulled it the wrong way. I cut the whole inside of my thumb, right where the thumb stretches to meet the forefinger—horrible pain, and blood everywhere. I dashed in the house and said, "I cut my hand real bad." Horace started screaming at the top of his lungs—"You ain't s'posed to pull it toward your thumb. That stuff'll cut ya." "Yeah, I know. I found out." So then I started doing the housework instead. As much as I could. But I had to take care of the baby too, and I never did feel I did my share. So when Gene came down a few months later, we went back together. By that time Gene's father was going into a sanitarium, so there was no worry about the TB.

Patsy was not only good to me, she was also good to her workers. She would have a lot of the farm people come in and she would feed them. And I learned a lot about the black people down there, about some of their beliefs and how nice they were.

So I came back to Maryland. But Gene's mother then put me out again. Said she couldn't take in both Gene and me. She wasn't mad at him—she'd let him sleep on the couch all day, which seemed strange to me. But anyway I had to go to Mommy again. I had a carriage somebody had given me, out of the trash, and I scrubbed it with Lysol. I put Eugene's clothes in it to make a little mattress, and I put a blanket over it and laid him down, and pushed the carriage down to Carmody Hills, which was several miles away. I was barefooted and pregnant. It was summertime and I had no shoes. Gene wasn't working. His mother wasn't going to buy me shoes. People laugh, "Aw, keep her barefoot and pregnant!" How many rednecks have you heard say that? It's not a funny line, not when you've been through it. I don't care if you've *never* been through it. It is not funny. It's a total disrespect for God, to talk about any human being like that. It was so hot out. There was no sidewalk, so I walked on the street. The tar bubbles were burning my feet, making blisters.

When I finally got there, Momma said, "We don't have much, but you're welcome to stay, anytime." Then, just before Becky was born, I found a place right up the street, in a basement for twenty-five dollars a week. It was really nice. It had a bedroom and a little living room and a small kitchen.

When I had Becky, I went into Prince George's Hospital. They took good care of me there. They gave me this new thing called a saddle block. They turned me on my side and put a needle in my spine and taped it there and poured in the painkillers. It was great. But I was so hungry. I said, "Can I get something to eat?" And the doctor said, "What do you want?" "I'd like . . . Can I have a piece of meat?" And they brought me up a steak, potato, salad, and peas. I ate every bit of it, much to the doctors' amazement. I thought, Hey this is cool, no pain, and I'm getting to eat! Then I was laying on my side and I started hearing music, like a thousand voices. Real angelic, though I didn't know the word at the time. It was like the heavens had opened up, and I saw big white wings all over the sky. I dozed off. Then it happened again, and I thought, Surely there's a radio on here somewhere. So I called, "Doctor, I hear the prettiest singing. Is there a radio somewhere around?" He said, "No, I don't believe so." He smiled. I dozed off again, and I heard it again. Real loud. It was like harmony with thousands of beautiful women's voices. And then I said, "Y'all better come in here. I feel the baby down there." And Becky was born.

I went home to my basement apartment. Gene was still at his mother's. And then the rains came. There was a hole in the wall, and the water got up to my knees. This was when I was three days out of the hospital. I took one of the overstuffed chairs that was in there and I piled it up with pillows, and put Becky safe in it in a little carrier. Then I put Eugene beside her in another chair, and I said, "Now, honey, you stay right there until Mommy can get rid of this water." He was so good. He stayed there—fifteen months old—knowing not to get down in that water. I was mopping and mopping, and wringing the water out in a pail and then emptying the pail. And then mopping again, exhausted and weak, just out of the hospital. I stayed in that apartment as long as I could. On the days it wasn't raining, the babies were happy. Eugene was playing on the floor. But it started raining again soon after, and I couldn't let him down into the water. So I had to go back living with Mommy again.

Why didn't I leave Gene? Well, there was no place to go. I couldn't make a decent living, on account of being a junior high school dropout, and I was sure no other man would want somebody with two little babies.

So Gene would be around occasionally, helping with the babysitting, and I'd get pregnant again.

Then I had a miscarriage. Momma said, "Now be careful, you can get in a family way real quick after you've had a miscarriage. You're very susceptible. Any time a woman has any cleaning out, she can get pregnant real easy." And, sure enough, I got pregnant with Barbara three or four months later.

I was occasionally playing music to get some money. I would play bass fiddle if I could get jobs in the honky-tonks around the Washington area. It wasn't much money but it was enough to let me rent a place up in Carmody Hills, a big old house that had been empty for about five or six years, which was why I could afford it. And Gene came with me. That's the way we worked it. I'd live with him off and on. Off, he'd go back and stay with his mother. I liked the house, but there was a road right there, and I thought, How am I gonna keep Eugene and Becky from running out on the road? Maybe if I fixed up the backyard. So I started picking up the trash. "Gene, can you help me?" I'd call. And he'd just sit in the living room on an old couch that someone had given me (I'd sewn on pieces of sheet to cover the holes). I washed thirty-six windows, scrubbed all the filthy floors, and I squirted down an old rug with a hose so the children could have a clean place to play on. Gene just sat in the house playing the banjo. I went through that whole pregnancy sleeping on springs covered with coats from the Salvation Army.

The baby was way overdue. I was hurting so bad they thought at first I had appendicitis. Gene finally took me to a specialist, who said that I had a kidney infection. But he wouldn't take care of me because I didn't have any insurance. About a week later I went to the hospital with severe pain. They gave me some pills and sent me home. I remember trying to take care of the two babies. I looked out the window and the road was going up and down, like a wave. The doctors were holding off my labor, I don't know why. About midnight I started bleeding and went back to the hospital. The woman there said, "What's your problem?" "I think I'm pregnant." Blood and water was running down my legs, and I'm standing there, pregnant as all the world could see. Then they took me in the labor room, and all these interns were gouging at me. I was in agonizing pain, hadn't even had an aspirin.

So finally in comes the obstetrician. By this time there are four interns on the left side of my bed. The doctor started working with me. The baby was just doing flip-flops. I was so thin you could see the whole imprint of it. And then he said, "Here, feel. What do you think this is?" to the four interns. There I am, in ghastly pain and they're taking a decision of what that was, sticking out of me! "I don't know." "Is that the bladder?" "You knot-head," said the doctor, "that's the buttocks." Well, the buttocks of the baby coming out—that's not the right way for a baby to come out. "Don't use the forceps, oh, please, don't hurt my baby," I cried. "I'm not, honey," he says, and he squeezed my hand. "We'll take care of this right away." He started turning the baby and he brought her out feet first.

I came home with Barbara, my beautiful, sweet-looking baby. What a lovely child she was. But I noticed she would stare at the light that I had on while I was changing her diaper. And she'd smile the weirdest smile.

After Barbara was born, I had another miscarriage.

I had had to give up the house, and now I was living in another basement apartment, with just a half-bath and two small rooms. I went to the lady upstairs, and I said, "Do you know where I can get something to do so I make sure that I pay you every week for my rent? I'll do any kind of work." She said, "Well, I run church bazaars, and I could use somebody to clean the clothes. We'd give you one dollar a basket for clothes, washed and ironed." So I'd go upstairs and pick up the baskets, and I'd wash the clothes by hand on a scrub board. I did that for three years. I did it well. The people at the church didn't know that I didn't have a washing machine. If they had known, they probably wouldn't have given me the job.

Then Mr. Sam Bomstein, who had seen me playing with Scott earlier, said, "I will hire you as a banjo player with Johnny Hopkins's band. I won't hire you as a bass player. Banjo is your instrument." So I would play at the Famous Bar and Grill, which was a raucous place right near the bus terminal. It was during this time that I got my very own Gibson Mastertone. Scott took me down to Fred Walker's music store, and he made sure that I got the banjo that was right for me. I paid eight hundred dollars for it, traded in the banjo Daddy had made me and arranged to make the payments in installments. But the saxophonist in Hopkins's band didn't really want me, so I didn't have steady work.

Well, there I am, in that small apartment, taking care of my babies, and doing laundry, and occasionally playing music at night. It was hard. It's all right when it's summer or spring because you can let the children play in the yard, but try to take care of children in a small room in the winter. The couch was a pullout, and you'd have to pull it out every day for you and your husband to sleep in. The children slept in a little cot in the corner and a baby crib.

One night, it was about 2:00 or 3:00 in the morning, I'd just finished feeding the baby, Barbara, and I sat down at the table. I had three chairs around that old table. I sat down and I took a pad and pencil. I thought, Oh God, Oh God, in Jesus' name, I need more money. Show me how to make a living for these babies. And I wrote down a whole list of things I could do—take care of children, take care of a house, wash dishes, cook, take in laundry. Then at the end of the list I put music. I started crying. I laid my head down on that table and I cried so severely. I couldn't make much noise because I couldn't wake up the children, but I cried and cried. Because I knew it was going to have to be music, and that I would really have to make a steady job of it. And when I thought of music, I thought of the honky-tonks. How the men'd be drunk, fall around, puke, try to dance in it. "Hey, honey, play such and such." And how the fights would break out. Those places were called skull orchards—for good reason. I would be being away from my babies for that.

So I talked to Sam Bomstein and he intervened with the saxophonist on my behalf and I started playing more regularly with Johnny Hopkins. Scott made me a pitch pot for the stage. I would say to the crowd, as Scott always said, "If you don't pitch in the pot tonight, tomorrow we won't have a pot to pitch in!" And I would sing my Kitty Wells songs, and my old songs, and the band would give me my share of the tips and I would be able to buy food for the babies and make my monthly payments on my Gibson Mastertone. But it wasn't easy. I played music 'til 3:30 at night and then I'd get home about 4:00. Six hours a night, six nights a week. In the middle of the night I'd take the bus and then walk from Seat Pleasant down to Carmody Hills, all through the bad section of town. When I got home, Gene would be just sleeping there. And then I'd wake up at 6:00 with the baby and during the day I'd take care of the kids and do the washing and ironing, one dollar a basket.

It certainly was hard times. But I don't want to leave the wrong impression. There were also a lot of wonderful times when I was raising my children. I just adored being with them. I would take them to the pond to watch the insects skimming over the water. I would get down on the floor with them and make dolls of sticks and toilet paper. I would always be hugging them and loving them and rocking them. There was a song I sang to each one, usually when I was in a rocking chair, holding and rocking them—"Old Shep." At first, when they were very little, I'd explain the song. *When I was a lad . . .* I'd sing, and then stop and say, "That means a little boy." *And Old Shep was a pup* ("That was his little doggie, named Shep. He was a tiny puppy.") And then I'd go on singing and explaining about how the boy and his dog used to roam around the countryside together ("'Meadows' means fields of pretty flowers"), and how Old Shep saved him when he was drowning ("The little boy was drowning, and the dog knew it and he jumped in and he pulled that little boy out and saved his life!"), and then how Shep got older and started failing—*His eyes were fast growing dim*—and the doctor said that there was nothing he could do. ("That meant Old Shep was going to die. The doctor couldn't stop it. That's the way life is.") As we were rocking, tears would be coming down the child's cheeks. And then I'd sing about how the boy tried to shoot Old Shep to put him out of his misery, but he couldn't make himself do it. And then we'd get to the last words of the song about how Old Shep was dead and the boy was missing him, but he knew that *Old Shep he has gone where the good doggies go* and now had a *wonderful home*. The children would cry and cry, but it was good, to teach them about compassion, to be compassionate. As they got older, of course, you didn't have to explain it so much. And their eyes would get brighter and brighter as I sang and hugged them and rocked them. They still talk about that song to this day. And so do I.

TWELVE

The Stoneman Family Band Comes Together

During the time I was playing with the Johnny Hopkins band at Sam Bomstein's Famous Bar and Grill, Scott had formed a new band. He called it the Blue Grass Champs because all the musicians had won contests. At first the band consisted of Scott, Donna, Jimmy, Porter Church on banjo, and Jimmy Case on guitar, but after awhile Jimmy Case left and Scott hired Van. "I want Van," he said. "He's my brother and he plays good enough to play with us." They were also playing the Famous. (Sam Bomstein really loved the Stonemans.)

I remember one night when my band was off and the Blue Grass Champs were on, coming down to listen to them. And they were brilliant. Brilliant. Donna was so good. She did "Rawhide"—de daddiddle di. Then Scott came in with that fiddle. And Jimmy riding the bass. And I'm looking one to the other. I couldn't decide which one I wanted to look at, they were all so good! I sure wasn't the only person to think that. They won the Warrenton band contest. And they got on TV, on the *Arthur Godfrey Talent Show,* and they won that.

I didn't think I was going to ever be able to play with the Blue Grass Champs because I had a bunch of kids and wasn't able to "woodshed" a lot—that means practice. But Bob Bean, who was managing the Blue Grass Champs, came into the Famous one night when I was performing, because he found he couldn't depend on Porter Church, the banjo player, unfortunately, though fortunately for me. And Bob said, "You're playing real good, Roni. Would you like to play with the Blue Grass Champs next week at the Charles Hotel?" So Sam let me off, said that he was glad to see me go with my family. But I was very insecure because I knew how great they were. I remember sitting in the car going to our first performance, and I was just silent, didn't say anything the whole trip, scared to death.

I did okay. The first times I played with them, I was timid, but they kept pushing me to take solo breaks. Donna would say, "Roni, you're going out there!"—and soon I got the hang of it and became a regular with the group. Then after awhile Pop joined it, and it became all Stonemans, the Stoneman Family Band.

Sam Bomstein was always in the corner of the Stonemans. He was even helpful with my clothes. When he first gave me that job playing with Johnny Hopkins, he came to me and said, "Roni, you've got to buy you a better dress." Because even though I would try to fix myself up, I still looked real shabby. He said, "Here's thirty-five dollars. Go buy yourself something pretty to wear." Well, Donna had a couple of dresses that I thought were really cute, and I knew Sam liked those. (Sam had also given her money to buy some new clothes, telling her he wanted her to look more "shapely." He knew Donna better than to say "sexy"!) So I gave her the thirty-five dollars to buy something new, and she gave me two dresses and a necklace and a pair of earrings. We killed two birds with one stone.

We really liked playing together. Donna always talks about how we had a . . . well, it was a message with our eyes. All we had to do was look at each other's eyes, and we knew what the other was thinking. She would look, and I would look, and we just knew. We would start giggling.

We had special fun with some of the husbands and wives in the audiences. Because I wasn't the pretty one, the wives thought it was okay for the husbands to look at me. But they weren't to look at Donna—then the wives would poke at them! "Don't you dare look at her! I know you're just flirting with her!" And Donna was so innocent and doing her thing, but those women were terrible to her. So I'd whisper, "Donna, see that lady over there. She really hates you. Look at her eyes, every time you move. And she won't let her husband look over in your direction. But she trusts me. Watch this! I'm gonna flirt with him now." The husband would look up at me, and I would wink and purse my lips. And the wife was so busy with Donna, she wouldn't even notice me. It was a learning experience, like a college course in psychology. Donna and I had all kinds of fun. I loved performing with her.

THIRTEEN

Opry

So we Stonemans were in Washington, playing regularly at the Famous Bar and Grill and around town. And in 1962 a man named Billy Barton, who was always trying to help us, managed to get us a guest spot on the Grand Ole Opry. Wow, were we excited! This was our big chance. We practiced and practiced.

Don Dixon, the man who married Patsy and was killed a year later in a car accident, drove us down in a bus. When we got to the parking lot, we were supposed to pay for the parking, but we didn't have any money. Daddy said, "Dadblame it, I'm Pop Stoneman. We came all the way down from Washington, and we don't . . . we barely have gas and food to get here. We ain't got any money for no parking ticket." The parking attendant said, "Right over here, Mr. Stoneman."

So we parked, and we all got backstage at the Opry. We're standing around, and I was holding my banjo. I'm several months pregnant with my fourth child, Bobby, but I don't show it because I only weighed 118 pounds. Me and Donna had these full skirts on, made of the material of a red handkerchief, and little white cowboy boots. I was getting real nervous because we were going to do "Orange Blossom Special," and that was Scott's showpiece number. I was thinking, Oh, God, I hope I can kick it off good. Oh, God, I hope my fingers go fast enough to keep up with Scott.

Then Billy Barton came over and took us aside—Daddy, Donna, Jimmy, Van, me, and Scott. He'd been talking to the big boys backstage.

"Let me tell you something," he said. "And I want you to remember this. Don't play too good tonight."

We all stared at him.

"What do you mean, don't play too good?" said Scott.

"You can't play too good because you can't make the stars on this show jealous of you. You make them jealous, you won't be asked back. Just don't play too fast. Just play normal."

"You're saying we're not supposed to play good?"

"I mean it, Scott. Don't do all those extra things. Don't play like you usually do. I mean it." And Billy Barton walked away.

Daddy was just standing there. He had his old cane and he looked so sad.

I was thinking and I was worried. I was really perplexed about what I was going to do.

"How do you not play good? How do you not play what you been working on?" I said. "I don't know how we're gonna do that."

"We're not," says Scott.

We all looked at him.

"We're gonna make a stompin' contest out of this," says Scott. "We're gonna play better than we ever played in our lives—just for them telling us that. We're gonna get out there and we're gonna show them what Stonemans' music is really like. We're gonna leave our blood on the stage!"

Then he said, "Now, Donna, when I hit that floor with 'Orange Blossom Special,' playing that fiddle behind my back, don't try to hold the mike down like you usually do, just keep that shuffle going. And, Roni, keep that banjo ringing. 'Cause there's a live audience out there. We're gonna play for that audience. And when the people out there in radioland hear the audience screaming for us, they're gonna say, 'What is going on there?' Then they're gonna know who that bunch is!"

Well, we were to be the guests on Hank Snow's portion of the show. And he announced us, "Here they are, ladies and gentlemen, the Stoneman Family." I get a chill, real goose bumps popping out on my skin, just thinking about it, how it was when I walked out on that stage and kicked off "The Orange Blossom Special." We were playing so fast and clear. And then Scott dropped the bow from his hands to his knees. Played the fiddle upside down on it. Dropped the bow again, perfectly, landed it right between his feet. Again played with the fiddle upside down against the bow. Grabbed the fiddle up, bent down on his knees, and played behind his back. Got back up, then jumped in the air, about two or three feet, and just kicked out, right with the music! I mean he flat out put it down the road. I was thinking, We're going to town, Dear God in Jesus' name, let my fingers keep up. Poor ol' Daddy just played as fast as he could go, that old-fashioned guitar lick, "boom chuck chuck chuck." Donna was really picking good. And Jimmy beat that bass. We were afraid that he was going to have a seizure because he would have seizures at the worst times. When it came time not to have a seizure, Jimmy would have one, and then he'd start walking around the stage like a zombie, or sit down on the floor, or drop his bass. But when we played that night, he was fine. And after "Orange Blossom Special" we did "White Lightning No. 2," which has impersonations of the top country stars.

People started screaming. They gave us twenty minutes in applause, a standing ovation. We came off the stage, wild-eyed. Hank Snow went out and he said, "Let's hear it for them, ladies and gentlemen, the Stoneman Family!" But as he passed us, he muttered, "You won't hear from them again." He didn't get to sing another song on his half hour of the show because the twenty minutes of applause took up his time.

So we didn't get asked back for many years. But it was worth it.

FOURTEEN

My First Love Affair: Glen Roquevort/Tony Lake

Only one guy here. I gotta say that before you get the wrong impression. His name was Glen Roquevort, though he called himself Tony Lake for his career, which he planned to be acting and singing.

Now, I basically considered myself separated from Gene, although he would occasionally be staying with us. But the children were still very small, really like stair steps. And I had nobody to care about me. Then Tony Lake walked into my life. He was a gentleman, had been trained right. His father and mother were Spanish and French, from New Orleans. Tony was a student, and he was real slick. He was voted as the Best Dresser of the University of Maryland at College Park, had a new car, was handsome, and played the guitar well. He also was a very good singer—he won the Best Singer of the Year in the contest at Warrenton.

We started dating. There I was, a one-room-shack girl with four kids, trying to raise them herself, taking in washing and ironing, and playing music all night. And I had this fellow come into my life, bringing me into this other world. It was just like going from a cave out into the sunshine.

Tony cared about me a lot. He tried to teach me how to sing. He'd sing *"Onnnnnce on a higgghhhhhh and winnnnnndy hill . . ."* or *"Whyyyyyy does the sun go on shinnnnnning?"* He was taking voice lessons at a Catholic university. I'd be outside in his convertible, sitting there and waiting. I'd be hearing voices singing "Ahhhh, ahhhh, ahhhh, ahhhh, ah, ah, ah," scales. I'd say to myself, why does he have to do all that ah, ah, ah, ah, ah? Well, he must know what he's doing. Then I'd get confused about myself. I'd see all these people going in, getting their lessons. And here I was, untrained and unlearned. But I was the one trying to make a living playing music. I didn't think of it as a career, or a business. I just thought I could go play tonight and make some money. Yet we Stonemans were so good that these same people taking the lessons came to see us!

Then one day Tony said he would like to go away for the weekend. I knew what that meant, but it was long into our friendship, and I really liked him, so I said okay. "Just pack an overnight bag," he said. I wasn't sure what an overnight bag was, but I borrowed my girlfriend's makeup kit, which was a good size, so I guessed it was like an overnight bag. I was real nervous and excited. He was Catholic, and first we were going to a Catholic church, the Shrine of the Immaculate Conception. Momma had made me a special outfit for that, a little skirt and vest, beige with green leaves on it, and she had sewn a little square thing to put on my hair. She was thrilled that I was going to the Shrine of the Immaculate Conception. I remember telling her about it—me with my four kids! And then from there we were going away for the weekend. She didn't know about that. For the first time I had a babysitter to take care of the kids.

We walked into the Shrine of the Immaculate Conception, and I was scared because I didn't know what I was supposed to do. "Just follow me," said Tony. I was seeing people pulling water on their faces as they went in. So I followed Tony in and flipped some water on me, a little spray. I thought that was okay, maybe. He didn't see me do it, anyway, because I was behind him. And as we walked inside, it was so beautiful, beautiful paintings in gold and blue. The ceiling was like heaven, just gorgeous. I was staring up, looking at it in wonder. Because my previous experience had only been with little country churches in the woods, places where you'd sing *Are you washed in the blood of the Lamb / In the soul-cleansing blood of the Lamb? / Are your garments spotless, are they white as snow? / Are you washed in the blood of the Lamb?* This was totally different.

I didn't know he was going to kneel. So I kept walking along, staring up at that beautiful ceiling. But he did kneel. And I stepped right into him. I fell. And . . . well, it was like I was rolling, because there was a downhill drag. I rolled head over heels to the altar, my legs up in the air. It took two choirboys and a priest to get me up.

And then when I came back to the seat, I sat down and he pinched me. He was real mad at me. I'm sitting there pinched, nervous, not knowing what to do, wanting so hard to make my best impression. That little square on my head is already turned sideways.

So afterwards we're driving to Virginia, and it's clear he's starting to get nervous too. I'm beginning to suspect it was his first time out on the track. He stopped and called his mother four different times on the highway, from little phone booths.

We got to this hotel. It was a nice hotel, but I was ashamed because I thought everybody in the world knew it was me coming in with someone I wasn't married to. It was also my first time on the track, so to speak, because I hadn't done this kind of thing before.

Then we went in the room. And . . . well, it took forever. It was just a nightmare of foreverness. By then I was sure it was his first time. So we discussed things—the children, was my husband a drinker? That kind of thing. We made love eventually, but it was nothing special, just basic sex, not wonderful sex.

I felt awful afterwards. I felt like I was bad. Even though I was separated, even though Gene was not a good husband, and even though Tony was a nice young man, I still felt I had done a terribly wrong thing.

The next morning we went to Mount Vernon. He wanted me to see it. He taught me about history there, about Martha Custis Washington. I learned she was George's second wife, or he was her second husband, and I remember that to this day. Tony made a big point of this not just being a one-night stand. He was a gentleman. I think that's why I don't have one-night stands—because he taught me to have pride in myself. He really cared for me, and so later things got better in the sex department. I hate even using that word. Because it seems to mean just a boy and girl, and what we had was intimacy and loving and caring.

He also taught me other things. He took me out to expensive restaurants, and he taught me about table manners. Because, well, if you're from a big family and you're sitting at a table with benches and homemade chairs, when are you going to learn table manners, like how to eat with the right fork and use a salad bowl? We were not such as that. We were lucky we had food. Daddy or Momma said grace and we went at it. Sometimes it was worse. Momma'd fix supper and we'd sit down. Then she'd go out on the porch to have peace and quiet for just a little while, and Scott would say, "Hit that key, Roni." And he'd pull his chair back and say, "All right now, when I say go, everybody start singing 'cause we gotta practice this song." And we'd sit there eating and practicing harmony. Then Momma'd come in with the hickory: "Stop singing at the table." "Momma, we gotta. We gotta get that part just right!" We'd be sitting at the table with our arms around our plates, shielding them. Because if you weren't careful, someone would go, "Give me some of that" and grab—even if you'd just sung a gospel song with the most heavenly harmony.

Tony showed me a different life. I remember sitting in one beautiful restaurant. He told me how to use my fork and how to cut with the knife. And then he said, "When you cut your meat, you put your knife here. Some people will put their knife like this, across the plate. But it's better to put the knife on the edge." Unfortunately there were some things he forgot to tell me.

Now, Tony's mother and father found out about me and naturally they wanted to meet me. So Tony arranged a dinner at a fancy restaurant—the Black Angus, downtown Washington. I guess he was pretty serious about us or he wouldn't have done this. Tony was about six foot one. His father was shorter, but a very handsome man. His mother had black eyes and black hair, was a beautiful woman. We walk to the table and Tony pulls the chair out for me. But this was one of the things he hadn't told me when we were doing the table manners. He pulled the chair out and I went oopp. And I almost fell on the floor. "I'm sorry," I murmured. He scowled at me with his Spanish eyes. His father smiled. His mother just looked.

So I'm sitting there, nervous and stiff, and the waiter brought the finger bowl—another thing that Tony hadn't covered in those table manners lessons. I drank it. This whole thing sounds like some *Hee Haw* skit, I know, but, believe me, it really happened. They all blinked their eyes.

Then we're eating away, and they're talking, and his mother suddenly said, "Well, Veronica, what do you think of Glen taking over his father's business?" It was a catering business, one of the biggest in D.C. She said, "Glen wants a singing career. But we want him to take over his father's business. What do you think about that?" I looked at her and I said, "I think he ought to make up his own mind. If he wants to be a singer, well, he's good now, but he's got a long row to hoe."

Tony kicked me under the table. His father was grinning at both of us. His mother probably was thinking, I'm gonna kill that kid.

How the affair ended? Well, the Stonemans were playing the Famous. Tony used to come down and see me pretty often and on one particular night he brought a friend of his, and they were sitting in the audience. Now I was really picking some good banjo. And in the door walks Bobby Bare: *I wanna go home.* Remember that, *I wanna go home?* And there was *Four winds that blow lonely / Seven seas that run high.* That was on the flip side. Bobby Bare, the handsome Bobby Bare, from Nashville and the Grand Ole Opry! He came in to hear us play! Whewww! Well, he was watching us, and then he came over to me.

"I sure like your singing, Bobby Bare," I said.

"Would you like to go to a party?"

"Yes." Wow, here I was, getting to go to a party with an Opry star! I went over to Tony.

"Tony, I'm going to a party with him."

"You better not."

"Whaddya mean I better not?"

"You better not go off with him. That'll be the end of us."

"But Tony, I gotta go. This is an Opry star. And I wanna go to the party. I wanna meet those musicians."

"You go with him, I'll never see you again."

So I said, "Bobby, I can't . . . my boyfriend . . . he don't want me to."

"C'mon, let's go," said Bobby. "You should be in Nashville. You'll never see him again. You got to be more interested in your career. It's gonna take politics and being around the people in the business." And

Bobby put his hands on both my shoulders and he steered me away from Tony.

Well, the evening turned out badly. The party was nothing much, and afterwards in Bobby's hotel room (I went there—that's how innocent I was!) I had to tell him I wasn't about to be a little fling. But I had no way of foreseeing all that. And, looking back, I can remember how I was thinking that night, why I did what I did. I was in a difficult situation. There I was with four children, and I had to work toward goals to better my career so I could get my kids out of Carmody Hills. I wanted to be around people who were from the Opry so I'd know what was expected of me when I got to Nashville for good, not just doing a one-shot guest appearance.

But I'll never forget it, that night at the Famous. Tony had that friend with him from the university, and I know what I did humiliated him no end. Because I wasn't pretty in the first place and he was such a handsome and nice man. He saw me turn and go off with Bobby. I looked back—it was raining, a kind of a drizzling rain—and I saw his feet running across in that water. He got in his car and drove away.

So I had somebody to care about me, and then I turn around and shuck it all. But in reality me and Tony . . . there was absolutely no way that could have continued. We were truly from separate worlds. He didn't know my world of hard times and stark naked poverty. And I could not have gone into his world. I know because later, with other men, I tried, but it never worked out.

FIFTEEN

Out West

The people managing the family band, Bob Bean and a new promoter-agent, Jack Clement, decided that we needed to perform in the West to get better known. So in 1964 we went out there. First stop, for some shows and some recording, was Beaumont, Texas, George Jones territory. In fact once George came around to borrow our bus. It was raining and he took it over to his house and got it bogged down in the ground, just ran it up to the axle in mud. It never did work right after that—every time we'd get in a rainstorm, it would quit on us. He was drinking when he did it, of course. That was before he sobered up.

After a few weeks, we went to California. Jack Clement had the boys dress in sweaters and slacks, and had us billed as "folk music," to take advantage of what they were calling the folk music boom. We played Disneyland and clubs like the Ash Grove and the Hollywood Troubadour.

We had some fun times out there, and caused quite a stir. People were always talking about this wonderful Stoneman family, with all these "amazing" children that played so well. I remember one time in particular in the early days when a TV reporter was interviewing Mommy and Daddy:

"Mrs. Stoneman, how does it feel to have such amazing children?"

"Aaaagh," said my mother, and rolled her eyes and sank down in the chair.

"Get her off that mike!" cried Bob Bean. "Get Pop on there, get Pop!"

So they moved the mike to Pop.

"How you doin', Pop?" said the interviewer. "They call you Pop, don't they? 'S all right if I call you Pop?"

"Don't matter to me a'tall," said Daddy.

"How ya doin'?"

"We're starving to death, that's how."

Me and Donna were backstage, doubled over laughing. And Bob Bean and Jack Clement were going, "Quick, quick, get Pop off there, put the camera on somebody else." They were really panicked. You gotta pretend like you're not hungry on a big television station in L.A.

And there's another memory I love from California. We would often play in California in the next few years, so I'm not sure of the exact date of this. Anyway, we were playing the American Pie club in San Francisco. The bands that went on before us were college students, about my age, trying to play country songs. I was a little peeved at them—well, let's come right out with it, jealous—because they went to college and I didn't. I was thinking, They don't have to do this and I do. They got other ways of making a living. Why do they want to play our music? And they were not doing it right. For instance, one band tried to do "Act Naturally," the Buck Owens song, and they would sing it *They are go-ing to put me in the mo-vies / They are go-ing to make a big star out of me.* Saying each syllable real clear. Instead of *They're gonna make a big star outta me.* I was thinking, Oh, how can anybody murder a song so bad!

We were standing around, getting ready to go on. Daddy and my brothers had on sweaters and slacks. Donna and I had on starched full skirts with ruffled blouses, red and blue, that we had made, and little white boots. And our hair was done just so. We were all so prim and proper.

Some guys came up to us, five of them. This is back when the natives weren't resting very well at Berkeley. These were students and they were rank, long straggly greasy hair and beads everywhere. Hippie City.

And one of them said to me, "Does she play that?" He was grinning and pointing to Donna sitting there so prissy with her mandolin. I said, "Uh, yeah." And I looked at them and I thought, Now they're gonna make fun of us 'cause we're hillbillies. So I said, "Yep, she's been playin' 'bout three, four weeks." I got real hillbilly, even more so than I naturally am—which is hard to do. And they looked at Scott, had rosin all over his fiddle, walking around the back of the stage, antsy to get on. And they said, "He plays that fiddle?" "Well, he don't have much hair on the bow 'cause it's an old used one, but he's been tryin' to learn to play." And Jimmy had his old bass, splinters all over the side of it, and one of the hippies said, "Guess he's learning that." "Yeah, he got it from a buddy of his." The hippie looked at Van, who had a hole in his guitar where he'd picked so hard and fast. "He's been taking some lessons," I said. And I told them I'd been playing my banjo "'bout a month."

Then I said in a real innocent voice, "We're gonna try and play good for you today. We're gonna work real hard for y'all." They looked at each other. One of them muttered, "This I gotta see," and they snickered. Then they went and sat down in the front row, crossed their arms, and stared up at us.

The announcer said, "Here they are, ladies and gentlemen, the singin', swingin' Stonemans." Well we cut down on "Cimarron" in the fastest way, ripped right into it, *Cimarron, roll on . . .* Scott was bearing down on that fiddle, Jimmy slapping that bass, Donna playing all those diddley notes. I took my banjo break, and I played as hard and fast as I could go, looking straight at them. (With my left eye, of course. My right eye, as usual, was doing its own thing.) And the hippies went, "Oh my God," and they slipped down into their seats, all five of them at the same time.

As I was putting my banjo away in its old beat-up case, the guys opened the backstage door, and all together they said again, "Oh my God!"

Then there was the time in California when we were playing, and the strobe lights were going, and Jimmy had a seizure on stage.

"Groovy," hollered the hippies. "Man, he's really grooving!"

The sound man, wearing an obscene tee shirt, came over and held the microphone in Jimmy's face.

"No, no, he's having a seizure!" I cried, trying to shoo the man away.

"It's a gas!" the sound man yelled.

And the crowd went wild.

Because people were liking us so much, we got to do a lot of television specials—the *Steve Allen Show,* the *Texaco Star Parade Starring Meredith Willson,* the *Danny Thomas Show,* the *Jimmy Dean Show.* That nationwide exposure from the TV shows meant we got more bookings in the East and we would go back and forth. Between shows I was living near Las Vegas, because Gene had started working with Judy Lynn's band there. Judy Lynn had called me, asked if I knew of a banjo player, and I had recommended Gene, thinking he'd be able to give me and the children some support if he had a steady job. So he was in Vegas, and I was traveling back and forth between California and Vegas and then sometimes going east. All that traveling was rough.

It was a rough time for another reason— Scott and his drinking. Scott started drinking real bad, a lot of wine and stuff. Daddy said, "Dadblame it, Scott, you gonna have to stop that!" He was really concerned about Scott because you couldn't depend on him, he might just take off. And in fact Scott did take off.

"I wonder where he's at," Daddy said to me.

"He's playing with the Kentucky Colonels. They took him."

"Why'd he want to play with them?"

"Because they let him drink."

And that was it. Scott went off with them because they didn't mind if he got drunk. Or if they did mind, they didn't feel they could get mad at him like Pop would. I know that's the reason—not that he wanted to play with them more than us—because with that band he did not have the grit behind him that he always liked. Now, the Kentucky Colonels was getting to be a well-known band. Their main players were Roland White, a wonderful mandolinist, and his brother Clarence, who was a really good guitar player, a great guitar player. But to have Clarence in the band and be your backup, that wasn't so good, at least to my way of thinking. Because he didn't give you enough rhythm. It was always diddling, all the time, deedle deedle dee dee deedle, playing individual notes.

And then the Kentucky Colonels put out live tapes and records from the shows. Now I know some people say that those recordings are legendary and that they influenced a whole generation of new musicians. But my opinion?—they should never have been released. Needless to say, Scott was drunk. It was very obvious that he was drunk because he did "Any Damned Thing," which is a song he wrote which was not a nice song. The reason he wrote that song was because he got mad. This was back when we were playing the Famous and Scott would take a bucket on the stage and, as I said, holler, "Pitch in the pot. If you don't pitch in the pot tonight, tomorrow we won't have a pot to pitch in!" Sometimes he would add, "If you got any requests, write it down on a hundred-dollar bill, and if we don't know it, we'll write it." Some guy came up, real drunk, and said, "Play any damned thing," and he threw ten dollars in the pot. Scott looked at him and hated him. So he said, "All right, I'll play any damned thing." So he started singing and he made this awful song up.

And those Kentucky Colonel showtapes were awful. Scott was playing that kind of song. And there'd be no solid rhythm background when he'd take a break. And the recording wasn't any good. They never should have put those performances out. I could pinch their heads off.

It was hard for the family band, Scott's going off like that. If you have the best musician you can imagine in your band, and he just takes off . . . My father, it hurt his feelings, hurt him bad. But he was used to Scott's drinking. We all understood.

Now, my mother would get real mad about all my brothers' drinking. I remember a time in particular, when we were still living in Maryland. There was one decent piece of furniture in the house, Grandma's old Singer sewing machine that Momma had brought from Galax. She'd wipe it off every day. I guess a lot of memories came to her with that old sewing machine. Well this day Momma was out at the grocery store, and my brother Gene staggered in drunk after work with a whiskey bottle and plopped it there on the sewing machine. It stewed over, and he passed out on the little cot we had. Momma came in, saw that bottle of whiskey, and grabbed it. It had eaten the paint off of her sewing machine, just ate the varnish off. Needless to say, that didn't make her very happy. And Gene laying there smelling of drink. Momma went into action. She put a sheet around him, sewed him up in it, and beat him with a stick of stove wood. I saw her do it. "Don't you ever bring another bottle in this house!" "God, I won't do it anymore, Momma, won't do it anymore!" An elbow would come up in the sheet. And she'd bang it down.

But with Scott, she couldn't do nothing. She would fuss, but Scott would say, "Ah, Momma, my little mother, the best mother I ever had. I'm sorry. You know I love you. Please don't be that way." That was Scott. You just couldn't stay mad at him. By the time he finished, you're the one feeling guilty and apologizing. He was a humdinger.

SIXTEEN

Nashville

After we were so successful in the West, it was decided that we should go to Nashville. Again it was decided by our manager Bob Bean and by Jack Clement, who was establishing himself as a producer in Nashville. And we agreed.

We got a job down at Printer's Alley, at the Black Poodle in late 1965. Incredible as it may seem, we Stonemans were the first ones to bring country music to the bars of Printer's Alley. There was an article in *Record World* talking all about it. Before us, the bars just had pop and rock. Actually, even more incredible, from what I was told, country music was pretty new to all of Nashville. Though we sort of think Nashville *is* country music, before the 1940s the only country thing in Nashville was the Grand Ole Opry. A lot of the country music songwriters and singers were in Hollywood where they were making those cowboy movies with Gene Autry and Roy Rogers. And the other country singers, the singers performing the old mountain songs, would play on small radio stations scattered all over the South, or, if they got lucky, on the two or three big ones. In Nashville there weren't any country recording studios or song publishing companies. Then during the forties the music business started to come to town, and it grew in the fifties. But it wasn't yet established like it is now.

Anyway, the Black Poodle was going to try us because we were kinda folk/pop after those performances in the West. Use "folk music" when in doubt!

Well, we were a big hit. The Nashville residents, the kids from Vanderbilt, the tourists, they would all line up around the place to get in. It was amazing. But we really were good, five or six musicians up there (Scott joined us after a few months), all working as a team. The other Nashville entertainers also came to see us. We played later than they did, and after they finished their shows, they'd straggle in—Tom T. Hall, Faron Young, George Jones, Johnny Cash, Waylon Jennings, Tompall and the Glaser Brothers, John D. Laudermilk, Kenny Price (just after he had finished doing *I'm walking on new grass / Singing a new song / Tomorrow you'll be calling me)*, Willie Nelson, Minnie Pearl, Mel Tillis with his band the Statesiders. All of them listening to us! I remember Tompall one time saying "The Stonemans don't play a song, they attack it!"

That attack was basically our bluegrass roots, I guess. Boy, we could drown in definitions—folk, country, bluegrass. And those bluegrass people go to the ropes arguing over what's bluegrass and what's not. Bluegrass to me is that hard-driving real energetic rhythm that Bill Monroe, the Father of Bluegrass, got when he had my hero Earl Scruggs in his band in the forties. We Stonemans had that drive. And we also had the traditional bluegrass instruments, all taking solos, and great harmony playing and singing. But there's a lot of overlapping with country and folk, which is why people argue about what is what all the time.

Anyway, Nashville for me was an incredible scene. First thing, I had never been accepted as a human being with any intelligence—until I came to Nashville. When I was in school, I was, as I said, out of my element. And at home I was never thought to be an intelligent one of the children, and Daddy always put a very high emphasis on intelligence. He would always have books around the house that the Salvation Army gave him.

And of course I wasn't a scholar. Sometimes I notice now I get things backwards. I once asked a doctor, "What is that? How come I do that?" "Dyslexia," he said. Even my sisters didn't consider me smart. Donna wasn't too harsh on me, but with Patsy and Grace I always felt intimidated. I was like a little kid to them. I wasn't trusted with anything.

But when I came to Nashville, I started thinking, Hey, I'm not a lost person. This is my place. For one thing my performing was being approved. We would be playing there at the Black Poodle and all those neat people would be looking at me and liking what I was doing. I was pretty good on the banjo then, fast and real smooth, and my comedy was going over well. Those people made me feel thankful that I was Roni Stoneman. And that made me more talented. I would be thinking, They're out there laughing at what I'm saying, so I must be pretty good. And that makes you relax and you just get better and better. (Or worse and worse. We used to say about Scott, "Don't laugh at him, you'll only make him worse.")

And then also Nashville in the sixties made you feel, Wow, this is fun! Everybody was creating something. I think maybe that was because country music was pretty new in Nashville. Singers and songwriters were just flocking to the place, but because the music business was only getting settled, there weren't these hard lines and rules. Everybody could meet everybody else and trade ideas. It was just casual and informal.

I'd go to the Nashville parties with the other pickers, and there would be all these creative people, like Hank Cochran and Jeannie Seeley. Hank Cochran wrote "Make the World Go Away" and Patsy Cline's "I Fall to Pieces" and *A little bitty tear let me down* and *Your hand is like a torch / Each time you touch me.* The rest of the Stoneman family didn't go to the parties, but I had a wonderful time at them.

Hank and Jeannie had an apartment and were great hosts. Sometimes we would pretend that we were in Hollywood. They'd set up a tripod and Red Lane, the writer who wrote a lot of songs for Dottie West, would say, "Now, take, take." And he'd act like he was turning on the camera, and everybody would go into these really clever acts. Hank Cochran—God what a genius he is. And Jeannie?—a great singer. They fought a lot, and they got 'til they hated each other and ended up divorced. But I loved Jeannie and I loved Hank.

And it was wonderful to feel accepted and be one of the crowd: "C'mon, Roni, get the banjo in here!" Or we'd have a guitar pull. A guitar pull's where you have one guitar, and a whole bunch of people get in a circle, and they talk and smoke a cigarette or two and drink a few drinks, and someone will say, "Hey listen, I got a great song." And someone else will say, "Play it." And he'll sing his song. And the other guy'll say, "Terrific hook! You finished? I got something here," and he'll pull the guitar away, and he'll start picking and singing his stuff. And everybody'll be listening to each other's songs. It was great. You'd just feel the creative vibrations. I think if you're an artist, a painter, whatever, if you surround yourself with other artists, you will climb in talent. If you're a singer and you're around a lot of singers, your voice will get better. If you're a poet and around poets, you get ideas, your soul is fed. For a musician, when you're around your own kind, people that like music and songwriting, you might hear a different note or a different key, and some time later you may not even remember where it came from, but it's there in your mind and you add it to what you're doing.

Now when they first booked us into the Black Poodle, it was a week with an option to renew. God, we were there forever. We were doing five shows a night and later we were also doing television shows during the day. Gene Goforth came down to the Black Poodle, went totally crazy over us, and got us a weekly TV show. Gingham Girl Flour was our sponsor. Just like Martha White's Self-Rising Flour was Lester Flatt and Earl Scruggs's, though we never did have a song for Gingham Girl Flour like the famous Martha White Flour song. But they put Gingham Girl dresses on Donna and me, with vests to match. They even had Roni and Donna dolls. The show, *Those Stonemans,* was very popular and soon it was carried in prime time by lots of stations, mostly in the South, but also in places like Chicago, Cincinnati, New York, San Francisco, and L.A. In one market it outrated the *Lawrence Welk Show.*

So Nashville was really exciting on the professional side. On the domestic front, well, at first I was living in a terrible apartment, all I could afford. Gene was only sending me fifty dollars every now and then—in spite of him doing pretty darn good with that job with Judy Lynn. I had seen a house that I wanted, but I didn't have the money for it. One day Gene called, said he was quitting Judy Lynn and wanted to come home.

"Well, Gene," I said, "like I told you, far as I'm concerned, we're separated. Now, I can't say I don't need help with the children, because I do, but I'm not gonna be a wife to you because all I do is have babies and you don't help me support them."

"I don't care about that. I'm coming home."

"Well, I saw this little house. You can buy it on the GI Bill, and we can get the children settled and they can go to this school right down over the hill."

The house was in Donelson, a suburb of Nashville. It had three bedrooms and a big yard. We moved there, and the kids were as happy as can be. Gene wanted to stay home and take care of them while I performed, like a housedaddy. Well, although nowadays that's accepted, it wasn't fashionable in the sixties. But it was okay with me, anything that worked. So that's what was going on with my family life.

I get real nostalgic when I think about all the talented people I met in those early days, the artists of Nashville. They were so interesting. I talked about Hank Snow and that scene at the Opry, where he said we wouldn't be asked back. But there was another side to Hank Snow. He really did a lot of good. He believed in doing shows for abused children because he was an abused child himself. We Stonemans all had a wonderful life compared to how he was treated. He was beat bad. So he did a lot of work for that charity, and we loved him for it.

Martha Carson became a great friend. She's the number one queen of gospel music far as I'm concerned. When I was a kid I used to listen to her on our little old wind-up Victrola. I'd put on her 78s and turn her loose: *I'm satisfied with my Jesus / When He knocks, I let Him in / He'll go with me to the valley / 'Cause I know He is my friend.* And when she hits the stage, well, Martha's my total mentor with that. She comes out there and she's got them frills on and she'll just rip into a song.

And in fact recently she was doing the *Midnight Jamboree* at the Ernest Tubb Record Shop, the show they always broadcast on radio after the Opry, and I went to watch. Eighty years old and that woman is still a-kicking butt. She had on a lavender dress, and she's got "Martha Carson" written on the neck of her guitar in mother of pearl. I sat in the back grinning up a storm. I almost cried because she's so good.

Now, I mentioned Johnny Cash and Waylon Jennings coming to see us at the Black Poodle. They were roommates then. That was a trip, to see them come and go and think of them having this apartment together. Waylon was as skinny . . . he looked like a spider monkey. And Johnny wasn't far behind. And they'd say, "Partytime is on, girls!" I think I'd just kinda grin at them—I mostly skipped their parties. Much later, after all his success, all those hit songs, Waylon went back and got his GED, to show his son the value of an education. We were awfully proud of him. Johnny of course, like Waylon, had hit after hit. And Johnny was fantastic. When we did his television show—we did a lot of his shows—I'd go out in the audience to look at him. Even when he was at his worst, the time he was partaking of chemicals, even then he had that proud Indian face. When he was talking about the native American Indians, I just stared in his eyes, and, well, everybody knows how low his voice can get. Very few entertainers have the effect on me he had.

John Hartford was another genius I knew really well. He would come and see us play all the time. And during that time I was separated from Gene, I used to run around with John. He had a little Volkswagen bug. John was about the same age as me, both in our late twenties. We never were intimate, but we were sweet, kissy facey. In the winter it would be so damned cold in that bug, you liked to died. One day he parked somewhere, and we kissed, kissed, kissed, and my feet were numb from us sitting in the front seat like two teenagers. He wanted to be intimate, but I said, "No, can't do that, no." So about three or four months later, he came up to me.

"I wrote a song for you, Ron-i."

"What's that?"

"I wrote it traveling from Kentucky." He was drawing it out.

"What's it called?"

"'Confused about a Simple Thing as Love.'"

Because I wouldn't do anything else but kiss him.

At that time John was sleeping on the couch in the office of Marijohn Wilkins. She's the one that wrote "Long Black Veil" and later the gospel classic "One Day at a Time." Back then she had just started Bucktown Music. John cleaned out the ashtrays and such for his keep. Well, I ran into him one evening on Music Row, and he said, "Roni, would you come up to the office with me? I got something to show you." I said, "Sure,

John." So we went up to the office and I sat down on the couch. And he said, "I'm going to play you a demo, Roni. See if you like it." It was a reel-to-reel thing. He turned it on and it was *It's knowing that your door is always open.* It was "Gentle on My Mind." I said, "John, oh my God," and tears started coming in my eyes, "My God, John, grab your hat and hang on. Really that is a monster! You've got a smash on your hands!"

And of course the song was a smash. One night we were playing down at the Black Poodle, and John came in. It was the evening of the country music awards ceremony and he was up for Best Song of the Year, Best Writer, and some other categories. He had a tuxedo coat on, bibbed overalls, tuxedo shirt, and a pair of tennis shoes.

I finally got off stage. "Roni, I'm going down to the awards, but I wanted to drop by first," he said. Now, I used to buy him hamburgers. I didn't have much money, but I knew he had less. So that night, when he came by the Black Poodle, he said, "Roni, you're the only one that ever believed in me in this town, you're the only one. I don't know if I'm gonna get the awards or not, but I'm up for five." I said, "John, you're gonna get them. And those five awards are just gonna be a beginning for you."

I had to go back on stage, and he left. But a few hours later he drove back, right directly from the Municipal Auditorium where they used to have the ceremony. He walked into the Black Poodle, and he had those five awards. He held them up to me. "I got 'em," he said. His face was just the way it normally was, dry, a straight face. But his eyes were shining.

So we went over to the Carousel. He said, "Let's go to the balcony, and we'll have some coffee, and just you and me talk." As we were going there, the people coming over from the ceremony were saying, "Congratulations," "Congratulations, John." Somebody touched him, and he jerked his arm. He said to me, "They never helped me at all, when I was climbing. Now it's all 'Good job, John, good job!'" And I said, "John, be friendly to everybody. You'll be paying them back—your success is your 'I told you so.'" (And in fact I read that some survey found that "Gentle on My Mind" was the fourth most often played country song ever!)

So anyway we had a cup of coffee, and we held hands, and got real close together, because it was private up there. Then my manager Bob Bean came over, and he said, "Roni, time to get back on the stage."

John and I never went out any more after that. I don't know, I guess we both just got busy with our careers and other people.

Just recently he died of cancer. Him dying was a real tragedy not only for me but also for country music—because he was so true to his music. I remember one time, just a few years ago, me and a friend went to a bluegrass event near Nashville.

"John Hartford's over there on that stage, getting ready to go on," somebody said, pointing to the stage.

"Oh, let's go and see him!" I said.

"Who's John Hartford?" asked my friend.

"The man who wrote 'Gentle on My Mind.'"

Now my friend really admires writers. He thought John would be somebody impressive, somebody real intelligent-seeming, a class act, to write such a song. We go over there and there's old John, wearing his shabby vest and his hat, his fiddle in his hand.

"You're gonna play in the contest?" I asked.

"Yep."

"What is a professional like you entering a contest for?"

"Well, I'm just playin.'"

And nobody applauded for him. He played the drabbest old tunes. And he would shuffle. He was playing just for himself. He was really true to his music.

Audrey Williams, Hank's widow, was another Nashville friend of mine. People used to badmouth her because of the way she bossed Hank Sr. around, and, later, the way she pushed Hank Jr. But let's give Audrey her due. We all loved Hank Williams Sr., but he was a troubled man. He was taking diet pills, speed, then drink on top of it. Which wasn't good. But he was a genius, and in my opinion, and as much reading as I've done about different geniuses, every single one of them has a flaw in their character. You just don't go through every day the same old same old and be happy with life and then turn around and produce great art. When our family would have a grandchild, Momma'd say, "Oh, we gotta pray them out of any talent. Maybe if we pray, they won't have it." In other words, if you didn't have talent, you had a chance at a good life.

Well, you're sure not gonna have a good life married to an alcoholic. And Audrey didn't. And then she got to drinking too. Doing the same thing.

She was kind to me. At first she wasn't, but I straightened that out. It was when we were playing the Black Poodle. I had just pierced my ears. Audrey came in and she was sitting there with five or six of her lawyers. I thought of her as a pretty woman, and very interesting. I went over, and I said, "Hi, Audrey, how're ya doin'?" "Hi, Roni. What's the strings in your ear?" I had strings because that's the way you did ear piercing then. You took a needle and shoved it in there, attached to a string with alcohol on it. Then you'd move the string to keep the hole from closing. I said, "I'm getting a little diamond earring to put in there, so I pierced my ears, and that's the string that came from the needle." "My goodness!" She said, "I wear diamonds"—she had huge diamonds on her fingers as well as on her ears—"and I don't have to pierce my ears." And then, well, sometimes these things come over me. I said, "If I had a ten-carat ass, I wouldn't need to pierce my ears either."

Audrey's mouth flew open, and the lawyers started laughing. And after that, me and Audrey were really good friends.

I remember one of Audrey's parties. It was over in Franklin, at Hank Williams's old house. It was the first time I was in the house and I was staring at the drapes. They were black and a kind of cream color, and on them was written out the words and the musical notes to Hank's songs. There right on the drapes was "Your Cheating Heart" and "Hey, Good Lookin'"!

Audrey was dating a young guy, a jeweler. I was thinking, She's going with that young kid? We were standing near the dining-room table and he started talking to me. Then Audrey came through the living room into the dining room. She was zonkered, I mean like out of her mind zonkered. She was carrying a drink, and she fell on the floor. She couldn't get up and her wig had slipped half off. So I raised her as much as I could with the jewelry guy helping me, and we got her in her bed. She was saying, "Noooo, I don't wannnnnt ta lay ddddown. I wannnnnnnnt ta get up."

There were a lot of sad stories in Nashville. Once Colonel Tom Parker, the guy who managed Elvis, stopped me.

"We listen to your family all the time. Elvis loves the Stoneman family."

"Well, that's real nice of him."

"Umm, Elvis'll be here in about, " and he looked at his watch, "in about five minutes. I'd like for you—would you like to meet him?"

But I knew Elvis was being bugged by everyone and I didn't want to be part of that, so I made some excuse and left.

They say that before Colonel Parker died, he sat in front of the window every day, all day, crying, tears running down his cheeks, because of what became of Elvis Presley. Elvis was used, absolutely used to death. A bodyguard of his once told me that Elvis never had a life. He couldn't go anywhere, he couldn't do anything.

There would also be touring musicians in Nashville, of course. I met one of them at the Carousel. He had a whole band down from Canada. I hadn't caught their name. "What do you do?" he asked. "I'm a mechanic for Piedmont Airlines," I said. We got to dancing and then we went down to an all-night coffee shop, my girlfriends and I and this guy and his band—we still didn't know who they were. Then we finished up at a pancake place, where we were all singing. I started "I'll Fly Away," and he came in doing harmony, and the whole place was singing "I'll Fly Away." When we finally said goodbye out on the street, the street washers were there—it was that late, that early in the morning, around four.

And then the next time I saw him was when the Stonemans were playing in Toronto. We were singing *In the early morning rain* and I said, "Ladies and gentlemen, I dedicate this song to . . . someone told me he's in the audience, the writer of this song, Gordon Lightfoot." Everybody started turning toward this guy sitting on the left-hand side in the front row grinning up at me. It was the guy I had danced with that night in Nashville!

Besides the performers there were other really special people who made Nashville what it was. Like Mr. Friedman, the gentleman who had Friedman's Pawn and Loan. One time when I walked in the shop, there was a guy playing the guitar sitting on the floor. And Mr. Friedman said, "Still feels good to you, don't it?" The guy had hocked his guitar about a month prior to this and he had not been paying his interest on it. But he wanted to feel it in his hands. "Yessir, it does." And he went, "Oh by the way, Mr. Friedman, I got a gig in Columbus, Georgia, and if I could play it, I'd come back and buy this guitar back from you." "In other words, you don't have a guitar to play?" "No, I don't, Mr. Friedman." "Okay, I'm gonna let you write a note that you promise to bring it back or bring me the money you hocked it for. I'm gonna let you take it." I loved that man. The store is right next to Tootsie's Orchid Lounge. His son's taken it over. But Mr. Friedman still comes in there sometimes.

And of course there was Tootsie herself, who ran Tootsie's Orchid Lounge. Tootsie fed a lot of the musicians, and she had an apartment upstairs over the restaurant, and they sometimes slept in one of the rooms. That's where Kris Kristofferson went after his wife left him, for instance. Tootsie helped a lot of the stars, but she would fuss at them too and get at them just like a mother would a child.

Now the great country singer Faron Young would go down to Tootsie's all the time. He called her "Tooootsie." Tootsie was a short little gal, kinda chunky, but not real heavy, with a round face and a darling high-pitched voice. She'd always be laughing and giggling. But when she'd get mad—"I'm not putting up with that dirty mouth around here, you son of a rat. I ain't putting up with it, Faron, no more!" And then she'd gouge him with a hatpin. And Faron: "Jesus!!!! Tootsie, you're gonna give me tetanus and lockjaw! That damn thing is rusted!!!" So one time he goes out on the road and he comes back with a beautiful box. "Tootsie, I got you a present." She opens it up and it's a gold hatpin, with a diamond, a ruby, and an emerald. "That's to stick me with," Faron said. "My private hatpin, so I won't get lockjaw. You can't use it on anybody but me!"

In Tootsie's Orchid Lounge there were booths set up along the wall and tall round tables and tall bar chairs. They have a good hamburger there, but the musicians would also drink, drink, drink all the time. And they would write and trade songs. In fact, the story goes that Faron got his big hit of 1961 "Hello Walls" from Willie Nelson in Tootsie's. And remember that song, "Please Don't Squeeze the Charmin"? That song was written in Tootsie's about a waitress whose name was Charmin.

Now from the Ryman Auditorium, where they did the Grand Ole Opry, you could go right across the alley, and you would be at the back door of Tootsie's. So Grant Turner, or whoever was in charge, would trudge across to Tootsie's to get the act that was coming out next. The musicians would be over there drinking beer, telling wild tales of the road, and trading songs: "Listen here." "Well, listen to this song." "When we were on the road with Tammy, you won't believe what she said." And Grant Turner would say, "All right, c'mon now, we gotta get . . . you're up next." And he'd drag them over there. Grant Turner was the real hero of the Opry. He was also of course an announcer there for many years.

Tootsie tried to keep the boys from drinking too much, to get them ready for their shows. She would say, "All right, here comes Turner. Get your ass up these steps and get to the Opry!" And if they got ornery and got to cussing, she'd gouge them with the hatpin, the one that wasn't Faron's.

Talking of Faron . . . Well, there was a girl called Suckin' Sue. She had an apartment off Music Row, above a store. She called it the Boar's Nest. Well one day I'm walking down the street, and Faron sees me. "Hey, Olive Oyl" (I was still very skinny). "Hi, Faron." "Olive Oyl, c'mere, c'mere. I wanna educate ya." He had a couple of beers in him. He'd been up to the Country Corner, another joint where all the pickers'd go to drink and feed off each other's talents and write songs. It was sort of like your local tavern. There was also another place, Wally's Professional Club. That's where I first heard Tom T. Hall's superhit "Harper Valley PTA."

Anyway, Faron put his arm around my shoulders, and said, "Olive Oyl, I'm gonna show you what life's all about." And I said, "Okay." Dumb, dumb, I was dumb. He said, "I'm gonna introduce you to a friend of mine, Suckin' Sue." Now in those days you didn't hear the word "sucking" unless it was a lollipop. "Okay, Faron." And he had another buddy with him. Well, we go trumbling up some stairs. And in the corner of the steps was dirt, lint, like fur balls. I said, "Well, somebody ought to sweep the stairs!" I guess he knew I was about to ask him if they could get me a broom and I could help out Suckin' Sue by sweeping the steps because Faron threw back his head and roared: "Ha, ha, ha. Olive Oyl, you beat all I ever seen."

Well we got up to the top of the stairs and straight ahead there was a little couch and a table. Off to your right was a bedroom. Off to your left was a little setting area, with a teeny chrome table and chairs, kinda raggedy looking. And there was this woman. Faron said, "Roni, this is Suckin' Sue." I said, "Hi, Suckin' Sue. It's nice meeting you, Suckin' Sue." And everybody laughed. So I'm sitting there, in one of the chairs by the table, just looking around.

"C'mere," says Faron. "I want to show you something. C'mere. Lookit. You see those little notches in the head of that bed? The headboard?"

"Ya mean them dug-out places, like a knife's been used on it?"

"Those are notches."

"Oh."

Well I didn't know what it all meant, though afterwards I figured it out. But I left right after that. There was too many men in there, and there was no need in my being there.

Now in general Faron was really good to me. When he came down to see us at the Black Poodle, he would always say, "I'm taking care of Olive Oyl, Pop." But he sure did like to tease me, and he sure got a kick out of somebody from the hills with so many children being so darned innocent!

During this time when we were so popular in Nashville, in the sixties and seventies, we were also doing a lot of recording, album after album. And I hate talking about our records—don't pay attention to our records—because they were really not us. The big guys at RCA would tell us what songs we were going to record. They took us away from our hillbilly roots and made us do more pop-like songs. This is good for you, you got to sing this to be commercial and saleable. We had no say, zero, zilch, none.

One reason we didn't rebel was because the situation wasn't like it is today where the records are all-important. In those days you did the records to make you more visible and then have more shows. The shows were where you expected to get your money from. Also, we weren't sure enough of ourselves because we weren't educated. Scott wouldn't record with us much because he hated Bob Bean. We thought we were working for Bob Bean. Later on, after I left the group, somebody told me, "Well, Roni, y'all had it backwards. Bob Bean was working for you all." But we didn't know it then. Anyway, we felt our managers were the educated ones, so we should do what they told us.

Bob Bean would say, "We gotta go over to Jack's. Here's a song that he picked out," and he would hand it to us and say, "Now learn it!" Like that stupid song—"Two Kids from Duluth Minnesota." Minnesota's a beautiful state, and I love it, but I hated that song. And we had to sing it the way Jack Clement wanted us to, separating each syllable—"Min-ne-so-ta," he kept insisting. I thought it sounded awful.

Now, I have to admit Jack Clement was really one of the most important forces in Nashville and in country music. He wrote some great songs like "Ballad of a Teenage Queen," and he discovered and produced some great talent. One of those talents was Charley Pride and I was in on the discovery. I was in Jack's office. A man came in, and he had this tall nice-looking black guy with him. He put on a tape. We all listened. Then he said, "What do you think of it?" And everybody's saying, "That's fantastic!" "You know who it is?" Everybody says, "No." "Well, that's this man here! We're trying to get him a deal with RCA." And I said, "If they don't sign him, they're crazy." So he said, "Well, you come with me." So we all trooped down to Chet Atkins's office.

Chet was an amazing man. He had performed all those big hits like "Mister Sandman" and had devised a guitar style all his own that everybody was copying, and he won instrumentalist awards year after year. By this time he had become a vice president for RCA. Well, we're all in Chet's office, and they put the tape on, reel to reel, and played it. "That's a good singer, a really really good singer. Who is it?" said Chet. And Jack said, "It's this young man, this guy here."

And Charley's standing there, kinda proud and kinda shy. I remember Chet studying, listening. And he pushed himself back from his desk, and he said, "How would we do that?" "You can put girls on the front of the album," I said, "beautiful girls, and don't let anybody know that's he's black." And that's what they did. The first two albums he made, they did not let anybody know he was black. Terrible, isn't it, to think that that had to be done? They did of course finally make it public.

Once, we were playing somewhere in Texas, the Stonemans and Charley. And we were riding down together in our limousine.

"I'm . . . I'm really scared," said Charley.

"My opinion, Charley," I said, "don't ever surround yourself with white women. With some of those people you don't want to even be near a white woman. Make sure your wife is with you at all times, or if there are any ladies coming around, make sure they're of your color. Just while you're getting started."

"They won't . . . Do you think they'll shoot me?"

"No, they won't shoot you, if you don't surround yourself with white women."

In those years, interracial dating was a big bad thing.

Chet Atkins was always on my side. I would normally go down to the RCA building every now and then to say hey to him. I'd push the button—daang. They'd say, "Who is it?" "Roni Stoneman. I've come to say hey to Chet." I could walk in any time I wanted to and talk to Chet because he was wanting some time out for foolishness. It wasn't sex or anything, never sexy with Chet Atkins. But I'd just drop in if I was downtown. And we would sit and talk awhile.

That ease of access is what I meant when I mentioned the freedom and lack of restrictions in those early Nashville days. I also used to go in the studios to watch the recording. For instance I remember one time when I went in to watch one of Charley's sessions. I sat down at the board on the right side of Jack Clement, and he was pushing the buttons up and down and directing. They had Buddy Emmons on the steel, Hargus "Pig" Robbins on the piano, and Junior Husky Sr. on the bass. And I was particularly interested in seeing them because we were good friends. They were seriously working at getting the arrangement they wanted. Now, that's about when the Nashville Sound was first being used a lot. A number system had been invented that named the intervals on the scale, so the pickers could just use a shorthand ("1, 4, 5, 5, 1") to tell each other which chords to play. And then the musicians could get more interesting arrangements, the Nashville Sound, because they could improvise more on account of knowing that number shorthand. (Later the term Nashville Sound came to mean something else—the fuller arrangements using strings and horns and vocal choruses to make it sound more pop-like. The fiddle and the banjo just about disappeared.)

So, anyway, Charley Pride was in the studio, and I was watching what was going on there. All the boys had written their numbers chart for the music, how to kick it off and so on. They studied on each other and would say, "How do you do that doodle doodle doo?" Or "I like that four in there. Keep it." Then, "We're ready, Jack." That's the way the session sidemen worked out the arrangements. It was really interesting. Audrey Williams would often come with me when I went down to the studios.

Back to Chet: he was a very helpful friend. He hired me to do a lot of shows. Once we played at the Hand Surgeons Association, nine hundred hand surgeons. And I played at his celebrity golf tournaments down in

Atlanta. He always encouraged me. I often played with the Boots Randolph Band, and I think Chet had a lot to do with getting me those jobs since he and Boots were friends. I would do "Dueling Banjos" with the piano and horn sections.

When I decided to leave the family band, he wrote me a letter to help me get jobs, saying what a great entertainer I was.

Daddy passed away in '68, of a variety of ailments, and three years later is when I left the family band. I left because I could not live on the money we were being paid. We had been named Country Music Association's Vocal Group of the Year in 1967, and that year and the next four years we were nominated for *both* Vocal Group of the Year and Instrumental Group of the Year. Plus our TV show was a big success. But even though we were sometimes getting a thousand dollars a show, and sometimes playing three different places in one night, the managers never told us exactly what we were making. They just gave us at the most $250 each a week. Then they went down to $200, then $165. They told us they were investing our money for us, and afterwards there would be the gravy train. Scott said they were crooking us but we didn't believe him. We just thought Scott was drinking.

When I first went out on my own in Nashville, I was playing by myself in Printer's Alley with the Nashville Cats. It was Jim Vest on steel guitar and Cliff Parker doing the lead guitar. And I would get up there on stage and I would play the banjo pretty darn good. But when I started talking, well somehow Vest would be playing around with the amplifier, or they would get down on the floor, looking around to connect the wires or moving pedals. And they would take my mind off of what I was saying. And one time my friend Pat McKenney was there. "Pat, what am I going to do?" I said. "Get up there and tell them to stop it. You be the boss on the stage, Roni!"

Pat McKenney was my hero. She was a girlfriend I ran around with. And a singer, the best you'd hear, and pretty, and she was dating all the musicians—Waylon Jennings, Roger Miller. Another friend, Dale Turner, would date Kris Kristofferson. They were modern girls. They did modern things.

We would all go downtown. And I wouldn't date a musician. It was always some businessman or somebody that wore a tie. I was trying to get more stability in my life. So they would say about me and my date, "Here comes Harriet the Housewife, and Herman the Husband." And I said, "What in the world is a 'Harriet'?" "That's a woman that has a bunch of kids. She's got a station wagon, going to the laundrymat with her laundry."

When I first started playing by myself, the main thing I was concerned about, after I got the sidemen to behave, was that I was not doing enough for the audience. What I missed from the family was . . . well it was like an obsession to put on the best show for the people. Scott instilled that into us. You can't let the audience get bored. If you see them milling around during your show, it means it's time to get off the stage. Scott used to tell me to practice in the mirror, so I'd really know what I looked like, with my body language, with my facial expressions, with my feet dancing, whatever I was doing. "Hey the audience, we've got to die for 'em," was Scott's motto.

I love Nashville. Later when my kids were growing up, actually in Smyrna, which is right outside of Nashville, I was taking Eugene over to the high school, and Marty Stuart came running out. This is *the* Marty Stuart, who's had all those hits, performed with so many of the top artists, and has a Martin guitar named after him. Then he was a high school kid. Now, I knew his mom and dad and his wonderful sister Jennifer—they went to the same church we did. But at that time and for some years after, I didn't ever think of Marty as being an entertainer. I knew he played a little mandolin, but we were used to that around that part of the country. You didn't pay much attention. "Well, he plays." "Oh, he do? Well, that's great. Well I pick now and then." "Okay, good, where y'all pickin' at?" "Wall, I don't know." "Wall, call me whenever y'all pick somewhere and I'll come over and see ya'." And that was it. That's how rich the Nashville area is in good musicians. I don't ever want to live anywhere else.

SEVENTEEN

George

The reason I finally quit the family band at the time I did was because I had gotten a second husband, and he was telling me to. He thought I could do better on my own. This is how that second marriage went.

Well, Gene and I were living in the same house in Donelson, but I had made it clear I wouldn't be a wife to him. He was taking care of the kids when I was out working with the family. Then the school authorities got into the picture. They called and said they wanted to come and talk to us. So we sat down at the table. And one woman said, "It's concerning your children, Barbara especially. We think it's having a bad effect on her, with her father at home all the time." The teacher had asked the children to cut out of magazines pictures of what their mother did and what their father did and glue them on a little poster board. Barbara had cut out pictures of a bus, an airplane, suitcase, and instruments—for her mother. For her father, she cut out a broom, a mop, vacuum cleaners, and dishes. They wanted to know what could I do about it. Well, excuse my language, what the hell could I do about it? But I didn't say that to them. I was gonna try my darnedest to do the right thing. So I turned to Gene: "Maybe you can get a part-time job or pretend to the kids that you're going to work. And when you pick them up after school, you can say, 'I just got outta work.'" Well, he sat there with those three teachers, and he said, "No, I'm not gonna do that. I'm not gonna go to work, and I'm not gonna pretend." He was the first Mr. Mom.

Now, as I said, I was doing some dating during those years. Actually they weren't all businessmen. There were some other real interesting encounters.

The Priest. He was at a show in Houston. He took a Polaroid picture of me, and I autographed it with my usual, "You really tear me up, Roni Stoneman." I guess he took it to heart. So we started having this little bit of . . . not real intimacy, nothing like that, just kissy facey. I'd call him at the rectory when my show was over, and he'd come pick me up in his car. He sang like Marty Robbins, and he sang all of Marty Robbins's songs. He'd go in this low voice: *I left you this moornin' / Couldn't taaake any mooore.* That romance ended when I was the one who left, off to California. He would have followed me, but I had started feeling like a Jezebel. l mean he was a priest!

The Jewish Feller. He was a fiddle player and I really liked him. That ended when I suddenly realized he looked just like Jesus! "I can't kiss someone who looks like Jesus!" I told him. I showed him a picture. "I do, don't I?" he said. (I encouraged him to marry a nice Jewish girl he knew who was studying psychiatry. If anyone needs a psychiatrist, it's a fiddler! He did look a lot like Jesus. But it wasn't a problem to her, good Jewish girl that she was!)

There were other dates. There was the guy in Boston who invited me to see where he worked. Turned out he was an undertaker and it was a morgue. There was the Blue Angel, who used to take me out driving in his car and invite me to parties the pilots gave, where there were all these beautiful delicate Polynesian girls—and clunky me with my country dresses. There was the psychology professor. "He just wants to pick your brain," said Daddy. "He wants to test you."

Then I met George Hemrick. I met him when he hired the family to play for a political rally. He seemed real intelligent, was a speechwriter for the governor of North Carolina, a school principal and an English teacher, was even in Mensa, which, he told me, is some kind of organization for supersmart people. In other words this was clearly the husband for me. He was the perfect person to help me educate my kids, right? Get Barbara on the right track cutting out the right pictures!

George was also a songwriter and poet and he had spent time at Carl Sandburg's ranch in North Carolina. Like a poet, George was very romantic with his words and his ways. He would write me love letters and love poems. He typed them from work. "Office of the Principal," the stationery said.

George was living in North Carolina, Winston-Salem, and I was in Donelson. He called me a lot and would come out to where we were performing, even if it was far away. And so eventually I got divorced from Gene, and George and I got engaged. It was 1968.

Now, one day the Stonemans were doing a TV show, and June Carter and Johnny Cash were there. I had known June awhile, since we had played some shows with them. And of course we knew *of* them forever, and Daddy knew the Carter family from the Bristol sessions in the twenties. But we were not real pals with them. The Carter girls were a different kind of girl than me and Donna. We were more sheltered. I also had known John for a long time. I had picked John up off the floor at Linebaugh's, and I'd seen him pass out in the middle of an aisle on an airplane. All this is in his books. And I remember June and John's "courting," such as it was, when June would come into Tootsie's—"Where's Johnny? Anybody seen Johnny?"

Anyway, that day we were all in California rehearsing the *Smothers Brothers' Comedy Hour,* with Glen Campbell. George had come out to be with me, and at one point he walked over to my brother Van.

"Roni, I need to talk to you," June said. She took me aside.

"Don't marry that man," she said. John was standing right by her.

"Why?"

"He's not good. He's evil, Roni."

"Well, he loves me."

"No, he doesn't. He don't know how to love anybody. He loves himself."

Well, I thought, I have those four little children, and he's an educator, and this will help me. June doesn't know where I'm coming from. I'm barely making a living.

"No, he loves me," I said, "and he'll be good to me."

"No, he won't, Roni. I know why you're like you are, so eager to be thinking that he loves you. You have that crooked eye. And your teeth is got a space in them. Like mine—I had buck teeth really bad. My dentist capped 'em, and put braces on 'em. Why don't you let me and John pay for a dentist?"

"No, I can't do that." I was proud.

"Oh, please let us."

And John says, in that low gravelly Johnny Cash voice, "Yeah, we can take care of it."

"No, no."

So we all went back to Nashville. The family was playing at the Black Poodle. I did my show and ran home to pack to go to the airport. I was getting married in a little town right outside of Winston-Salem.

June Carter and John came into the Black Poodle. Donna was there.

"Where's Roni?" said June. "I don't want her to marry that man. I'm gonna stop her from marrying that man. He's no good. He's violent." And then when Donna told her that I had left to pack, she apparently just sank down in a chair and went, "Oh my God!"

Well, the day before I was getting married, I was staying at a girl-friend's house down there in Winston-Salem. I was in the bedroom, combing my hair. There was a big glass door. I went to the mirror and I looked in my eyes as I was combing my hair, and all at once something in my mind says, "Run! Open that door and run. Get outta here." That was my woman's intuition, and I should have followed it (or June's), but I didn't.

That night, right after the wedding, George and I were driving back up to Nashville because I had to tape a TV show. I knew something was wrong on the way because George started drinking a lot of vodka. We rode with a couple of friends of his, lawyers and politicians, and George was awful, got very belligerent to me. I just sat there real quiet. When we got to Nashville, I had to go right away to the studio.

Pat McKenney had given us the key to her apartment to stay in while we were in Nashville. By the time we got to Pat's apartment, after the taping, George was drunk. I didn't know it because I was used to the loud drunks in nightclubs—"Hey Rooonnnni, playyyy a song!" I wasn't used to a soft-spoken southern gentleman with perfect English getting drunk.

So we're in the apartment, and I said, "Honey, want me to put your clothes in this closet here?" He got up from the couch and he came over. And he slapped me in the face! He kept beating me and hitting me real hard! I had no idea why. I was crying, sobbing. I ran back in the bathroom, and looked in the mirror. There was a huge bruise coming up on my cheek. I was shaking all over. I thought, Oh, God, what have I done? I made a horrible mistake. What . . . what am I going to do?

And I know this sounds ridiculous but I saw my grandfather's face, my Grandfather Frost. He said, "I didn't raise you to . . . That ain't what I would want you to put up with, young lady. Not for one minute!" So I went back into the living room. George was sitting down on the couch and he looked up at me. Now he weighed 250 pounds. I weighed at that time about 100. I said, "Why did you hit me for?" And he says, "I'll hit you again if you don't stand still." So I took my fist, and I hit him so hard in the nose that the blood poured out all over the place. He had to go back and get a towel, and I was cleaning up the carpet with cold icy water. I had a terrible wedding night.

I called Gene the next day: "Gene, I made a terrible mistake. I need to have the children stay in the house so I can get something done about this." "They can't," he said, "I already sold the house." And he took the equity. This was in spite of he hadn't put a penny in the house.

So I went on back to North Carolina with George, and we were going to find a place to live in. The next day I was sitting on a bed in a motel with my arm under my chin, looking at a soap opera, and George was sitting on the other bed. He got up and hit my head, and my neck popped. Then he dragged me out into the parking lot, said he was going to have me run over out there. I don't know how, but I got back into the room. And I thought, Don't argue with him, he's not well, something is very very wrong. I didn't know that besides the vodka he was gulping amphetamines.

I had to go back to Nashville again a few days later because I had to do another television show. George took me to the airport in Winston-Salem. And as I walked up the gangplank to the little prop jet, he said, "I'll be waiting for you, darling." I looked down at him and I thought, Oh my God! I got on the airplane, trembling.

In Nashville I told Pat McKenney everything. I laid down on her bed and crawled up in a fetal position and cried and cried.

The next day I performed with the family on the television show and I had to pretend like I was okay.

But things got worse and worse.

We found a house down in North Carolina, and George moved his furniture in. He had a bedroom set, and as I was trying to clean the bureau, I saw the top drawers were full of pill bottles. "Why do you have all these pills?" I asked. He jumped up and ran to the bureau and told me to leave my hands off his things. The pills were for his back, he said, prescribed by his chiropractor.

Gene brought the children down to North Carolina one or two weeks later. I never felt so alone and lost as when he left, when I watched him pull out of the driveway.

I thought that if I had a baby, George maybe would be closer to me. But he beat on me even when I was pregnant with Georgia. One time Patsy had to call the cops. She was back in Tennessee, and I phoned her, crying, scared to death. He had beat me, and blood was all over where he busted my mouth and all over my maternity suit. There was a knock at the door, and a policeman said, "Are you Roni Stoneman? Your sister . . ." But I told him everything was okay. I wouldn't let him in because I was afraid that if he got after George, George would beat me worse when he left.

I was always bruised and my face had that drawn look, and my hair . . . well, stress can cause your hair to go bad. It just seemed like it was coming out in handfuls. George would get into an argument, or fight with me, and I would be saying, "I didn't do nothing! I didn't do nothing!" He would even accuse me . . . he accused me of Georgia not being his. Of course I'd never been with anybody else at that time but him. I would say, "Yes, she is, honey. I swear to God she is! I swear to you!"

I think a lot of his money was going to drinking and pills. I'm not sure, but me and the children were definitely suffering. I was not playing that much music since it was a lull time with the family. I wanted to quit and stay home and be a mom to the children and a housewife. Later George would want me to quit, but at this point he wouldn't hear of it. When I suggested it, he beat my head on the wall. We were starving. It was real hard times. And then George had convulsions from his drinking and had to go to the hospital.

I had no food in the house. I knew I had to buy some groceries, the kids were hungry. So I looked at my banjo, the Gibson. I thought, I'm gonna have to hock this banjo. Only thing I had in the house that was fit. I didn't even have a dresser for my children's clothes—I was using boxes.

So after George got out of the hospital, he drove me downtown. He parked way up the street from the pawn shop so nobody would see his car there. It was drizzling rain, and I had a scarf on my head because I didn't have an umbrella, and I came walking down the street crying. And I thought, I gotta stop crying, gotta have pride. The rain was hitting against my face, and I said to myself, Well, they'll think the tears is raindrops. So I wiped my face and I went in the shop. "I need to hock my banjo," I said. The manager offered me a hundred dollars. "A hundred? Is that all?" He said, "Yeah. I want you to get this back." "Well, I guess . . . if that's all you're gonna give me." "It's only because I really want you to get it back. I don't want you to lose this." I went out the door and I walked up the street crying.

I cooked a big dinner that night, meatloaf and mashed potatoes and peas. The kids were real happy, sitting at the table, swinging their legs under the chairs. George was in the bedroom. He never ate with us.

That was the banjo that I bought in 1956, the one that I played in all them honky-tonks to support my children. The banjo had scrapes on the bottom, where at the end of the night, after playing five or six shows, I had to drag it off the stage because it was so heavy, and I was carrying a baby, and I'd be too tired to hold it up.

The banjo had a mellow sweet sound. And it was perfect for playing outdoors—because in the old days when you had bad skin heads on the banjo, if the weather got just a little bit damp or the sun came out, the banjo went totally out of tune. But there was a very good skin head on this. And then for me to lose it for a hundred dollars . . .

I couldn't do gigs. George did drive me to this one bluegrass festival, and people were saying, "Oh, Roni Stoneman, you're the greatest."
I said, "Well, thank you." But I was thinking, Oh yeah, right! I was just
weak, weak in my body. But I was weak emotionally too, because along
with that kind of physical abuse, as so many women know, you also get
the mental abuse. You're not only beat and punched, you're constantly
being put down by someone telling you you're stupid, ignorant, just a
hillbilly, just a piece of trash. You don't know nothing, you're incompetent. I learned words like incompetent. And that's a technical term.
George said if it wasn't for him, I would lose my children. Because he
had an education and I didn't. (And I had heard of that happening to a
woman down in Mississippi.)

Then all of a sudden I'm at this festival with everybody making a
big deal of me, telling me how wonderful I was. There was one person
there—him and his wife had an RV. "Did you bring your banjo?" he
asked. "No, I left it at home." "C'mon up here, I wanna show you a
banjo." So he took me to the RV. And so I sat there on a couch with a
cotton dress and a leather vest that was twice my size. And I played a
banjo he had handed me that was made out of aluminum painted green.
The man said, "This friend of mine makes these banjos and I'll have him
send you one and he can sponsor you." "Oh, will you?" I said, because
it was the only way I was gonna get a banjo. "That'll be wonderful!" So
the friend sent me a banjo, a little green banjo. It didn't have the tone it
should. But I was thankful to get anything. I played it for a long time,
pretending like this was what I wanted. And I truly am to this day grateful to the man in the RV and his friend.

We moved back to Nashville. Why we finally left Winston-Salem?
George drove into some parked cars, coming home from school drunk.
Well the school board told him either resign or they were going to fire
him. Dale Catlett, a friend, helped me leave first. It was so dangerous for
me because I was really isolated in North Carolina. George was telling
everybody *I* was on pills, *I* was drinking, because he was making excuses
to cover his own irresponsibility. Dale got a truck for me to get my things
moved up to Nashville. Then George followed. There's a picture of me
with Eugene at that time, early 1972. I look like death.

I didn't get my banjo back for nine years. Nine whole years later, I get a call from my "cousin," Bill Stanley. I think of him as my cousin because he's as close as any relative I've had. Bill Stanley says, "Roni, yer banjer is . . ." He talks country and he plays guitar, banjo, and fiddle, but he's real smart, a wonderful man. He was known as the best car salesman five years running in the whole state of North Carolina. And his wife Peggy's my dear dear compadre. Well, Bill called me and he said, "Roni, there's a woman advertising your banjer in the trades. I know it's your banjer. It has the work your father did on the neck and that peg your father put in." The banjo broke when I was flying one time. They made me check it, which is ridiculous because I could have put it above. It came off the conveyor belt and hit neck first. (I can just see all you musicians out there wincing.) Well, rebuying the banjo wasn't all that easy—there were complications—but eventually I flew down to North Carolina and Bill drove me over to the woman's house and we retrieved it.

I got in the car, and I didn't even put the banjo in the back seat. I sat in the front and hugged it. I was just ecstatic. I was so happy, I was out of breath. And the reason is . . . that banjo . . . well, sometimes you have to learn to carry on. You can't let emotions eat your soul. You can't let the love of a thing . . . Now a child, an innocent child, is a whole new ballgame. They come first before everything. But a banjo? You know, like hey, that ain't no big deal. But you know what I thought when I saw it? I thought, It's got the laughter of people in it. You could feel the audiences inside the resonator, thousands of people. And it had not only the good times. There was all the dirt around the brackets, the smoke from honky-tonks. It also had in it every cigarette and every drunk yelling out, "Helloooo, play me another banjo number!" All the laughter, good, bad and indifferent. That banjo had my life in it. And when I got it back, I suddenly had this vision of myself—I would be with my stomach out, in a family way, 'bout ready to have a baby. So I'd be playing the banjo over on my hip. And the banjo paid for the baby's birth.

Back to my marriage. Abusive men . . . well, in my experience, it's unlikely the man that has an abusive heart is ever going to get better. Now they can claim they're gonna go to therapy, but it's real hard to change their already made-up stuff.

George was always calling me names, and accusing me of things. It was a standard speech—I was incompetent, stupid, etcetera. Finally, in my own way I rebelled. One day I said, "George, I've written down some words that you haven't used yet to me. I was on the road and I found this Chaucer book and here's some new words that will help you."

I was fighting back, I guess. I had thought of every kind of thing I could do to assert myself. But he was still pounding it to me. Anyway, that time he got quiet, turned around slowly, and walked back to his bed and picked up a book.

I tried to get the children involved in a lot of things outside so they didn't hear so much of the abuse. I would "cover," like every woman in that situation will do. I would cover in the way I acted and I would use Max Factor pancake makeup. It's water-based and it will stick to your face better and stay longer. I put that on and then a darker makeup over it. But even so, when the kids were getting ready to leave for school the morning after a beating, I would be keeping my cheek turned away so the kids didn't see it. Women hide things from children partly because they're embarrassed. But most important, they don't want the children to be afraid. It doesn't always work though. Georgia got nightmares. She got nightmares a lot.

EIGHTEEN

Scotty

Every time anyone in the family is asked about Scott, it's just like an awful flashback, like a Vietnam flashback. It was so sad. He was so talented. Lots of people say he was one of the greatest fiddlers ever—he just had a genius for it. I remember a time when he was a teenager. He had been out to watch some fiddle players in Washington, and he came back, and he was practicing those rolls on the fiddle bow. Momma said,"Lord God, Scott, where've you been? I was worried to death!" And Scott said, "I've been downtown, Ma. You don't know what I've learned . . . that sound. But I can get it even better. I can double note it."

The learning just went on all the time. I heard something about this from a guy who was a Secret Service man. But at the time he was talking about he was a policeman. He said that Scott used to go out every night in the alleys when we finished playing in Washington. He would be going after bootleg whiskey. And he would play all night for the people who couldn't afford to come into the club, mainly black people. My opinion, it was an equal thing. Because I bet it wasn't only the whiskey Scott was after. Music professors are always talking about how important the African beats and rhythms are in country music, and I bet Scott was learning from those people. And playing for an audience like that, well it really draws the art out of you. The policeman said he and his partner would go there, not to arrest them or anything but just to listen to the music.

From early on I knew that Scott had started drinking. He would vomit violently whenever he drank. One night, when he was young, he came home from playing some joint, and he had been drinking. The moon was out, full bright, and Momma was downstairs sleeping—after praying for hours for Scott to get home safe. I heard Scott out in the yard and I went out and helped him up to this old tree. He threw up for about an hour. I held his head, and then we got him quietly into the house to hide it from Momma.

That's how he died. He died in his own vomit. Some people thought Scott killed himself. That's not so. Scott wanted to live too much. What happened was that he had been at Central State Hospital, the alcoholic ward. I remember me and Mommy had gone to see him and we took him some candy bars.

A few days after that, Scott got out of the hospital. But they had filled him up with Antabuse. Antabuse makes you very sick if you drink any alcoholic beverage. So Scott was staying at Donna's house, and, well, he got ahold of some alcohol, and he got sick from the Antabuse. Patsy, who lived across the street, found him in a pool of vomit. He was unconscious.

They took him to the hospital. They called me, but I wasn't that upset because I had seen Scott sick before. I thought, Well I can go visit him later. So I left to go play a show. I stopped at a place on the road to call the hospital. And the person I reached said, "Scotty Stoneman? He's DOA." I said, "DOA? Is he all right?" And I knew what DOA meant, but I was just so shocked, it didn't register. There was a silence. Then, "No." But I could not get it into my head. And I went on, and I played half the show, thinking, Well, he's DOA, but he's gonna be okay. I just couldn't imagine he could die. Not my Scott.

My mother buried her son at forty years old. I looked over at her when she took that clump of clay and sprinkled it on Scott's coffin. She kept saying, "'Now go on, Scott, go on, just go away, go on, just go on.' That's the last words I ever said to my son." She had said those words the day before he died. He had come over to the house and he was aggravating Momma like we all did, and she had said, "Now you just go on, go on."

A preacher came to Scott's funeral and told us a strange story. He said that he was in the church the night before Scott died. He was working late in the office, and the church had been left open, which was very rare. He said he saw this young man come down the aisle and go to the altar and get down and pray for God in Jesus' name to forgive him for all of his sins. It was Scott and he apparently almost went into a convulsion. The preacher said he'd never seen anything like it. He said, "Your brother Scott knew Christ before he died."

Scott carried a Bible for about two years. He had quit playing the fiddle, thinking it was his fiddle that was making him drink. He decided it was putting him in the wrong environment. So he stopped performing and started doing roofing. A friend was going to teach him. Scott said, "Aunt Roni, I got my hammer, I got all my tools, and I'm ready to go work today. I'm gonna really work hard, and I'm gonna keep this job."

But all of Scott's buddies, people that Scott was trying to teach to play fiddle, they came over there. While he was up on the roof hammering, there was twelve of them, down below, and they were applauding Scott. He looked down, and he said, "What . . .?" And they said, "That's for Scott Stoneman. We're here to applaud Scott Stoneman on!"

They were Scott's people. If you saw Scott Stoneman one time perform, you'd be his people. If you saw him perform twenty or twenty-five minutes—even ten minutes, he was that great—you'd be his people. From then on, you would never forget Scott. People come up to me now: "I remember your brother Scott. Booooy, what a musician! What a showman!" Scott sang good too. But he was so brilliant on that fiddle. He would come, 4:00 or 5:00 in the morning, knocking on my door: "Aunt Roni, can I come in and play my fiddle?" I'd say, "Well, the kids are asleep, but you can go right in there in the kitchen." And he would play. It sounded like from outer space, he would get so far out. It sounded like nothing I ever heard before.

So his "people" were mad at him. There he was hammering and ruining his hands. They were mocking him, trying in that way to get him to go back to the fiddle.

Scott came in that evening and he said, "Mom, you know what they did? They 'plauded for me." Momma said, "Well bless your heart, Scott. Just don't pay no attention to them." He said, "They're embarrassing me, Mom. The boss of the construction said, 'Why don't ya just skip a day?'—since I couldn't do good on the job with them 'plauding. But they told me they're coming back every day." And he just laid his head down on the table. So he quit after only working a few months.

Now, I was on the road somewhere years later, and Benny Martin, the great fiddler, told me a strange story.

"You know what sobered me up?" asked Benny.

I shook my head.

"Well, Scotty was my friend. We were rivals, but we were also friends. This is how I found out about his death. I had been out drinking a lot, was real drunk, and I went over to Dickerson Road, where this guy had a service station, which was also a bootleg joint. At that time Nashville didn't have liquor by the drink, and you had to go buy your bottle. I knocked at the door, but nobody answered so I kicked the door open. There was a cot in the back room, and the guy was asleep on it. I kicked him and said, 'Get up and git me a drink.' Well, the man shot me in the foot with his gun. It was dark and he didn't know it was me. I cried, 'Jesus, you killed my foot,' and the blood was flying everywhere. So I went into the bathroom, and I stuck my foot in the commode—it was filthy, stinking—and flushed it several times to take the blood away.

"A few days later I started having severe pain. Gangrene was setting in. I was still drunk, reeked of alcohol. But somebody took me down to General Hospital. They put me up on a gurney and the doc came in and looked at my foot.

"'Well, we can fix it, but you're going to have to stay off it for awhile. What do you do for a living?'

"'I play fiddle. And I'm damned good!'

"So the doctor says, 'Well, that's funny. We just took a guy right off this same gurney straight to the morgue. Was a fiddle player too. Scott Stoneman. You know him?'

"'Scotty Stoneman dead?'

"'We just got him off this gurney. We just now put some clean paper on it.'"

And then Benny said to me, "I sobered up immediately and I wrote a song about it."

But I want to leave you with something sweet about Scott. This incident—I can see it now. I put myself in that one-room house, and it makes me want to cry. Well, Scott came in—he was young, fourth or fifth grade—and he said, "Aunt Roni, guess what? Everybody likes my fiddling." "Yeah, that's good, Scott." Because we were kids. We didn't pay much attention at that time to how good he was. And he's sitting there at the table. He said, "I gotta practice my name." He got a piece of paper, and he started practicing autographing it. He put lots of curlicues on the S." "How does that look, Mom?" he asked. And then, "Look, Roni, ya see how I did that Y? See that S?" Signing his name. Over and over. And when he got it the way he wanted, it was like a piece of artwork. "Idn't that good? Idn't that good, Roni?" "Yeah, that's good, Scott. That's real nice."

The irony of it. Because soon all these sophisticated people would be showing up to hear him play. And there he was, working so hard learning to write his name pretty, like an artist, so he'd seem more worthy. I think that everybody ought to know about that, that Scott wasn't all drink. He had ways about him that were so sweet. And he was lost, bless his heart.

NINETEEN

Hee Haw

Before I left the family band, I had an interesting talk with Ernest Tubb. We were doing a lot of shows with him, Ernest Tubb and the Texas Troubadours. Well, I remember one time going on the bus—that same bus that's now on exhibit at the Ernest Tubb Record Shop in Nashville. We were playing at Sunset Park or someplace like that. I had just about crawled into that bus because I was so hot and tired. I'm sitting there, and Ernest Tubb was sitting across from me.

I sighed.

"What's the matter, Roni?"

I looked to the window, and I said, "I can't stand this. I hate it."

"Well, what do you want to do?"

"I don't know. Maybe get into comedy? Maybe on television? It would be so much easier. I know that from when our TV show was still running. I could be with the kids more, just go in for the taping and then come home. And still do better than what I'm doing."

He reached over and he patted my hand. "You got the talent, girl," he said. "Don't dream small, reach for the sky. You want to do comedy? Go for it. There's a television show—*Hee Haw* . . ."

"Yeah, I know. I'd like to get on it."

Hee Haw had just started. No one realized then that the combination of quick segments of cornball humor, beautiful girls, and country music would end up being so popular, would sweep the nation. No one realized it would become the longest running syndicated show ever.

Anyway, back then Bob Bean said if my brothers and sisters couldn't go on it, I couldn't. And at that point I didn't want to leave the family band. I was bringing home some money, and in those days it was enough to get by on, at least feed the children and buy my place to live.

Ernest Tubb was great. Not only because he was a terrific performer and Opry star, but also because he was always helping young musicians. He'd showcase them on his *Midnight Jamboree* radio show and advise them as he did me. God, I loved him. Years later, in 1982, I played the last show he ever did, when he had emphysema. He was so sick he'd get on the bus and use oxygen. Everybody in the audiences adored him. They knew he was terribly sick. His face was all sunk in and his eyes were hollowed, and he was gasping. And he got up there and did his "Walking the Floor over You."

So now let's back up to about 1970, a little while after that conversation about *Hee Haw*. I said I knew I couldn't get on the show because of Bob Bean. But I got a call from Bud Wingard, who was one of the *Hee Haw* writers. He said he was working on something for the show, and could I come down and talk with him about it? I was staying with Bob and Donna, but I sort of went down to his place secretly. I got all dressed up as fancy as I could, did my hair, had on a nice black dress, perfect makeup and all. I walked in the door, and he said, "Yes, you're exactly what we want. We already have enough pretty girls." Hmm! And he talked a little about the Ida Lee character they were creating. But nothing really came of that.

When the money I was making with the family band got really bad, that's when, as I said, George started telling me to quit, and I did in 1971. But *Hee Haw* was still not something I seriously went after. We were living on an ex–military base in Smyrna, a cheap little place. I was raising seven children, four of my own, and me and George had Georgia, and then his two boys, Bart and Eric. And I was trying to get jobs wherever I could.

After quitting the family band, I had to start all over again, and it wasn't easy. It was not only that I didn't have the musical support I was used to. It was also the responsibility. You're out there entertaining the people, and you know you've got to keep them satisfied in order to keep working. It's all on you, the pressure and the stress. That's what it was though I didn't use those words. People didn't contemplate about stress in those days. You just did your work. And you'd worry—worry about the food, worry about the rent, worry, worry, worry. George wasn't working, and I didn't have nothing. I was in no state to imagine that I could go after a TV show.

I did get that job in Printer's Alley, where I had to learn how to get the sidemen to stop distracting the audience. That job, however, soon ended, and then I went with Buddy Lee Attractions, a talent agency. But they never booked me in six long months. Finally they said that I could perform at a party they were giving. I was desperate. I got the kids to bed, and I took off.

The party was at one of those huge hotels. I walked into a main room, and there was a long table with all kinds of hors d'oeuvres and little teeny sandwiches. Tom T. Hall was sitting in a corner, by the table. Everybody else was standing up and mingling. And there was a door leading to another room where there was a whole bunch of other people. I looked down at the table. I was starving because I didn't hardly eat anything—I gave it all to the kids.

Tom T. Hall saw me look at the food.

"What's the matter, Roni?" he said. "You hungry?"

"Yeah, sure am."

"Get you a plate, big plate. Pile it up." Now, this is not long after Jeannie C. Riley recorded Tom T.'s "Harper Valley PTA." He was *the* Tom T. Hall with a huge hit record.

"Here, take a plate," he said. "Pull a chair up."

"You're not supposed to sit down at the hors d'oeuvres table."

"Who cares? Sit down. You're hungry, eat. Eat all you want. Do it."

Tom T.'s got a soul and can really understand downtrodden folk. He deserves his name, Nashville's Storyteller. He's written one hit song after another about ordinary people just living ordinary lives. I perform a lot of those songs—like "Clayton Delaney," about the old drunken guitarist and the young boy he encouraged, and "Old Dogs and Children and Watermelon Wine," about a janitor's advice about life.

Anyway, I sat down and Tom T. filled my plate up. I ate sandwiches and more sandwiches and all kinds of little hors d'oeuvres. Then Tom T. leaned back in his chair.

"Roni, you should be on *Hee Haw*," he said.

"I'd like to be on *Hee Haw*. Yeah, I'd like that."

"The producer of *Hee Haw* is in that room there. His name's Sam Lovullo. You *are Hee Haw*. You should go in there and say, 'Hey, I'm Roni Stoneman. You need me.'"

"Oh, I can't go in there and bother him."

Now at that time I still had a big space in the front of my teeth and I had my crooked eye. Besides being skinny as a rail, I could walk up to a wall and my two hipbones would hit the wall before my tummy hit. And I was just weakened down, beat down.

"C'mon, I'll take you in there," Tom T. said. And he did.

Sam Lovullo was talking to three other men.

"Sam . . ." said Tom.

"Yeah, Tom, what can I do for you?"

"I want you to meet Roni Stoneman. She should be on *Hee Haw*."

"Oh?"

"Yeah, she should be on *Hee Haw*. *Hee Haw* needs this girl."

"Hi," I said. And I grinned.

Sam looked at me.

"You *are* just what we need," he said. "We have all the pretty girls we want."

This was something of a common refrain with those guys!

"You oughta come see us," he went on. "We need a character actress."

I didn't know what a character actress meant. I didn't know anything about that kind of thing. I was just stark-naked stress, walking around in a stupor.

I left the room in a daze. Later, I took some sandwiches home, and some other food. Tom T. packed me a bag. "Here, take it," he said.

Six months afterwards Sam Lovullo contacted me to come do a "reading." I didn't know exactly what a "reading" was, but I told George that I had to go down for it. He drove me to the producers' office. And all the way down there from Smyrna to Nashville—it's about thirty-five miles—he was yelling at me, "Don't act stupid! Don't act dumb! Don't use bad grammar." In fact everything he told me not to do was what they wanted. But I didn't realize this.

By the time I got down there, I was a wreck, scared to death. When I walked in the office, there was Sam and another producer and the director, and the people who created the show, John Aylesworth and Frank Peppiatt. George went in with me. The producers said, "We want a skinny Marjorie Main." "That's Ma Kettle, isn't it?" I said. "Yeah." "Well, she used to be my favorite actress." So they gave me this paper and told me to read some lines. I said, "Umm, umm." And then I tried to read, with good grammar and all. And I said, "Is that all right?" I didn't ask them. I looked at George. Because I didn't want to get yelled at.

I was in that room for about an hour, reading those lines and knowing I wasn't doing a good job. It was a horrible experience. Sam finally said, "Um, that'll be fine. You'll hear from me."

George cussed me all the way back to Smyrna. How dumb I was, how stupid of me not to do anything right. We got home and he went into the bedroom and drank 'til he passed out.

He was still asleep the next morning after I got the older kids off to school. Georgia was a little baby. I fed her and gave her a bottle and put her back in her crib. Then I went into the closet in the kids' bedroom and I started praying. This may sound corny but this was my prayer: "Dear God, please help me. If I had this job I wouldn't have to play nightclubs and honky-tonks. I'd have money enough to buy food and things that the children need for school. And I wouldn't have to be away from them so much. In Jesus' name, help me to get this job. Make the man call and give me a second chance." I prayed for about an hour and a half right in the clothes, tears streaming down my face. Then I quit crying and got up and did all the housework and picked up Georgia and played with her.

Two days later Sam got in touch with me again.

"I want you to come down here without your husband," said Sam.

"I don't have no way to get down there unless he brings me."

"You can't get down here?"

"No, sir, I don't have a driver's license."

"Okay," he said, "I'll tell you what. Come with him. We have a suite up there at the Ramada Inn, and Gordie, who's the guy that will play the character's husband, can take you up there to read with you. We'll pretend that we need to see George for business and keep him here."

So that's what happened.

Me and Gordie sat down at a little table in the suite at the Ramada Inn.

"Now Roni, like we said before, this is a Marjorie Main, Ma Kettle kind of character," Gordie explained. "So we want you to sound like that."

Well, I knew her voice because I remembered her so well in *Ma and Pa Kettle Go to Town*. And I used to imitate her when I was a child. But it wasn't only Ma Kettle that I would imitate, it was also a woman who sounded just like her, Mrs. Crigger. Mrs. Crigger was a neighbor. I believe she was originally from West Virginia, from the mountains. She had seven sons, and they lived in a place called Miller's Bottom, not far from our house in Carmody Hills. Momma would get after my brothers for going there because the Crigger boys drank and were wild.

I loved watching Mrs. Crigger. Momma would say to me, "Now, don't go and bother that poor old woman. I don't want you causing her any more problems and being in her way." Then Momma would say, "Poor thang, she just don't know any better." And first chance I got, I'd go sneak off over there to watch. Mrs. Crigger dipped snuff—sometimes it was dry, and sometimes it was wet. She would yell, and a big puff of it would come out of her mouth. She would be trying to control her sons, but they were all doing awful things, drinking, hollering, stomping around. She'd say, "Fightin', you ornery cusses . . . ?" And once she got the shotgun and she shot the chimney of the old wood stove right out of the roof. Sparks went everywhere and the house caught on fire, and they had to call the fire department down. But she was just trying to show her sons that it wasn't a fitten thing to do, to celebrate Christmas by getting drunk and fighting. She would say, "Dadburnit, I don't know what makes you boys all do like this! Dadburnit!"

She was a total joy to me. She was short and she wore brogan shoes, and, as I grew older, I thought she would have been perfect for *Li'l Abner*, as Mammy Yokum. I dearly loved her. So when I walked home, I'd be practicing her voice. I'd say, "Dadburnit, git outta the way!" to some squirrel or chipmunk. "Dadburnit, don't you hear me? Quit actin' like that!" I was about nine, ten years old. And I would practice her body language, her gestures. She would take her forearm and swipe it across her mouth. She'd just sling it, and the snuff would fly right onto the long apron she wore over an old cotton dress.

Anyway, back to Gordie and the Ramada Inn.

"I can do that Ma Kettle voice," I said, "'cause I used to do that for drunks fighting when I was playing honky-tonks."

"Well, let's hear it."

"All right: 'Dadburnit, settle down y'all! I mean it now! Pa, git over hyar.'" It was the voice of Ma Kettle, but of course it was also the voice of Mrs. Crigger.

"That's just what we want!" said Gordie.

He was holding a paper, and he said, "Can you do a reading of . . . ?"

"I don't know how to do a reading, but I know how to read."

"Well, just do these lines with that voice."

And I did.

We walked back down to Channel Five, went in the back door, and Gordie said, "She's perfect, Sam."

Well, that was the way Sam Lovullo was—he had known that I was so beat down and intimidated by George I could never do anything right with him around.

So I was cast as Ida Lee Nagger, the mountain woman at the ironing board. And that gesture of wiping the snuff by slinging my arm across my mouth became one of my trademarks.

What I tried to get across with Ida Lee is a funny mountain woman that's standing up for herself. Laverne'd badmouth me about my cooking, and I'd say, "What are you talkin' about? My cookin's the best in the world!" Most of our skits took place in a kitchen. They would bring in pork and beans and cornbread from Cracker Barrel. And Gordie'd sit there and stir it on this tin plate. And he'd say, "Dadblame it now, Ida

Lee, get it right this time. I've eaten half my beans. I'm eatin' the props here!"

The ironing board was always sitting there with this old eight-pound flat iron. I had it where it had a rag over it, like it was awfully hot and I was having a hard time picking it up because of the heat. One time they had misplaced my rag, so I said, "Aw, it don't matter. We'll do it without." And then I got letters—"Where's the rag?" "How come Ida Lee's not using the rag over her iron?" I immediately got a rag. The fans of *Hee Haw* were the most loyal, wonderful fans in the world. They noticed everything. Another example, my way-too-big socks that I had on with bedroom slippers—the fans would write in if one sock was dirtier than the other one.

We'd get letters all the time about Ida Lee and Laverne. They were really beloved characters. And people would come up to us at shows and say, "That's just like my husband and me!" "My Gosh, that's just like us!" I felt that I did that part well. Why? Because it really was my life. And what wasn't, I had learned from watching Mrs. Crigger. Ida Lee became a hillbilly icon.

We taped twice a year, June to July and October to November. It was very concentrated. They'd give us our checks on the last day of the taping. We didn't tape much on weekends, at least I didn't. I did shows in some nearby state, air shows, country fairs. I'd be coming back late Sunday night, and still have to be ready early Monday morning, on camera by eight, seven if we were going to overdub our voices to make it sound fuller. We'd sometimes do twenty-eight Ida Lee and Lavernes in one morning, just one after another, the best we could.

I had other parts besides the Ironing Board Lady. I was Mophead, the hotel maid, with the mop head. And then sometimes I was Roni, with the pony tails, playing the banjo. And then they had me as the exercising gal in a skit called "Fit as a Fiddle." The girls would get up there and they would dance around, looking gorgeous. I had a 1920s type bathing suit on, and a bathing cap. I was supposed to look awful, and I did. But I could do anything I wanted with my exercising. So I'd jump up and down, sort of mocking the gorgeous girls, but mainly creating my own daffy character. I was having all kinds of fun.

But one of the funniest experiences occurred when I was doing Ida

Lee. I was late for work. I'm thinking, Oh my God, I'm running late. I took the baby to the babysitter, now I gotta get back here, and I got this to do, blah, blah, blah. Anybody who's been a mother knows what that's like. I thought, I might as well wear Ida Lee into work. That'll save me some minutes when I arrive. And maybe Sam will think I've already been there or I wouldn't be dressed like that.

So I put Ida Lee's outfit on, and I put the darkness under my eyes—on the place that nowadays I try to lighten up! When I walked in, they were breaking for lunch, that's how late I was. I think somebody like Roy Clark had to do their songs over. They did all the filming in segments. Then Sandy Liles would do the editing, putting it all together. That was the talented part. The other part, what we did, was all foolish and fun. But, boy, little Sandy was some editor!

Anyway, back to that day at *Hee Haw*. The girls were going out because the fire department was going to give us a brunch. Well, we had that brunch with some mighty handsome firemen. The other girls had their cute little dresses on, with their chests pushed up. And I'm sitting there dressed as Ida Lee, in the old robe and the wig with rags in it.

On the way back, the girls somehow got a little ahead of me. And just as I reached the edge of the curb to turn in to the *Hee Haw* studio, three plainclothes policemen jumped out and they grabbed me by the arm.

"Wha . . .?" I cried. "What are you doing?"

"Police Department," said one, showing me his badge. "Who threw you out the car, lady? Who did it?" (This was in the early days of *Hee Haw* before everybody became so recognizable.)

"Nobody threw me out of a car! Nobody!"

"Oh yes, somebody did. C'mon now. Just tell us who it was. We'll take care of it for you."

"No, sir, I promise with all my heart, nobody threw me out. I'm getting ready to go on stage . . ."

"You don't have to be afraid. Who did it? Who's treatin' you this way?"

"No, no, really. You come down to *Hee Haw*, right over there. They'll tell you."

Someone finally said, "Okay," and they marched me over to the studio. They had me under both arms, practically dragging me.

"See?" I said. "See, there's Kenny Price. See, there's Gailard Sartain. Kenny, tell them I'm here to do a part in the show. They think I've been thrown out in the street."

"No, no, no, she belongs with us," said Kenny. "She belongs here."

Now Kenny Price was a great big heavyset guy. But he was wearing a little boy's cowboy outfit, sheriff's department, with a great big ol' tin star, short britches, knee socks. And Gailard's wearing one of his hillbilly costumes.

The policeman looks at Kenny, and then he looks at Gailard.

"I'm not so sure about you two either," he says.

Then Archie Campbell comes out.

"No, Officer," he says, "she really does belong with us." Archie had his barbershop outfit on and that cigar in his mouth.

The policeman stares at Archie.

"I'm not so sure about you either."

In the end they had to take me inside and talk to Sam. Everybody laughed about that for years.

I want to talk a little about some of the other actors on the show because they are beloved by millions of people all over the country. The girls were wonderful, the *Hee Haw* Honeys, with their chests, like whoa, Dolly Partons, and always a diamond or pearl in their cleavage. I never heard of the word "cleavage" until I got on *Hee Haw*. Archie Campbell told me what it meant. People would always say, "Those beautiful girls," and they *were* beautiful. In one skit the girls laid on the porch, and there would be Grandpa Jones, and they'd say, "Grandpa, do you think . . . ?" And the camera would pull back from these beautiful girls laying there, focusing on one after another, laying sideways, with them bras that was just tight as they could be around them. The girls suffered a lot to get that look. They'd come running backstage and throw the bras in a box where there'd be laundry. They'd say, "Oh, God, this bra—I'll be so glad to get it off." I kept thinking, How come I'm not fluffy up there on my chest? I'm just a boneyard. What can I do to get that look? There must be a trick to this. So I tried one or two of the bras on. It didn't work. The pushups really did nothing but bring up what the girls already had. And I just had the bone.

But those girls were wonderful in spirit and soul also. And they were great actresses—they knew how to read their lines and they were total professionals.

Misty Rowe was the one who had that high-pitched voice—"Hi, everybody." Sometimes you wanted to pinch her head off, it was so cute. All the fellers liked it—"Now, it's time for me to tell my bedtime stories." But Misty's real personality? Well, she's the kindest, most giving, gentle gal ever. She took care of her grandfather up 'til the very end, never had him put in a nursing home. Then she got married to this guy named Jim, a soap opera star, and they had a little girl. Misty had gone to acting school and had lived in L.A. And she was smart. She would give you advice like a lawyer.

One day she said, "I'm working up a show, Roni." And I thought, What is she gonna do after she does the "Hi, everybody"? But I encouraged her, and we did some shows together. She sang, *Oh you stepped on my heart / and squashed that sucker flat,* and she sounded good. She wore a little cowgirl outfit that she had made herself, pink satin, and a hat, and boots that came way up high, and rhinestones all over. She looked just darling. The audiences loved her.

Then there was Gunilla, Nurse Goodbody. She was also beautiful, she could sing very very good, and she was funny. Just by giggling herself, she could make anybody giggle and not be able to stop. She was also never insecure with herself on stage. She was married to a guy named Allen that had his own construction company. Last time I heard she was living in Boston. She had two boys, and adopted a wonderful little girl named Amber, who she sent to the finest schools. Gunilla is a mother type. She looked so beautiful, but she had a mother's mind, and a caretaking way about her.

Lulu, who played the fat girl, was also very talented. I really liked her work, and I would try to learn from her. I would watch her expressions, her eyes, and think, Ah she's good. She was sensitive too. I felt sorry for her because she wanted so desperately for a man to love her like a man should love a woman. And Lulu was a beautiful woman. There was none that had prettier eyes than Lulu, none that had prettier skin, none that had prettier hair. She dressed wonderful. She would wear the highest styles, even with her size.

Lulu was not happy with her size. On camera you'd think she was okay. She knew how to put that over. But she was never satisfied with her weight or her love life. Her love life had not been good—she had been taken advantage of and hurt a lot. One day I came in the dressing room and Lulu was sitting there alone crying her heart out. I said, "Lulu, is there anything I can do? I hate to see you so sad." So she told me a terrible thing that had happened with one of the men in her life. And she said, "Don't tell anyone." I said I wouldn't, and I hugged her, and I said, "Just pray. That's the only thing you can do. Just pray."

Linda Thompson. The most gorgeous woman in the world. Everything on her body was tan. Sometimes I'd get embarrassed and go into the bathroom to change because I had been raised in a modest environment—you don't look at your body or you don't show it much. But the *Hee Haw* girls, well their bodies were also their job, so they were more casual about not being covered up. Linda always wore gold chains around her waist. She became a very good mother when she married Bruce Jenner. She had two boys by him. When the kids went out to play at the Opryland, they would sneak through the door. They had to sneak out because she was a famous person and so was Bruce Jenner, and she was scared that someone was going to kidnap her children. When Marianne Gordon married Kenny Rogers, they had little Christopher Cody, and one time Christopher took off with Linda's two. Three little boys on the loose. The parents were really scared. They were out hunting for hours for those children. Finally the kids came back—"Hi, Mom, we had fun today!"

I loved Minnie Pearl. Everybody did. But she was a powerful woman, and you had to know where you belonged. No mugging when she was on stage. That was understandable. You don't get into people's way when they're stars. And Miss Minnie was truly a star.

She always considered herself Mrs. Henry Cannon, and Minnie Pearl only when she was working. She was from an upper class family, very proper, and had been trained in a finishing school like a true Southern belle.

She thought of herself as not pretty. She'd say, "I know what I look like." But she wasn't jealous—she treated the pretty little girls on *Hee Haw* like they were her own children. And when she'd sit in the makeup room to have her makeup done, all the girls would gather around her,

Miss Georgia, Miss Tennessee, Miss This and Miss That. They would make it a point to be there early enough to hear Miss Minnie's stories. She would talk about when she was a young girl and what she had learned in her life.

A lot of the advice was about men. Although she always told the girls to be careful, not to believe everything the menfolks said, she really didn't badmouth them. She would declare, "I had a wonderful time in my life." Miss Minnie was a man's lady, she truly was. She loved to be around where all the boys were.

After the stories, when she'd gotten her makeup and her hair done and put on her dress with the safety pin and her little Mary Jane shoes, she'd come cruising onto the set and she'd go right to her spot: "We're gonna play now. *Hee Haw*'s All Jug Band." Then we'd start playing. Miss Minnie would sing—*Oh love, oh love, oh careless love*. And she'd just beat the piano. She was a great character actress, and by then I understood exactly what that was.

Although I got along real well with the girls on the program, I didn't have much in common with them, other than Gunilla and Misty Rowe. I was not in the world of the girls on the show: Look at the beautiful dress I bought, or Here's my new fingernail polish. I was in a world of take care of babies and work to bring home baby food.

So in the studio I hung around with the men as much as the girls. Buck Owens always seemed to me like a businessman. He was 100 percent professional. He would say, "All right, boys and girls, let's get this thing going. Let's cut this chorus." And he'd gather us all around the microphone. I never saw him drunk, or pilled or cocained up. He wasn't that kind of guy.

Now, when it came to his love life, he maybe had a weak moment. Anybody that talented usually does. So he might have had trouble with his lady friends. Like little Jana Jae, the fiddle player. And he might have followed her around the country, staring up at her when she did a show, like everybody said he was doing. Stare at her and beg her to come back home to him. She wouldn't. She was married to him for about a week. But from what I was told, he had been living for a long time with this other woman, who had been on the road with him before. And when she found out that he married Jana Jae, she threw a big fit. And what I heard, and I don't know whether it's true, but that's what everybody was saying, was that she beat him up, and he was in the hospital from it. His story was that he fell off of a horse in distraction when Jana Jae left him. The rumor was that Jana Jae left him because she didn't know that he had been living with this woman, so it made her look like a fool.

Gailard Sartain was the funniest man I ever knew. I loved to watch him perform. And I fell in love with him like a woman with a man. But I was also scared of him because he would change from one minute to another. He was extremely intelligent, a genius. But sometimes this is a problem. You're more sensitive than the average bear, you sense all these emotions in other people, and you have to cope with that.

On the side, he painted. His southwestern paintings were just beyond compare. But whenever Gailard had the blues, he really had the blues. One day he looked extremely sad.

"What's the matter, Gailard?"

"It's my little girl."

"What happened?"

"Well the other day I thought, Well, I'm going to draw something for her. So I drew a pair of socks and shoes on her bare feet with a magic marker. I even drew shoestrings."

"That's real cute!"

"Well, she went to her friend's house, and when she came back, she was all upset and crying. She said, 'My friend's father told me you were silly, a silly man.'"

And Gailard was hurt about that real bad. He loved his children so much. (He said it took about three months for that stuff to wear off his little girl's foot.)

Roy Clark I knew before joining *Hee Haw*. We were friends back in the old days, when we Stonemans were playing the Famous Bar and Grill in Washington. Roy would often play our nights off. Which is what makes this story I'm going to tell you strange. I still don't understand it.

Now, after awhile I was not only playing the comic parts, but was also in the Banjo Band. And one day we were going to film a whole bunch of banjo songs. So we were messing around before, five or six banjo players, all walking around, tuning and warming up. And I went over to Roy, and he looked at me: "Hi, Ronald J." And he went cha na na cha na na on his banjo, and I went cha na na cha na na, "Dueling Banjos." Then I got faster and faster, because that's what I always did. Well, Roy was picking along with me. Now Roy is one of the greatest guitar players in the world. On the guitar nobody could catch him, nobody, never. But he hadn't been used to playing this particular tune on the banjo. So I'm zooming along. And then Roy holds my hand up, like "The winner, the champion!"

"Thanks, Roy, that was fun," I said.

And Sam Lovullo came up and he walked me away from the group of people that was picking.

"Roni, you shouldn't have done that."

"Done what, Sam?"

"You shouldn't have outran Roy."

"I didn't outrun him."

"Yes, you did. He even held your hand up."

"That was just in fun. It wasn't taped anyway."

"Oh yes it was. We taped it."

"You did? Well, erase it, just erase it. Don't use it." I was scared. Roy was the star. I didn't want to lose my job.

"No, no, it's all right. We're gonna let it go."

"Don't do that, Sam! I didn't know you were taping."

"Yeah, we were. It's all right. But don't do it again."

So they went ahead with the rest of the taping, and, needless to say, I was real subdued. In my family it didn't matter who got the applause just so somebody got it. But when you were with a group of people like the *Hee Haw* bunch, you had to be extra careful. And I hadn't realized that enough.

That was June/July. Then the fall taping time came around, and I got a call from Al Gallico. Al Gallico was an Italian from New York, and he had a publishing company, Al Gallico Music, with offices in Nashville, L.A., London. At that time he was publishing everything that Tammy Wynette and George Jones recorded. Gallico was an old friend and he knew about my family and he knew how hard we had worked. He was always encouraging me.

So Al Gallico calls.

"Hey, Dollface . . ." That's the way he talked, with an exaggerated

Italian accent. He was warm and funny, a wonderful man. "Hey, Dollface, come on down to Mario's. I'm gonna tell you somethin' important. I'm gonna buy you some dinna, and tell you somethin' important."

So I went down to Mario's.

"Dollface," said Gallico, "you gotta listen to me, Dollface. They're so damn jealous of you down at *Hee Haw* they don't know what to do."

"What's the matter?"

"Well, I rode back from L.A. with one of the writers of *Hee Haw*. He told me that some guy connected with managing Roy came into a meeting, and he said that he did not want for Roni Stoneman to ever play beside Roy Clark in the Banjo Band again."

My heart went down to my stomach. I just felt that I had lost my job. I thought, Roy won't do me that way. But I felt that Roy did not know about it. I would like to think he didn't, that he's not that kind of a person. Because, God knows, he was the king. I was just one of the workers. I worked hard on that show, I would lose fifteen pounds every time we taped, but Roy was a star.

So I said, "Oh, my God, what am I going to do, Gallico?"

"Don't worry about it, sweetheart, don't worry about it. Just be careful."

The fall taping started about three days later. I was walking on eggshells, moving very quietly in the hallways. I was keeping my distance even though I hadn't seen my friends for the whole summer, and we had a lot to talk about—what's happened to you since I saw you, I want to tell you something funny, such stuff.

So then it came time to film the Banjo Band segments. Now the Banjo Band would always stand on a flatbed truck. The rest of the cast would sit on bales of hay, watching the Banjo Band and clapping their hands to the music.

Well, I started to go up there on the flatbed, and they said, "No, no, no, no, you come here." They sat me down on a bale of hay. Then the floor manager came over with a piece of that white Red Cross tape, and he taped my banjo strings!

I sat there and I almost cried. But you don't cry. Crying girls don't make it in such a place. So I just sat. And I stared straight ahead, and I thought, Well, what do I do now? I wanted to get up and walk out. But

I thought of Daddy, and I heard an echo in my mind say, "You stay right where you are, girl, you got children to feed."

But they weren't finished. Then they came with paper tape, and they made an X on the floor and put my foot on it, made another X and put my other foot on it, so I couldn't dance while I was sitting down. I could just swing my knees a little. And then I had to pretend to play. No one ever said anything to me about it. They told me my story with showing me.

Now, as I said, I always felt that Roy himself wasn't really in on that whole thing. Because Roy's a great guy. One time he said to me, "Ronald J., you know back when I was a kid and you lived in Carmooody Hills"—that's the way he pronounced it—"I used to hang around outside, just to listen to your brothers playing."

"Well, why didn't you come on and join 'em?"

"Well . . ."

That was Roy. In spite of being such a big star, he was real modest, and private. And he's always been super-generous. He recently got a big humanitarian award for his work with charities.

Anyway, the men I hung around with most were Grandpa Jones and Stringbean. With Grandpa and String I felt a special kindredship. They seemed like, I don't know, I guess my Grandpa Frost mixed in with Daddy. I talked about Grandpa Jones and how nice he was to me at the Constitution Hall contest. Well later I guess Grandpa sort of forgot about how old I was because he tried to fix me up with his son Mark. Afterwards, I tried to fix Mark up with my daughter! Is this getting confusing? Reminds me of that song "I'm My Own Grandpa." That was one Grandpa Jones often sang. He never actually was a natural grandpa though he did have stepgrandchildren. The age thing was bound to be confusing with him of course. He had been making himself up to look old since he was twenty-two.

Stringbean would be wearing those rolled britches, the long-waisted pants, and he would really look funny. He and Grandpa were good friends. I would follow them around. One day they were sitting there at *Hee Haw* talking about hunting and fishing. Stringbean was always telling about how during the Depression years up in Kentucky, they didn't have any food at all. He said, "I used to take my slingshot and kill crows.

Every time I see a crow, I think that's what kept me alive those years." Well, they were talking about hunting, and then they started talking about this set of books called *Foxfire*.

These books came about because there was a man who was teaching in Georgia, and he didn't know how to reach the mountain children. So he decided to teach them about their own culture, and he started writing the *Foxfire* series. The books tell you how to do everything that they did in the mountains. Any New Yorker or person from Chicago could learn the mountain ways just by reading these books. They teach you how to hunt, how to live off the land, how to make a fiddle, how to get cane for chairs, and how those old ladies would make their butter like I saw my grandma do—you skim off the top and you dip down deep and start churning and churning. Well, String would say, "Yeah, I been reading that *Foxfire* last night." They were so proud that someone from Johns Hopkins University wrote about our culture.

After I heard String and Grandpa, I went out and got the books, and I read them all, every one of them. And I think a similar kind of teaching maybe would work in some of the city schools where there's a lot of bad things going on, people beating up on each other because there's all different nationalities. The teacher could say, "I want you all to go home and talk to your mother and father about your family background and the story of their lives." And then the kids would get some pride in their heritage. Because this *Foxfire* series really made me feel proud of my culture. And the different heritages would be interesting to all the kids and make them understand each other better.

Stringbean was the first one to mention my name on *Hee Haw*. I worked there awhile before anybody knew who that Ironing Board Lady was. And when I held the banjo, I would just stand around and hope for a turn because I wasn't hired for banjo music. But String got me playing more, and he would introduce me, "My little friend from woman's lib, Roni Stoneman!" It made *Hee Haw* look more up to date to have some woman up there. So I was able to get in with the Banjo Band because of String.

Then when String was murdered, I took his place. I can't even remember the exact year that happened, it was in the early seventies, because it was so tragic and so emotional to me. He and his wife Estelle were just the most delightful human beings that lived on this earth. Now, whenever String would come in the back door of the studio, Roy Clark would say, "String how much you take for your britches?" And String would say, "Oh," and he'd pat the bib of his bib overalls, "about seventy-five." And I'd say, "What do you mean by seventy-five?" And he'd say, "Well, just seventy-five," and he'd pat his bib overalls again. Then one day I went to Roy. I said, "Roy, how come you're always asking String how much he'd take for his britches?" And Roy said, "He's always got sixty-five to seventy-five grand in them."

String said that was in case some of his friends needed money. "I don't believe in banks since the Depression years," he would add. Estelle also carried a lot of money on her. The musicians all knew that, and String and Estelle were never harmed. Of course we all also knew that he could shoot good because he was a hunter, as in those stories of him killing the crows. Though there ain't a Kentuckian alive up in those hills that don't consider themselves one of the best shots that ever happened. You take a mountain man, and you tell him that he's not a good shot, he'll come after you to prove you wrong!

I was talking to String one day, at *Hee Haw,* sitting on a bale of hay, during a break. I said, "String, why don't you take some of your money and go with Estelle to the Riviera? Just think, you could take a photo and say, 'Stringbean and Estelle at the French Riviera.'" And then I went on, "From what I was told, they don't wear bathing suits over there." He took his pipe out of his mouth, looked at me sideways, kinda cocked his right eye, and grinned a little bit. I said, "Don't you ever want to take her somewhere romantic-like, and put her in one of those little gondolas around the river? That would be fun. Spend some of the money you carry around in your bibs." And then I said, "String, seriously, honey, you ought to be real careful." He said, "Well, I've been doin' it for many years. I have my protection," and he patted his chest, where he had his gun.

The last night I saw String, I was backstage at the Opry. Jimmy Dickens came over to him and said, "String, be careful going home, be careful drivin'." This was so strange, that he would say that. And I went over to him, and I said, "String, we're gonna walk you all out to the car, you and Estelle." We got to the car, and I said, "Now you be careful." "Oh,

I got my little baby with me," he said, patting the gun. I said again, "Be careful." And him and Estelle drove off, with me and Jimmy Dickens waving to them. And that was strange too. We didn't usually do that.

Grandpa found the bodies. He was to go fishing with Stringbean about 4:30, 5:00, the next morning. String was lying on the porch. He had set the banjo Uncle Dave Macon had given him down at the door. Evidently he sensed something was amiss. He probably said, "Get out! Go!" Estelle must've started running to the car. They shot him before he even got in the door. And she was shot in the back of the head four or five times.

People put out rewards. And everybody started getting dogs for their places. I think Jimmy Dickens had five Doberman pinschers in his yard, and a fence around it. Detectives and the FBI, the federal FBI as well as the Tennessee office, worked on the case. And next thing you know, they caught the robbers.

The robbers didn't take a bit of money. They couldn't find any. It was on him and on her, and some of it was in an old costume bag, and some in the freezer. The robbers were not Nashville people who knew that String and Estelle kept vast amounts of money on them. They were just three men from Greenbriar, Tennessee. They had been waiting at Stringbean's house while he played the Grand Ole Opry. They were listening to him on the radio and waiting for him to get home.

The funeral was the saddest one I've ever been to in my life. The fire department and the police had on their dress uniforms. They stood with their hats over their hearts. And of course the mountain people, that loved him so much, were there, standing silent as the coffins in the procession went by.

There was no music at the funeral. I just couldn't believe that. But String belonged to a church that didn't believe in it. They had singing. The thing that made me sad too was that they buried him in a suit. Everybody in Nashville said, "He's not gonna rest! He's not gonna rest in peace in a suit!"

A particularly tearing thing was the flowers. Stringbean did not know how to drive a car, but he bought a new Cadillac every year. He said that was for Uncle Sam and because the fans expected it—he never used it except to go play music in. Estelle was the one did the driving, and at the funeral, to honor her especially, Audrey Williams sent a huge flower arrangement in the shape of a steering wheel.

Well, when we came into the studio the first day of taping for the following season, everybody was real quiet. And then Roy said, "We sure are going to miss String, aren't we?" And that was it. You didn't have to say anything more.

When we were doing the Banjo Band, they had me stand exactly on the spot where String had stood. I felt the hair raise on my arms, and I felt weepy, like it was hallowed ground. It makes me embarrassed to tell what I was thinking, it sounds real sentimental, but I bet it's what anybody in my place would have been thinking: I won't let you down, String, I'm gonna do the best I can.

String was our leader, him and Grandpa. People may have thought Roy Clark and Buck Owens were the leaders because they were the big stars. But really String and Grandpa were—just on account of being the kind of people they were. And I adored them.

⌒

The other day I took a friend to see the Nashville studio where we filmed *Hee Haw*. We wandered into one of the rooms and there was a guy named Larry, who had worked on the set, on the technical side. Those people on the technical side and those people on the production side, they really made the show. I can't say enough in praise of them. Anyway, Larry gave me a big hug, and he said to my friend, "Those were great days. The people who worked on the show—well, we were just like family." And I was practically crying, remembering, because it was true. We had our tragic losses, we had our little petty squabbles—just like family. But we also had fun, and wonderful caring and companionship—just like family.

When we'd first come in to start each session's filming, there'd be that big buzz of conversation I talked about, with everyone asking everyone else what they did in the past six months, and how their families were. And we'd tell each other what plans we had for the future. I'd say something like "Oh, and I think I'm gonna get me out to L.A. and see if I can get some shows at the big places there." Everyone would listen, really listen to each other. And be encouraging about your endeavors, just the way I was with Misty Rowe and her plans for her show. No one would say, "Well, that ain't gonna work out" or anything negativistic. Thinking back, that's what I remember most, everybody really listening and being respectful of each other.

We'd encourage each other about small things too. There was one particular incident that sticks in my mind. The *Hee Haw* people were going to a big elegant party, and we girls were all wearing real fancy dresses. I was wearing the only one I had, and it was okay, but needless to say I didn't fill it out. I was feeling real bad about the way I looked, all scrawny and ugly, and I was thinking, Well, I'll just hide away. Being around all those beautiful girls could be depressing. I was playing ugly characters, that was my job, and I understood that, but still sometimes it was stressing on my soul. Well, Marianne came over to me and she said, "You get right out there. You look beautiful! You have the figure of a model. You just go right out there!"

We were also considerate of each other's family problems. I talked about my consoling Gailard when he was sad about his daughter. And there was once when Cathy Baker was especially sympathetic to me. She knew I was going through a difficult time (with my kids), and she said, "C'mon. We're going to have dinner, just you and me, and I'm going to talk to you." She was a very busy girl. That's partly because she never thought she did enough as an actress on the show. So she'd also work on the wardrobe, be a Gal Friday kind of person. But in spite of all Cathy had to do, she took the time to go out to dinner with me and tell me about a friend who had a similar situation to mine.

And everyone treated my kids kindly. When Georgia was ten and wrote a little book called "My Mother, The Entertainer," lots of the *Hee Haw* people signed it with nice messages. One of them reads "Georgia, someday you'll be a great writer. And then I'll say I knew her when she first started and I'll get your autograph. Love, Minnie Pearl." When Georgia graduated from high school, Gordie sent her a present with a note saying it was from her *Hee Haw* father.

We fed off each other's compassion and each other's sense of humor—we were always having fun. To give one more example, and this may seem strange, but this was at Junior Samples's funeral. Junior was a wonderful comedian and friend, and we were all very upset when he died, none more than Diane Goodman, one of the most beautiful of the *Hee Haw* girls. She and Junior had had a special sort of relationship because she was a former Miss Georgia and he came from Georgia. She was crying, crying.

"I can't go in there, Roni. I can't look at him. I just can't."

"Now, you don't have to, Diane, if you don't want to. Junior would understand. But if you think you can, I'll go with you, and we'll look at him together."

"Would you, Roni?"

And then we joked for a minute about how people are always saying as they peer into the casket, "Waalll, now don't he look natural!" When that's the last thing the poor victim looks after the embalmers have finished with him! And I promised Diane I wouldn't say that. So we go into the room and gaze in the casket at poor Junior. And after a minute along comes a prominent female member of the *Hee Haw* cast, who shall remain nameless, and looks down real solemn-like and drawls, "Waalll, don't he look natural!" Diane and I burst into giggles. And we knew wherever Junior was, he was laughing too.

Larry was right. We were like family, and those were great times. I was a very lucky lady to be a part of that.

After Daddy died, Patsy often performed with the band. She's a great auto-harper . . . autoharpist . . . autoharp player? Well, she really plays the autoharp good! (From the collection of Patsy Stoneman Murphy)

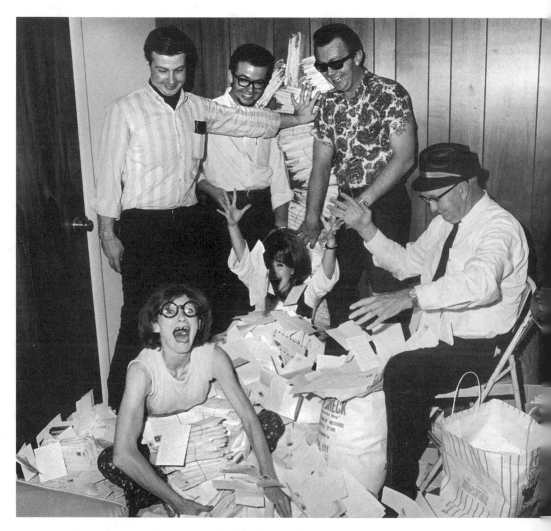

Here we are with some of the hundreds of letters that came in every week when we had our TV show. See the huge stack behind the boys? The letters became a segment of the show. Someone would read a few of them, and we would make comments. It wasn't rehearsed in advance. (Imagine producers allowing that now!) (From the collection of Patsy Stoneman Murphy)

Performing at the Hollywood Palace. A lot of glitz! From left to right, Daddy, Jerry Monday, me, Scott, Van, Donna, and Jimmy. (From the collection of Donna Stoneman)

Performing on the *Glen Campbell Show*. From left to right, Don Lineberger, John Hartford, Glen Campbell, me, Steve Martin, and Mason Williams. And then standing, Jimmy, Patsy, Van, and Donna. At the time I didn't know Steve Martin was a comedian, but I fell in love with his gentle soul. He's also a very good banjo player. We banjo players played "Cripple Creek," and there were dancers who jumped from behind us, over our heads, landed on the floor and slapped their thighs in an L.A. director's idea of what country dancing was. It might not have been authentic country, but it sure was a great scene. (From the collection of Roni Stoneman)

Opposite page: Me on the night the Stonemans won the Country Music Association's Vocal Group of the Year award. It was 1967. The dress was gold lamé. (From the collection of Eugene and Angela Cox)

Ida Lee Nagger, the "Ironing Board Lady," was my most famous role on *Hee Haw*. In this picture, it looks like I'm contemplating taking action—probably with a rolling pin against my husband Laverne. (Photo courtesy of Bill Zimmerman)

Opposite page: At the reception after the wedding to my second husband George, who is right behind me. You can see the difference in our weights. That really mattered when he would beat me, which he did regularly, including that night. (Photo courtesy of Cookie Snyder and Tom Pitts)

Me and George Lindsey sprouting corny jokes in one of *Hee Haw*'s "In the Kornfield" skits. (Photo courtesy of Bill Zimmerman)

Opposite page: I was also part of *Hee Haw*'s Banjo Band. That was mainly because of Stringbean's support. He would announce me as "My little friend from woman's lib, Roni Stoneman." And the producers liked it because it made the show look more up to date. (Photo courtesy of Bill Zimmerman)

Backstage at *Hee Haw,* getting ready to go on. (Photo courtesy of Bill Zimmerman)

My daughter Georgia (the blonde) and a friend on the *Hee Haw* set with Minnie Pearl, Cathy Baker, and Lulu. In the background are the *Hee Haw* Honeys. Georgia got bit by the drama bug. Now she's studying to be a drama teacher. (From the collection of Donna Stoneman)

I played several characters on *Hee Haw* besides Ida Lee. Here I am as Mophead, the hotel maid. (Photo courtesy of Bill Zimmerman)

My all-girl band, the Daisy Maes. Corny name, huh? I formed the band after I lost *Hee Haw* and couldn't get work. From left to right, Melissa Smith, Beverly Nolan, Terry Lee, and Jessie Morgan. (From the collection of Roni Stoneman)

TWENTY

George after *Hee Haw*

The best George ever treated me was after I got *Hee Haw*. We had more money, of course. We bought a big fine house in Smyrna and leather furniture and all the brand new things that we could get. We had Frigidaire appliances which we thought was high dollar. Of course I paid for the house and everything that went in it.

George became a gourmet cook. We would have little groups of people come over. I had a swimming pool and I'd put candles in it and let them float. George would mix frozen tequila sunrises. He would be real cordial to all my guests, and everybody just . . . well, you couldn't find a finer host than George Hemrick. He would talk so properly, and he would get his guitar and sing in a sad voice, *Ah yesterday, when I was young*—and he would miss that C chord every damn time. I thought to myself, How does he play that song a hundred thousand times and never hit that chord right once? He goes duh duh duh, and he'd hit it, on the fourth try. Every time, for fifteen years of being married. I never said anything. I was trying not to get punched in the face.

Why did I stay with him? Well, I didn't want to, but I kept thinking he would get better and stop the abuse, and he was my second husband and, well, if you're on your second, you really try harder.

Another reason I stayed with him was that in some ways he was good with the children. For instance, he would play word games with Georgia when she was two or three. While he was shaving in the morning, he would say a word. Then he'd tell her, "Now go get your secret box." And we'd write the word down, like "doctor" or "baby doll," and then she'd make sentences and put the word in the little plastic "secret" box. Every day she'd learn one, two, maybe three words.

George also was fond of Eugene. He thought he was very bright, and would try to teach him, watching classic films with him on TV, handing him books to read like *War and Peace,* buying him a telescope when he got interested in astronomy, and encouraging him when he showed talent for drawing. In other words, in some ways I was right about George helping me educate the kids.

Because of *Hee Haw* I was being hired for many fair dates and shows. I was away from home a lot, out on the road, but as long as I was bringing in enough money, that seemed to satisfy George better. It didn't stop him from drinking or taking pills, but he didn't beat on me as much. Sometimes I could go a week without getting beaten up. I would feel pretty good about that. And I was feeling better about other things, about *Hee Haw,* and all the show dates, and the fact that the kids were growing up and they had everything they needed.

TWENTY-ONE

The Kids

The kids were growing up real nicely. My kids were all-important to me. If I knew ahead of time that I would have to go through all that stress that I had with Gene not supporting me, and the abuse I had with George, I still would have married them to get the children that I have today. I would do it all over three or four times. I want to tell you now a little more about my life with them, and how even though I wasn't educated, I tried to do things to be a good mother.

So we have to go back to the early years. And it was then I got the best compliment I ever got in my life—when we had moved out to Las Vegas because Gene was playing with Judy Lynn and I was doing shows in California with the family. We rented a house, and I thought, Well, now things will be better. He's got a job, and it's something that he likes to do. Turned out, as I said, that he hardly gave me any money. And then he took off, traveling with the band, and left me in the middle of Clark

County, with my four raggedy kids. I didn't have a car, didn't have a telephone. At night when the wind blew and the bushes scratched the wall, it was scary. I'd sit up all night long.

The compliment came about because every day I'd walk the kids to the end of the road, where there was a little store, to get them a penny candy or something. I just walked them up and walked them back. Carry one, let it walk a bit, carry the other one, carry two. That's the only thing we had to look forward to. And one day the man at the counter said, "You know, we were talking about it the other day. We see you comin' up here, every day with your children, walk way up the street, in that hot desert air! I never seen such clean children, and well behaved." That compliment meant more to me than any compliment I've ever gotten.

They were wonderful children. And they were all different. When Barbara was real little, I noticed that she couldn't speak plain words, and I said to Daddy, "Daddy, Barbara's a little different. What's the matter?" And he repeated what he always said, "You can have a house full of children and each one of them's different. Some can learn faster than others. But don't let the ones that are a little slower feel bad. I had a bunch of children and every dadblamed one of them was different." And that's true. Every one of my brothers and sisters was different and every one of my children was different. The trouble with some teachers is that they try to force kids in the same mold. Or parents expect their kids to act like grownups. Children ain't gonna be grownups, and all you're gonna do is cause emotional problems when you push them to be a grownup before their time.

So now I'm going to try to explain some of my kids' differences, and how I tried to deal with them as they were growing up.

Eugene was a really smart kid, and he was interested in music when he was young. But because our family had had such hard times in the music business, I was encouraging him to develop this other talent he had—for drawing. The last thing I wanted was for him to be a musician. Yet even so, when he was little, I got him a saxophone. That's because I was desperate. He had developed bronchial asthma. He had it so bad that he couldn't even run outside and play. He'd go "Hagggh, agggah." When I was in Vegas, I had to take him to the emergency room every day. They'd say, "Boil some water and hold him over it." We didn't have vaporizers, didn't have money for that kind of thing. They told me to give him Primatene. I went back to the doctor and I said, "The label says it's bad for the heart." "It can be," he answered. So I threw out the Primatene.

Now when we were on the road, I used to read a lot of books. So I was reading about one of the Roosevelts, and he had asthma and the boys used to beat him up because he was so pale and thin and couldn't do the things they could do. It was the Roosevelt that said, "Walk softly and carry a big stick"—Teddy. So his mother bought him a trumpet. Well, that takes air. It built his lungs up, and he outgrew the asthma. So I thought, I'm gonna get Junior, which is what we called Eugene, a wind instrument and that will probably help him get over it. That's how dumb I was, dumb! I bought him a saxophone and I just let him blow it as much as he wanted to. The amazing thing was it worked! He doesn't have asthma anymore.

And he's a good saxophone player to this day. But his main job is as a design engineer for Nissan. I am so proud of him and his wife Angela and their three sons.

Becky, the next born . . . well, wonderful is the way to describe Becky. I put too much of a load on her when she was growing up. I know that now. She is such a caring and compassionate person. Even when she was young, I would confide in her if I was sad. We were living in that crummy shack on the military base, after George lost his job, and I had nobody else. She was maybe sixth, seventh grade, and she'd sit there and listen to me, and then give me the most levelheaded advice. One time I went and got some old material, and she helped me make curtains to cover up the shabby windows. She helped me with everything.

Particularly with Barbara. Well, for awhile I was in denial about Barbara's problems, the fact that the slowness in talking was part of her just not developing like the other kids. You say, No, she's just immature, and you make excuses. And then one day, you stand up straight and say, "I have a special child. Now what do I do, God?" So, after seeing a lot of doctors, I realized that Barbara had to go to a special school. I was back in the bedroom, wondering how I was going to get her there, since I had to be on the road so much. And Becky came into the bedroom. "Momma," she said, "I want to go to that school where you're going to send Barbara."

"What?" "The school has regular classes too. And if I switch there, then I can take care of Barbara on the bus and make sure that she gets to her right classroom." And she did. My Becky did that for her. They have a real strong bond, Becky and Barbara.

Becky married the wrong person—and I tried to prevent that. But she can be stubborn. I begged and begged for her to take a year off—I would pay for her to take a year of school in Europe. I wanted so much to get her away from this boy and then go to college. But she married him anyway. It was a horrible marriage, but she got two great children from it.

She is now the secretary to the head man of Nissan in Smyrna, and always gets glowing job reports (and is finishing up college!). And she has a real nice boyfriend. If everyone were like Becky, the world would be a wonderful place.

Barbara's my special child. (But of course they're all special.) As I said, I first noticed that there might be problems when she was a baby, because of the way she focused on lights, and then later when she had trouble talking. Then when I was in L.A., I woke up at about 3:30 in the morning, heard a noise, and ran into the kids' room. She was in convulsions. I thought she was dying. I had never seen that kind of convulsion before—Jimmy's seizures were different. She had four other seizures that night.

I took her to the hospital the next day. I sat there for hours, along with people who had running sores on their legs. I'm looking at them, and trying to keep my kids away from them. The kids would say, "Momma, I gotta go to the bathroom." How do you tell your child you can't go to the bathroom? So I'd go in there and take some paper towels and try to clean it up the best I could and pray they wouldn't get any germs on them.

Then the doctor said, "Well, this baby is an epileptic." Just as cold-hearted as could be. And he just gave me some phenobarbital, without explaining anything at all.

Later, when we moved to Donelson, I had Barbara in the public kindergarten. And three teachers came to me at the end of the year. "Barbara's not ready for the first grade," they said. And I said, "I didn't think she was." Then they recommended we get her tested. We had her tested at a hearing center and at other places too. And this stupid child psychologist, he took Barbara in the room, talked to her a little bit, and came out and said, "She's retarded. Don't bother spending any more money on that child." I'll never forget that. I was young and I didn't know what to do. I just stood there crying.

But when I talked to Peggy Shannon, Barbara's teacher at that little public school in Donelson, she said, "Barbara can be taught a lot. We'll keep her in the kindergarten again and that'll be all right because she's small." I said, "That's fine." Ms. Shannon went on, "Barbara has a lot of talent. She's got perfect timing. Nobody's got the timing in this whole class like Barbara. She marches the band around and she sings so beautifully." There Barbara was, five years old, with perfect timing!

Ms. Shannon assured me that you could be "special" in more than one way. She was really capitalizing on the talents Barbara had. Ms. Shannon was right, by the way. Barbara's a great singer. If I was traveling and she was with me, I'd get her up on stage. She would do one of Tanya Tucker's hit songs: *What's your mama's name, child? / What's your mama's name?* She was terrific.

But in general Tennessee has a long way to go when it comes to special needs children and young adults. I was honorary chairperson for special children for the state of Tennessee for three and a half years. So I learned a lot from that. Let me give an example. I was doing a show for the special children. But they also had people in the same place that were so-called normal. They seated the special children in some bleachers and the "normals" in another. And they wanted me to stand in the middle and perform facing the "normals"! Well, of course I didn't do that. I turned completely around, and I said, "You're my little darlin's, and I'm playing for y'all. I love you dearly." Then I said, "If any of you want to come up and sing with me, feel free to do so." And I got a couple of little kids to come up, some of them severely handicapped physically as well as mentally. I may not be real smart, but I do know special children's needs. By the way, you can't use a banjo with special people. It makes them nervous. Upsets some "normal" people too of course—that's why we have all those banjo jokes! But for a special child, particularly an autistic child, it's awful. They often have special hearing. For them I'd use a guitar or an autoharp so it didn't sound tinny to their ears.

I taught Barbara to read through singing. I saw she was having problems reading. So I'd write the words down to a song and then point them
out to her. This was before *Sesame Street*. "Help me write that song," I'd
say to her. "You've got to help me." And that's how she learned to read
and to talk more clearly. Someone came up to me the other day and reminded me that I helped a child with a speech problem when I was performing at the bluegrass festival in Bean Blossom. I couldn't remember
it right away because I've done the same thing often. Generally, I'll just
choose a cute song. "Ducky Duddle" is a good one because the child has
to use their tongue more. So I'd sing with the child *Little Ducky Duddle
went wading in a puddle / went wading in a puddle quite small / He says it
doesn't matter / How much I splash or splatter / I'm only a ducky after all.* That
song's easy and it's funny, so it makes the child lose his inhibitions. Also
kids love little animals, and the song's got a nice message.

Bobby's my last child by Gene, and he's a musician. No matter how I
tried to steer my kids away from the music business, it didn't work with
Bobby (maybe because he's the one I was pregnant with at the Grand
Ole Opry!). He's a wonderful guitarist and singer.

Now I was working in Chicago on this book on September 11, 2001,
the day that horrible tragedy happened to our country. Bobby called and
said: "Mom, I joined the National Guard last week."

And he thanked me. Because about a month before I had made a
suggestion. Now, I knew Bobby was real good at soldiering, and I had
always encouraged him with that. In high school he was in ROTC, also
in the drill team. Well, I had met this guy who was a general in the National Guard. So I said, "Bobby, you ought to see about getting into the
National Guard."

Bobby's patriotic. All of us are patriotic. We'd die in a minute for our
country. Without even a second thought.

Back to September 11. I said, "Bobby, I feel like I gotta get home. I
just gotta get home." He was in Mississippi at the time, playing with his
band. But he offered to come up and get me. We decided not to do that.
But ain't that sweet? That's Bobby.

Georgia thinks deeply about things and worries about them. Maybe
because of the way her father drank. Once, when she was little, I saw
her coming down the hallway and she was crying, just shaking all over.

She had found one of her father's bottles under the bed. I picked her up in my arms and I cuddled her.

"Oh, honey, you got it all wrong," I said. That's an old bottle that your daddy had a long time ago. He don't do that anymore."

She was panting. "Momma, are you sure, Momma? Are you sure?"

"Yeah, honey, I know that to be a fact. I just haven't cleaned under the bed in a long time. Daddy's working now, and he's doing really good. Don't worry, he's not going to have convulsions anymore."

A baldfaced lie. But the most important thing was to calm her. She went outside and started playing.

Maybe because of her sensitivity to other people, Georgia's really talented as an actor and a writer. She's also brilliant. And she's got perfect pitch. There's a whole bunch of music teachers who we left wringing their hands when she stopped taking lessons, violin, piano. But you can't force a child.

And now she has a lovely daughter and she's studying to be a drama teacher. I'm so proud of her.

I'm so proud of all of them.

TWENTY-TWO

The Real Thing

I was at a bookstore recently and I went "Whoa, wow!" 'Cause there was a book called *Big Stone Gap,* a novel about a small town in Virginia, by a woman named Adriana Trigiani. And I read some in it and I kept saying "Wow." 'Cause I know those people in the book. I don't mean I know those people like I know how it is to be from the mountains and all. I mean I know those actual people! And they turned out to be a big part of my life.

Well, there I was, married to George, and living in that nice home.

I get a telephone call from George at his work. He was working for the Adult Continuing Education program of the state of Tennessee. After years of not having a job, he finally got one.

"Roni, a man called here. Name's James Smith." (I'm not using his real name here.) "Wanted you to play in Big Stone Gap for the opening of a new business. I told him you'd do it. He'll be phoning."

Twenty minutes later he did, and I arranged to go.

So the time came. I got to the hotel in Big Stone, and I thought, Well, I gotta rest some. I lay there on the bed and I was watching television—Grizzly Adams, that big grizzly bear-man.

I was half asleep, and there was a knock on the door: "Miss Stoneman?" I went to the door and opened it as much as the chain would go, because I looked so bad, I was so tired. A man said, "Would you come down to the room at the end of the hall? Miss Virginia wants to meet you." "Miss Virginia? Okay. But I gotta fix up some." I had just bought a salmon-colored dress with fluffy sleeves, a real pretty dress to wear at the show. So I put the dress on and combed my hair and went to the room. That same man opened the door, and he looked at me real funny and said, "C'mon in." I sat down. There was also another man that he introduced as D. (Again, I don't want to use his real name.) Sweet little Miss Blue Eyes, Miss Virginia, was laying on the bed, resting with her feet on the covers, the counterpane, as Momma would call it. She had a chaperone with her. I sat at the foot of the bed on a . . . it was like a big chest for you to put quilts in.

Well, they started asking me questions. The first one was from Miss Virginia, and she said, uh, "Miss Stoneman . . ." "You can call me Roni." "Roni . . . how many's in your family?" "Fifteen." "Oh, really?" she said, in this odd voice. James laughed. I looked at him. I didn't know he was James at the time. I just knew he was the guy who had invited me to join them. Then they asked me some more questions. I answered, and every time I said anything, they would laugh. I thought, they're laughing like I'm lying. Then James said, "Well, I don't believe that for a minute," which made it pretty clear. I looked at him and said, "Mister, If you don't believe anything I tell you, why ask me? I don't know what kind of friends you're running with, but it sounds as if you can't trust anybody, sounds as if you're hanging with the wrong bunch. You're asking me questions, I'm telling the truth, and you're acting like I'm lying." I walked up to the door, was going to leave.

He said, "No, no, we're sorry, we're really sorry." "Don't ever call me a liar," I said. "I don't like it, and I'm not gonna put up with it!" He said, "Please accept my apology." Told me he was James Smith, brought me back and was more respectful. Then after awhile I got up, said "Bye," and went to my room. I wanted to go to bed early because I had worked so hard at home, getting ready to go.

Then there was another knock on the door. Was James Smith again.

"Would you like to go to dinner?" he said. "There's a place down the road, a pizza place."

I got back in the dress.

We went down there, and we were having a good time. And after a little he started getting romantic with me. Needless to say, I really enjoyed the attention. I wasn't used to some man treating me like a reasonable human being. I didn't know him much, but he didn't have a wedding band on. And after I told him off about calling me a liar, he seemed to be very very nice. I said that to him.

"Do you know why I talked to you like I did in the room there?" he asked.

"No, I don't have any idea."

"Because when I called to hire you, your husband told me that you would do a good show if I could keep you sober. He said that you had a severe drinking problem."

I sat there stunned. I hardly ever drank!

"We thought we were gonna get a drunk coming up here," James said.

So James and I were talking and having dinner and I start to get involved with this man. I start to fall in love. He was really courting me that night, and when he took me back to my room, he encouraged me to go further with the situation. I . . . I just couldn't. Even though I felt really warm and loving and sensuous with him. What was stopping me was my morals. Even though my husband was so abusive and had told James I was a drunk. "What kind of a husband do you have anyway?" he said. "What kind of a man would do that?" So of course I would like being loved and kissed and petted and understood. And then James was a classy man, I thought, a Virginia gentleman. When I said no, he stopped.

The next morning, about 7:00, he came knocking at my door again. "Roni, Roni," he said. And he was really upset and shame-faced. These mountain people do have their ways, and even though he was a successful businessman, he was still a country boy, been raised in an atmosphere of morals and values.

"Roni . . . my God, I don't know how to tell you this."

"What is it?"

"My wife is at the restaurant. She's gonna be having breakfast there with D and me and you. She's come up here 'cause she's pretty thick with D."

I went, his wife? My God! Now, although there was no ring, I had to admit I had seen a color difference on the skin—I just hadn't let myself think about it. So this was partly my fault. I can hardly say how I felt. Here I was going down to have breakfast with the woman whose husband I'd been kissing just a few hours before!

I got to the restaurant and I had to pretend like nothing was wrong. James sat across the table from me. D sat at the other end. The wife Lureen (again not her real name) was setting there so high and mighty and cocky. Her and D were more than "thick." But I didn't know about it then.

Then I had to go out and get ready to perform. I was still furious. James was inside his office, taking care of things there. A bluegrass band went on, started doing their show. I came up by the stage and I was looking out in the audience. I like to look at the people. I like to look at them maybe more than they like to look at me. I just love people. The whole shopping place was packed, and over to my right was a beautiful sweet-looking old lady with a cane, wearing those little mountain shoes that lace up. I wasn't used to that—not in Nashville. Reminded me of my grandmother. (And I was more affected, I guess, because my mother hadn't long been dead. She died in 1976, after having survived nine heart attacks!) With the woman was this younger guy. It was Mama Griggs and her son, Otto, who's in this book, *Big Stone Gap,* though I didn't know their names at the time (and actually I've changed their last name here). I looked at her, and I thought God love her, she's out there in all this heat and she doesn't have a chair.

So I went inside, got a chair, and brought it out to her.

"Here, Mrs. . . . ." I said. "My name's Roni."

"I'm Mama Griggs."

Then when she was thanking me for the chair, she said, "I want you to come up to the house after the show and have dinner with us. We'll feed you some good food."

That sounded great to me. I wanted to go home with somebody that looked like my grandma, up there in the hills—specially now, with the way I was feeling.

"Well, thank you," I said.

While I was performing, she would take her cane and beat it on the ground when I'd dance around or whenever I played fancy. She just loved it.

After the show I went back to the hotel, and this guy, let's call him M, who was supposed to be responsible for showing me the town, took me up to the mountain. Mama was up there waiting. For dinner she fed me all kinds of homegrown vegetables and cornbread. Besides Otto, she also had a son named Worley. Worley was about fifty-two years old, never married, just like in the novel. Well there's stuff in the novel that I won't talk about (don't want to spoil it for you), but Worley later told me that stuff wasn't true—"The lady made that up," he said. But they are real, Otto and Worley are real. Because I know Otto, and I know Worley, and I knew Mama. (In the novel the Mama character seems to be the mother of someone else.)

Mama invited me to come up and stay with her. I didn't tell her anything about James because I thought he's got a wife, I'm getting outta this mess. But I moved out of the motel and went up on the mountain to be with her.

It wasn't 'til three days later that James found out where I was at. And then he came up to see me, all the way from another town, about thirty miles away. He had a business in that other town before he opened the new place in Big Stone Gap.

"I pretended that I had to be over here for work, Roni, but I really wanted to see you," he said.

"I'm leaving in the morning."

"My God, I didn't know what in the world happened to you!"

And I thought, What did he think would happen to me?

"I heard you went off with M," he said.

I knew what he was thinking.

M was a single man. And Mama Griggs couldn't stand M because she said some relative of his had been seen making love to a cow. I said, "You gotta be kidding me!" I think she was.

But I wasn't sure. She did have some strange ideas. She kept a pistol under her pillow in the bed—like mountain grannies often did. She'd see a car come up that driveway.

"I wonder what that old so-and-so's comin' around for," she'd grumble.

"Well . . ." I'd say.

"He's after something."

"Don't you sell hay? Bales of hay? I betcha that's what he wants."

"I got my pistol in my pocket."

She'd walk to the door and say, "What can I do for you?"

"I come to see about getting some hay."

So then she'd be taking money from him, and she wouldn't let him inside the door. I would stand there and watch her with her pistol. She was wonderful.

I fell in love with James, head over heels. George was always drunk. And the constant abuse. He used to say to me, "You don't know nothin'. Anybody can just twirl you around three times and push you toward a microphone. That's all you're fit for." And here I was supporting nine people! Even when he was working, he never gave me a cent. So I thought, I'm not really married to that man. That's somebody I don't need to be married to.

I told him.

"George, you don't love me, and I know it," I said.

"You sure know more than I know." And then he thought for a minute and said, "Well, you're right, I don't."

"Okay, I'm not going to be intimate with you. As long as you drink and take those pills, I've got nothing but a drunk lying beside me. I'm getting tired of hearing you grunt and groan all night when you're high and out of it. I'm just . . . I'm not your wife from now on."

At least I didn't cheat on him. Just like with Gene, I told him that I was no longer his wife.

Then I would go up there and see James.

The affair went on for about a year. We'd go places together, like, for instance, the coke burning. That's when they burn off the extra coke from the coal mines. They do it in huge ditches, and it seems like there's just miles and miles of fire. It's a real spectacle. James sent me his credit card, first credit card I ever had in my life! I'd fly into Tri-Cities airport, rent a car, and drive on up there and we'd meet and we'd stay together and he'd talk to me, tell me about his situation. I had a beautiful affair with him. The thing about it was he had not been with too many women. He hadn't been a rounder. He was caring and loving, and sex wasn't the only thing on his mind. He wanted comforting, understanding, and talking.

He made me feel very important to him. The situation he was telling me about wasn't the best. He truly was hanging with the wrong bunch of people—there were some real shady dealings going on. He'd call me from Virginia and say "Roni, somebody is after me."

But many times I would go up in the mountains of Big Stone not to be with James but to be with Mama Griggs. The Griggs's place was real primitive. I'd be in the kitchen with Mama, and we'd be fixing food. She had a wood stove and it got real hot in there in the summer. "Mama, it's awful hot in here!" I'd say. She said, "Yeah, I know it is." They didn't have fans or anything.

Old Worley would wake me up in the mornings, and he'd knock on the door, bang, bang! I'd leap. "Get in here for your breakfast!" he'd yell. And Mama would just laugh and call from the bedroom we were sharing, "Now, you leave that little thing alone. You just don't worry about us, we're having more fun." Because Mama would start talking about her young days, and it was like a story in itself. She said she used to like to dance, and her husband Wilbur wouldn't let her. "He was so mean to me," she said and then she paused a second, this sweet old lady, "so I just said, 'Fuck him!'" I went Aaaghh and started giggling. When she told these stories, I'd be in old pajamas and an old robe, and we were like mother and daughter in there.

I would go to see Mama Griggs to get away from the drinking and the abuse. At first I had a babysitter, but soon the kids were in junior high school and high school, so if I had their clothes all put out in the drawers with their names on them, everything done, then I felt I could leave for two or three days, usually combine it with a time when I was out on the road. Things were good for the kids. They had their own bedrooms. And Becky was very . . . you could depend on Becky. Becky helped me a lot with Barbara and Georgia.

At Mama Griggs's I would often get out early in the morning, and sit on the porch and watch the sun come up on the mountain and feel the wet grass under my feet. It was like it was down by Grandma's house years ago, those summers in the Blue Ridge. I guess I was trying to go back to my girlhood.

I gave Mama perfume, Chloe. And I bought her a new stereo so she could hear music, and because she'd want me to dance for her because she couldn't get out easily. I bought her some of Ralph Stanley's records, and an album by the group called Chicago, and I'd dance for her every evening.

They gave me Wilbur's change purse and his watch and some gold coins to put in the purse. Mama Griggs said, "I want you to have them." I knew that, in spite of Wilbur's meanness, that was the biggest gift they could give me. Wilbur had carried the purse all through the coal mines.

When it came time for me to leave, Mama'd cry. I'd say, "Mama, I got a family. I got to go home." And she'd say, "I know, I know." But she'd cry so hard. She didn't have nothing but nails on the wall to hang up her clothes, so when I went away, I'd leave some of my clothes hanging there on a nail, just to make her feel better.

Then one day I get a call. From James. George picked it up and he's drunk, and he's pilled up, and he starts telling James horrible things about me. I just walked out of the house. I was devastated. And then later on, I went to my minister, Brother Moore, at the Lord's Chapel. I said, "Brother Moore, I have a problem. I'm involved . . . I'm having . . . kinda having an affair . . . Not kinda . . . I'm having an affair and I'm in love with this married man. I know it's not right." I said, "The only way I know to get out of this is to pray it out. Would you pray with me?" "Certainly I will, Roni, of course." So we prayed.

Less than an hour later I get a call from James.

"It's awful!" he said. "You can't imagine what just happened. I was sitting here at my desk and the blood just squirted out of my nose. You wouldn't believe how much my nose has bled. I got enough . . . I got enough gauze in my nose to make you a gown."

I'll never forget him saying that.

"Well, James," I said. "I just got back from the minister's. I said a prayer that you and I wouldn't see each other anymore. Because it's not right for you and your family or me and my family. I can't go along like this. It's not me. God's gonna help me to get away from this, help me stop loving you like this."

He was quiet a minute. Then he said, "I understand." And he never called me again, and that was the end of that story.

Except that it took me about two years to be able to drive down a road without crying when I got to thinking about him.

And then it also became clear that I was going to have to stop going down to Mama Griggs's. Worley was always so kind to me, in his way, and I didn't want things to get out of hand. One day I was helping Mama pop beans. And Worley came in with a copperhead, one of them great big copperheads, wriggling around, doubling over a stick. "Hey, Mama, look what I found up there in the garden patch. Dontcha go up thar now, Ronnni. Dontcha go up thar." As sweet as he could be.

Worley was always trying to help me. He took me out and taught me how to shoot a 38 Smith and Wesson and then gave it to me. He said, "You oughta have this if you're ridin' through these here mountains." I refused it. I never had had a gun in my hand except for the time I dropped one when I was a little girl. It broke my toe into several places, and I ended up with a terrible fever.

I treated Worley like I was his sister, and once talked him into getting his teeth fixed so that "maybe all the mountain women'd come hanging around." Otto was good to me also, showing me all over the farm. They were just real nice. And they knew I was seeing James. But then one time Worley said, "Now where do you want me to put a cabin? I'll build you any house you want up here." I didn't know Worley's true feelings, whether he thought of me as a sister or something else, but I thought it was time to leave. It was time to get out of Dodge.

Mama Griggs would always say to me, "Now, Roni, I don't want them boys . . . I don't want one of them takin' a likin' to you. And I tole 'em plainly I don't want 'em ever getting jealous of you. 'Cause I know what it was. I had a husband that wouldn't let me dance or do anything. And I ain't gonna have it. D'ya hear? I'm not gonna let them boys . . ." And I said, "I know, Mama, I know. Everything's fine, everything's fine. We'll handle it." Because I certainly wasn't going to get involved or hurt them. She was absolutely right. I just left and I never went back, though

I have had some nice phone conversations with the boys over the years. Mama has since died.

I never talked to James anymore, but my affair with him was one of the most wonderful things that ever happened to me. It sounds kind of dumb, like, well, Roni Stoneman, there she goes, in love again, the romantic of the world, dumb dumb. But it was the real thing. I think that there are some times in life that something is real for you in your emotions, but it can't work in real life because there's other people you gotta think about. But in its way it was so real and wonderful.

And my time at Mama and Otto and Worley's house was also real and wonderful. It was pure peace.

TWENTY-THREE

My Bronze Uterus

Well I loved having the children, as I said, but years passed and the pain of my monthly periods was getting to be too much. I hated every bit of that part of being a girl. I never saw anything joyous in it. I had a bronze sculpture of my uterus made from a picture of the real thing—after I got it out, of course!—because I was so glad to get rid of that son of a gun! In fact I was thinking of putting a photo of it on the cover of this book. It looked like a bronze pear. And we could draw a neck on it, like a banjo neck. The picture would be sort of a symbol of my lives—my professional life and my personal life!

Well I took my bronze uterus into the dressing room at *Hee Haw.* All the girls gathered around.

"Here's my uterus, girls," I said. "I had it bronzed."

They gasped. "Did you really?!!!" "Roni, I can't believe it!"

"Now don't tell anybody else I showed you this," I said. "Don't tell any of the men. Just you girls can see it. I feel so much better it's out. I'm having the best time. I'm going to grow into a *real* woman now!" And I mugged my "real woman" sexy face.

Next thing you know, I'm walking down the hall, and Roy Clark says, "Ronald J., come here. I want to ask you something."

So I went over.

"Ah . . . um . . ." He was having trouble getting the words out: "Do you . . . do you have a . . . a bronze uterus?"

"Who told you?"

"Uhh . . ."

"The girls were not supposed to tell anyone."

"Can I see it?"

"It's in my overnight case."

"Well, go and get it."

So I brought it to him.

"Here it is," I said. And, again, there was a whole crowd gathering around.

Roy stared at it.

"I'm supposed to do the *Tonight Show*," he said. "I want to take it on with me."

"My uterus don't go anywhere without me. You gotta take me with you."

He frowned. "Don't think I can do that."

"Well, you can't take my bronze uterus. You might lose it."

"I'll wear it around my neck."

"My uterus is much too heavy to wear around your neck, boy!"

TWENTY-FOUR

On the Road

Well, what with the popularity of *Hee Haw,* I had an easy time getting work, and I was out on the road a lot, traveling from show to show, all over the country. That's a whole new ballgame, being out on the road, and it's a real big part of any country musician's life. So here's a little about what it's like.

At times it can almost be dizzying. Sometimes you're traveling so much that you would sort of lose track of where you were. I remember one time back when I was with the family and we were playing some grand auditorium. I sang Hank Williams's "I'm So Lonesome I Could Cry" and got a standing ovation. I said my standard line, Scott's line, "Hot dang, I'm good!" Then I went off the stage, and I said, "Daddy, wow, did you see that? I got a standing ovation!" And he said, "Well, you darn well oughta. This is Hank Williams's birthplace!"

Aside from those times when you were totally "out of it," you really did get an education on the road, learning about people and places. Like when we went west and learned about those California hippies. Another learning experience was when I was booked into a little place in Alaska, in Fairbanks. Now, at the time I gotta admit, this seemed like the gig from hell. It's only in looking back that I can appreciate it. Anyway, ice all over the roads. Every piece of car that came to town was wrecked, had a hole in the side or the front or the back, or both sides would be crunched in. People would drive ninety miles an hour and slide on that ice, and I don't know how they kept from killing themselves. It was like the 1800s or something, like a pioneer town.

It was winter, January. And what did I know about the weather in Alaska? So I'm in little cotton dresses, because Nashville is not really that cold. And when you're on stage, it's a lot of hot lights up there, so you wear cotton clothes, something maybe with rhinestones in it, something pretty, but as far as wearing warm clothing, you don't want to do that.

The thing was I had bought that house, that beautiful house made of Tennessee sandstone with all them bedrooms and that swimming pool shaped like a big kidney where we floated those candles. So when I got the chance to go to Alaska, I thought, Good, the money will buy all the extra things that I need to go into the house.

When I first got to Fairbanks, I went out to the place I would be playing in, to see it and hear the band I would be performing with. And there was Merle Travis doing his last night. He did his last show and fell off the barstool from drinking. And I don't blame him at all. Because the place . . . it was just one room, an old square, with a little bar.

Merle's drinking put him there. I mean, this guy was so far above me or anyone else, and his drinking got him down to a point that he actually had to play in a place like that. Anyway, I helped him up off the floor. And I played there the next night, and the next night, and the next night.

I played three sets a night, three sets with a band that couldn't hardly boom chuck chuck chucka chuck. Oh sweet Jesus! But anyway, the second night the guy that owned the club took a liking to me because I didn't drink, I didn't smoke. I just got up there and I did my show the best I could. And the guy decided he was going to find me a good husband. I said, "No, I'm married! I don't want a man, no, no, no!" He wasn't listening. "Oh, you gotta have a good man to take home with you to Tennessee. Or you could move up here."

The next night this Eskimo who won the dog-sled contest across Alaska came in. He had teeth that were worn down from chewing blubber! And the club owner said, "Now he's a little dude but, Roni, he is just the one you need." This Eskimo didn't seem all that small, but then he peeled his muckaloks and his parka off, and he melted. You get real skinny when you shed all them clothes. He wanted me to come out to his igloo! And I said, "No, no, no!" Then he suggested a dog-sled ride. I could just see it, me out there freezing my butt off in a little cotton dress on the back of a dog sled, going all through the cold flat land of Alaska!

The pipeliners were there, though, and I got to learn about pipelining. On the airplane going over, I ran across a lady whose husband was a pipeliner. She and her husband were kind, picked me up early, it was still dark, and drove me out to the pipelines. They showed me the steel drillings and how the pipes went across the ice.

Well, I learned a lot, but I kissed the ground when I got back to Nashville.

On the subject of kissing, one of the things every woman musician on the road gets is a crash course in dealing with men. Of course, dealing with male musicians can be tricky anywhere. But it's even trickier when you're traveling. I was one of the boys. Purposefully. I never messed with any pickers. I got a key bit of advice about that from Mother Maybelle Carter herself. I was sitting on her bus one day, just talking with her. She was a quiet woman, but she liked humor. She had a round face and big eyes, and she wore long dresses, like prairie dresses, with lots of lace.

"I don't know what to do," I said. "I'm separated from Gene, and I want to start to date, but I've got the kids and, well, you gotta be careful when you date with children." And that's true. You have to be extra careful because you want your children to have a safe atmosphere. Mother Maybelle pondered a minute and then said, "Well, just don't date no musicians. Don't do anything naughty with the pickers. 'Cause they tell."

I came off the bus, and I thought, Well she's got a point. They're always telling war stories of being on the road. And then I started laughing. Because it was as if she was saying, "Don't worry about your reputation with God or anything, just watch that the boys don't hear."

But there would of course be propositions, and you had to learn how to handle them. One of the ways that worked well was to joke about them. For instance, there was the time I was doing an Opry package show with Jeannie Shepard's band and some other folks. Huge auditorium. And there was this nice-looking young man and we were just talking in the afternoon while everybody was checking out the hall and the sound system.

"You know, Roni," he said. "Music today is changing."

"Yeah, it is kinda different. Yeah, I'd have to say it is."

"I think it's really getting bad."

"Yeah, it's getting pretty bad, but some of them pickers sound good, and they got some awful cute little gals out there that are singing real good."

So we're having this philosophical discussion about the state of music. And I thought this is nice, the guys are talking to me like I'm one of them, a professional and all.

And then, out of a clear blue sky, he said, "Roni, what would it take to get in your britches?"

I just looked at him. Then I stood up and walked away. But I got to thinking, Well, I can't let this get the best of me. I'm gonna have to come up with something.

So later when I got up on stage to perform, I was wearing some pantaloons I had made to go under my full dress. They came down to just above the knee, with a little ruffle and lace. I'm on stage, and Jeannie Shepard's band is backing me up. That guy was sitting there in the front row of the band, a piano player. The audience is listening hard, and I say, "You know, gang . . ." And then I stop. "No, I can't tell you that." Now, you start off like that and what's an audience going to do? They're gonna holler, "Yes, yes, we want to hear! Tell us, tell us!" And I said, "Well . . . I don't want to offend anyone." So then of course everybody yelled, "We want to hear! Tell it!"

"It's something one of the boys up here in the band said to me." Then all the band is saying, "Who is it?" "What was it, Roni?" And the audience all started applauding. The piano player was shrinking a little bit. I said, "Well, I was talking to . . . You really want to hear this now?" "Yeah! Yeah!" "Well, okay. It was him, the piano player. You know what he said to me?" And the audience said, all at one time, "WHAT?" I said, "Well, I was sitting there talking to him before the show." Now he was really sinking down. Spotlight came right on him. "And," I went on, "he was talking real nice to me, but then suddenly he said to me, 'Roni, what would it take to get in your britches?'" I looked at the audience for a moment, to let it sink in. And then I pulled my dress up to show the pantaloons. I faced toward the piano player, and I said, "Honey, I don't think you want to get in these old britches!" Here I am, Roni Stoneman, measurements 9–10–11, and wearing a training bra, and those pantaloons. Well, Jeannie and the band were in hysterics. There was fifteen minutes of applause. I guess Maybelle Carter was right and the boys do tell because I was never asked that again.

Speaking of "romance," one of the more, well let's say interesting, characters you run across on the road is the "snuff queen" or "diesel sniffer."

I did a whole tour with my friend from *Hee Haw*, Junior Samples. This was another time when I kissed the ground when I got home.

We were going to play Coffeyville, Kansas, and we stopped in Fort Smith, Arkansas. The boys said they wanted to go to a certain club. I didn't want to, but Junior said, "Roooni, you gotta go with me." He had that drawl. Bless his little heart. Well, he wasn't little, but bless his heart. So I agreed to go.

We get to the club. Junior's sitting there with me at a table and we were listening to the band, and people were saying that the steel guitar player was the ex of Sammi Smith, the "Help Me Make It through the Night" girl, a friend of mine.

Before Sammi made "Help Me Make It through the Night," which was written by Kris Kristofferson and which got her and him Grammys, I used to help her—not through the night but to move her stuff from one friend's house to the next because she'd have to be living with different people. She came from a . . . I guess you'd say it was a deprived background. Her mother was married eleven times, and Sammi grew up in a flophouse. Anyway I loved to go out to hear her play her songs. Daggone they were good.

Back to Junior. We're in this club in Arkansas, and all these girls started gathering around Junior. They were kissing him on the neck.

And I'm sitting there beside him, thinking, This is awful. But it was new and wonderful to Junior. He was a country comedian, overweight, in his bibbed overalls. He hadn't had someone to constantly tell him he was handsome. He had a beautiful wife, I thought, was named Gracie, a sweet lady. But he hadn't been out on the road before and he wasn't used to this kind of thing. It certainly was different from life back in the swamps of south Georgia where he came from.

When he was a kid, Junior told me, his father was making moonshine and they caught him and put him in jail. The family lived in a little shack out in the middle of nowhere, had holes in the floor, big cracks in the walls, and mosquitoes. They didn't have any water in the house and the mosquito eggs were on top of the bucket of water in the yard, and you'd have to scoop off the mosquito eggs with your hand in order to drink the water. You do that and of course you're inviting malaria. Well, the authorities came down to look, to see how the family was doing, because they were worried there might be no food in the house because they had his father in jail. What they saw was all the rest of the family laying on the floor, unconscious, from malaria. "We almost died, Roni," Junior said.

The family lived in a tenant house. And when Junior got *Hee Haw,* he built a large new house. He had silver dollars writing "HEE HAW" in the driveway, with polyurethane poured right over them. "Junior, that's beautiful," I said. He built the house right in the middle of all them tenant houses. In Cummings, Georgia. They were nice enough little houses, and they were clean because the people were hard-time workers. But you know you don't get your money back from your house when you build it in the middle of that. But he wasn't going to move. Those were his friends, and Junior never let his friends down.

Okay, we're back at the nightclub. And all these girls were slobbering all over Junior. I went, Oh my gosh, I want out of here. The place was so bad it brought back memories of those bars in Washington, D.C. So I got Sammi's ex to take me to the hotel. He was a nice enough guy, but steel players will be steel players and he wanted to play a little bit, but I wasn't interested in singing his song. He was a gentleman about it.

The next morning, about 9:30, I go down in the coffee shop in the hotel, and Junior's down there and this girl's sort of latched onto him.

Junior said, "Roni, she really loves me!" Well daggone if she wasn't a diesel sniffer! Now I've got to explain this. The men singers often had female fans, and we called them different things. The "gherms" are female fans that go "I love you, I really love you!" in a high squeaky voice. "Diesel sniffers" (sometimes called "snuff queens") are the women who follow the buses of the entertainers from state to state. Most of them take their vacations at the time their favorite star is going on tour. They go to the shows, and then they go to the hotel rooms and party. We had been through four states, and this diesel sniffer and some of her friends were following us.

So there we were eating breakfast, and this girl's trying to cuddle up with Junior! And people kept coming over and asking Junior for his autograph. He sold his picture and autograph for two dollars. He'd just put "Jr." Or "Junior." Later somebody taught him to write "Samples."

That evening, before the show, we're back in the tune-up room, and Junior said "Ronnnni, I went shopping." Everybody in the world had been used to Junior Samples in his bibbed overalls. Well, he had gone out and got a new shirt, a pair of Levis, and a plastic vest. He was like a little boy at Christmas with his first cowboy vest—"Ronnnni, how do I look?" He also had a belt with a big buckle and a pair of cowboy boots!

I just stared at him. The vest was brown, made out of Naugahyde. And he had that big belly. How he looked was like a barrel. He said, "Ronnnni, I respect you. Your family's been in the music business for years, and I respect what you say. Tell me, does this look all right for me to perform in tonight?" "Well, Junior," I said, "you look mighty handsome, you look very very handsome. But you gotta think of that audience." And I paused, "Now you can put this on after the show. But my opinion? You should wear your bibbed overalls, 'cause that's what you get paid for, honey. The audience wants you in bibbed overalls."

Coffeyville, Kansas, was where those old cowboys did a big robbery. Not the James gang. The Dalton Boys—last raid of the Dalton Boys. Historical town. Well, I wanted to see everything that the cowboys was into, so I wanted to stay overnight and go to the museum the next day. All right, after the performance we pull up at the hotel. And a lady says, "Mr. Samples, Mrs. Samples is here." Junior says "Oh, God! Lord have mercy! Lord gosh!" He thought Gracie had come. Fortunately, he come to find out that the diesel sniffer had introduced herself as Mrs. Samples.

To know Junior was to love him and understand. I was lucky. My mom and dad had stepped out into the world, so they taught us a whole lot. But with people like little old Junior, you didn't have those parents who stepped out into the sunshine, so how were they going to teach their children any better? He was a good sort. That was a good family. But they were just backwoods. I understood him. I understood everything he was going through and what he was saying in his heart.

Those long long drives are a big part of the musicians' road experience. Now, I really in my heart believe that the bus or van drivers had to take something to stay awake because they were driving so much. It's well known that they took pills. That was the time in the sixties and seventies when Dr. Snap in Nashville was giving them out. I think he was a good man who loved musicians and he saved a lot of lives. Because, well, this is how it worked. You had to do a certain amount of Saturday nights at the Opry in order to keep staying on the Opry. But it didn't pay well, I think it was sixty-five dollars a night, so you had to book dates for the rest of the weekend. And as soon as you'd finished your Opry appearance, you had to run and get on the bus, and the driver, who was often a sideman, would take off, and he would drive all night long through snow, sleet, hail. It was like the mailman—the band must go through.

So the bus driver took a pill or two to keep going. And then he would start talking, and he could talk you to death. We called it a talkathon. The drivers wouldn't use coffee because then they'd have to make a lot of pit stops. So it'd be an "old yeller," or a "blackie," or an old "benny." They'd say, "I think I'll let old Benny drive awhile."

Well, one time we Stonemans were on a tour with Kitty Wells, her husband Johnnie Wright, and her daughter Ruby, Jim Ed Brown, George Hamilton IV, and the Stonemans. We were going through Iowa in the wintertime. I remember it was winter because the wind came whipping around those corners in Des Moines. We were on an Abe Hamza tour, and if you were on his tour you were number one. So we were proud of that.

We were going to be on this radio program, Mike Hoyer's. It was about 2:00 in the morning and Mike stayed on all night. The program was a musician's dream because Mike was a fun guy to communicate with and the station was like WSM, but it seemed like it was even larger, seemed like it broadcast all over the United States. So a lot of entertainers would go through there from the Opry, and Mike would interview them live.

We got to the studio for the radio show, and we were talking to Mike while he took a break during the weather report. All the boys were discussing what they were on, the pills they'd been taking to keep them driving all night: "Boy, I can drive all the way to Canada on this!" "Just give me a West Coast Turnaround!" That was the "blackie," and the whole idea was you could take one and drive to the West Coast and back on it. A lot of the pickers were talking about Dexedrines. Dexedrines were very popular, and a few of the musicians had taken them. One guy's eyes was staring like he was on them right then. Anyway, after the weather, Mike was introducing Kitty Wells, and he said, "Miss Kitty, and what are you on?" She looked at him and said in this incredibly sweet voice, "De . . . De . . . Decca." And the whole room busted out laughing.

That was Miss Kitty Wells. She is truly the best lady. I remember we were playing a fair with her in Springfield, Illinois. The people from Illinois never let us down. They came there in droves. We Stonemans performed first, playing so hard and jumping around. We were all over that stage. And then after we got off, they said, "And now, ladies and gentlemen, the Queen of Country Music, Miss Kitty Wells!!!!" She walks out on the stage, just walking, taking her time, such a lady. The people roared. And she said, in this tiny little voice, "Thaaaannk you." Roar, roar, roar. "Thaaank you. Thaaaannnk you." I stood and I watched her. And I thought, God, ain't she fantastic! I thought, I'm doing this all wrong. I'm up there jumping around doing crazy things, and she just says "Thank you," and the audience goes wild. But of course even at that time I realized that you have to do what you do best, act like people expect you to act.

Kitty Wells was my hero. Without her songs I would never have been able to feed my children. Because that's what I used to sing back at the Famous Bar and Grill in Washington. I learned to sing just like her because the people always wanted Kitty Wells songs: *As I sit here tonight / The jukebox playing* . . . Recently I was able to sing at her combined anniversary and birthday party. She and Johnnie have been married some sixty years. Johnnie was from the team Johnnie and Jack—*Goodnight, goodnight, sweetheart / Well it's time to go.* But after Patsy Cline got killed in that air crash, Jack Anglin got killed in a car accident on the way to her funeral. Johnnie's still a class act, and Kitty can still outshine any newer girl. Well at that party I got to sing one of Kitty's religious songs. They picked it out for me to do and I didn't know all the words to it, but I faked it because I wasn't about to lose my part in the celebration.

Once I did the Ralph Emery show, *Nashville Now,* and Kitty Wells was on the show. I'm sitting there beside her, and she looked at me and said, "That's where I got my name." I said, "Where?" She said, "Your father's song. I was named after 'Kitty Wells,' your father's cylinder record." My eyes got real big, and I said, "Ralph, did you hear that?!!!"

Here's another story about one of those long drives. Now if you go out on the road with Faron Young and the Deputies—and I did—you got yourself a heap of trouble. Faron was really funny. As I said, he called me Olive Oyl because I was so skinny. Faron would say, "Olive Oyl, c'mere, Olive Oyl." And there I'd be so skinny and with my crooked eye, onstage with Faron, so handsome. Gee, was he handsome! And so full of impish goings-on. True, he would talk tacky. There wasn't a sailor from the furthest of seas could talk rougher than him. But if he really liked you a whole lot, he'd kind of cool it, the real nasty stuff.

Now, Faron always treated me with respect. Though he would joke with me. One time I wore a short dress, and he went, "Olive Oyl, stay the hell out of Clarksville with them bird legs." That's because Clarksville had a lot of blackbirds, and they had to have this campaign to kill them because they were causing lung diseases from the droppings. In other words, somebody was going to shoot me, mistaking me for a bird. And I laughed. Faron had a way of loving you at the same time saying something that would kill anybody's feelings. He was adorable.

I traveled a lot with Faron because he liked the way my banjo playing would give the show a slightly different flavor, different from just steel guitars and drums. This was when I had just started doing *Hee Haw,* during the seventies. Faron was called the Little Sheriff because he was once a sheriff. So he called his band The Deputies. Faron was tough. Especially when he'd get to drinking and . . . All right, I was in the bus. I forget where we were exactly, but we were riding along. The boys had been playing cards and drinking beer, and then they all went in the back to sleep it off. And the driver was driving, just driving along.

Most often someone would be riding shotgun. That means you would sit up by the driver, in this sort of well at the front of the bus, down where the steps to go in and out of the bus are. There's a little seat that pulls out. And you'd do that either because you wanted to get away from the rest of the band or because you wanted to make sure that the driver stayed awake. You'd talk to him—or you'd be listening as he was going through the talkathon.

Okay, on this particular night since the boys had been up drinking for hours before they went to sleep, the trash bin was full of beer cans and there were others stacked up waist high against the wall near it. Now, Faron wanted his bus kept clean because he did have a nice bus. But the band's thinking, Oh hell, we'll just get rid of this stuff next stop.

So everybody was asleep. And I thought, Well, I'll get up and ride shotgun with the driver. We're riding along, just talking quietly, and then we heard Faron stir out of his room. Had a little star on his door. That was usual. Sometimes the musicians will put the star on for the bandleader and sometimes he'll do it himself. It's sort of a joke because although the bandleader would have the only private room, it wasn't luxurious or anything. It was cut real short into the wall. The rest of us had bunks.

Okay, so we heard Faron get up and open the door and he starts yelling to the driver (I was invisible down in the well, so he didn't know I was there): "Hot damn, ****###&&#**&&&&. What've they been doin' in here?! Them son of a bitches! Look at this trash! Look at 'em cans! Son of a bitch! Well, I'll fix em! I'm gonna put this shit . . ." And he picked up this big trash can and threw it right down into the well where I was sitting. He dumped all this stuff on me. Beer came running down over me. And the food they hadn't eaten, sandwiches and stuff. And cigarette butts. I had worked hard on my hair, trying to make it look nice for the next show coming up, fixing myself up real good. I just sat there. And then I slowly raised up. And I kept raising up, and I said, "Faron, why'd you . . . ?" "What the hell!!!!! I didn't know you were down there!!" He started laughing, and he got all the boys up to come look at me. "Look at 'er. Look at Olive Oyl," he said, "Look at old bird legs herself!! Hot damn. I just . . . I'm sorry." That's the first time ever I heard Faron say he was sorry about anything!

Now, Faron was a great performer. When he walked out on stage and started *It's four in the morning,* well, the girls would go "Ahhhhh-hhh." I could see why. He always looked so nice, and he had a whole lot of energy on stage. Offstage he was also always doing something, and it usually pertained to girls. Later when he did get married, he really adored his wife and his daughter. One of his wives was called Hilda. He would call her Brunhilda, I guess because she was pretty tough on him in the divorce.

Everybody in Nashville knew that Faron was the cat's pajamas. If he liked you, he was always on your side. And if I'm gonna give you the full picture of Faron, I gotta go back to Nashville for a second. One time we were down at Channel Five filming *Hee Haw,* and this man was there to watch. He was kind of cocky. And someone said, "Faron Young's going to come in today and do a guest spot." So this guy started talking about Faron. He said, "I heard he was such and such," badmouthing him.

I said, "Let me tell you about Faron. He is such a giving soul. You can go to Faron and say, 'Faron, I need eight hundred dollars.' He wouldn't ask you why. He would just give it to you."

"That's hard to believe," said the know-it-all guy.

"You don't believe me? Okay I'll prove it."

Faron came in the back door and went into the studio area and started taping his part.

I said to the guy, "Make sure you're standing right here when he gets through. He'll come out this way and say hello to everybody."

The guy stood there and soon Faron came along.

"Faron," I said, "I gotta have one thousand dollars. I just gotta have it."

"Okay, one second," he says, and pushed around in his pocket, about to get it out.

"No, Faron, it was just to prove a point."

And the guy was amazed.

"That's the kind of man Faron is," I said.

Believe it or not, the arrival at a venue after a long trip could have its own set of problems. Back when I was playing with the family, I often traveled separately from them, if it was more convenient. In the late six-ties we were performing with Eddy Arnold. He was known as one of the greatest singers of our time—any time, as far as I'm concerned. He could sing, oh brother, and he was such a gentleman and so sweet and calm. It was particularly amazing to me because I was so hyper. We'd open the shows, "the singin', swingin', stompin', sensational Stonemans," and then later on, calm, gentle Eddy Arnold would come out. He'd croon "I'll Hold You in My Heart (Til I Can Hold You in My Arms)" and "Make the World Go Away." Again, like when we opened for Kitty Wells, a terrific contrast.

Well, one time we were playing in some big auditorium in North Carolina. I got there before the family because I rode with some friends. And I had always been told, if you're part of the band, don't get there ahead of the rest of them because everybody'll be asking you all kinds of questions in a worried voice: "Where they at?" "Why aren't they here?" Even though they're not late. So I thought, What am I gonna do? Maybe if I get into the dressing room, I can hide from the promoters.

Now we used to kid among ourselves about Eddy Arnold's manner. It was very formal. He'd put his hands together, grasping them, like holding hands with himself. And he'd say, veeery sloooowly, "How are you, Mr. Stoooonnneman? And how are yoooou, little Donnna?" And each time he'd say a name, he would change his hands. He was really funny with that.

Okay, so there I am in this dressing room, really a locker room, but I'm still worried that someone will come in asking about the family. So I shut myself up in a locker. But then the tin bottom of the floor bent to where I couldn't open the door! I started banging, "Help! Get me out of here! Help! Help!" So someone walks inside the locker room, and he hears me bang, bang, bang, and he manages to open up the door. I stare out. It's Eddy Arnold, looking me right in the face. And instead of saying "What the hell are you doing in there?!!", he grasps his hands and he says, very calmmmmly, "Hellooooo, Ronnnni. How are youuuu? And where is the rest of the familllly?" It was real tempting to say "In the other lockers!" I didn't.

I guess one of the best things about traveling was just being with the other musicians, performing with them and getting to know them, and watch them in, well, different-from-the-usual circumstances. So now some stories about them.

Patsy Cline

I first met Patsy Cline when we were part of a show with her. I was about ten years old. We were on WARL in Arlington, Virginia, performing outside on a flat-bed truck. The audience was huge. Patsy was young, had a cowgirl suit on, a long-sleeved western shirt, and a navy blue skirt with a fringe that touched the top of her boots. The boots were white and on the front of them was a gold eagle.

Connie B. Gay said, "And ladies and gentlemen, the young lady coming out here now, she just got out of the apple orchard. She's been picking apples all day, and she's gonna get up here and sing, and her name's Patsy Cline!" We knew to respect her because we'd heard her sing before. I thought, Well, she don't need an old stupid banjo in her band, so I started backing off. And she said, "You get right back up here, and you pick as hard as you want to!" She sang real loud, in this clear voice, and I'm staring at her face, trying to chop rhythm on the banjo. And about that time there's this "whheeeeeeeeee," a loud siren, over on the Lee Highway. It was a police car. She stopped right in the middle of her song. "Sic 'em, boys!" she said. "Sic 'em!" And I thought, God, she's so great!

I wasn't paying much attention to the songs she sang. I was mainly just watching her. I thought, One of these days I'm gonna get me a pair of boots just like hers. And I did. I have some pictures of me wearing them, with the gold eagle on the front. My legs look like sticks. I look like Minnie Mouse on a bad day. But I had those white boots all polished up.

By that time Patsy Cline was getting pretty well known. She hadn't come to Nashville yet, but she was working a lot in Virginia. Because her voice . . . it's as if as soon as she started singing, she was famous. There's some people can do that. They are immediately famous by the way they play or sing.

I never became close friends with her because, well, my sister Donna would say about a number of singers, "Now, Roni, don't spend a lot of time with them. They're kind of rough." Patsy Cline knew how to party hearty. Just like the girls of today will go out and have a drink with the boys. She was ahead of her time, that's all. Because young girls in our world didn't partake of alcohol, as I said. Whenever we'd see a woman drink, we felt that she was rough, she's been there, she's done every-thing that boys do, and that wasn't good. I now think it was the double standard and it was unfair. After all, what's going to happen when you die? God will say, "Oh, you're a boy, well you're going to heaven. You're a girl. Even though you did the same thing, you gotta go to hell." In my opinion, God don't see it that way.

Loretta Lynn

Well, while we're on the subject of boots, as I guess it's clear, I love them—and so does my friend Loretta Lynn. And one time we were do-ing a show together in Toronto, Canada. Loretta had a pair of boots she had bought in London that I wanted so bad. So this must have been back in the late sixties because that's when the boots were in, the mod boots. Donna and I wore white boots on our television show, white boots and cotton dresses. It was a sort of go-go-dancing-with-country-music-and-folk-music look.

Loretta's boots were a light blue-gray, real pretty, with a charcoal band at the top. No zipper—they were a soft glove leather. And I said, "Oh, I really like your boots, 'Retta." She said, "Ya dew?" in her southern drawl. And I said, "Yeah." And I thought, How in the heck am I gonna get them boots from her? Because I kept watching those boots every-where she went. Now Loretta is slightly bowlegged. She couldn't catch a greased pig if she tried. That's why she wears those long dresses.

I said, "'Retta, you know, you're an awful pretty woman." Of course that's true. She's a gorgeous woman.

"Oh, thank you, Roni."

"But your legs . . ."

"I know, these old legs . . ."

"I'm gonna tell you something," I said, "you're like a sister to me . . ."

"I know, we're two of a kind." And that was true too. She had a bunch of kids like me, and a sorry situation.

So I said, "You know, if you didn't wear them boots . . . Well, they got a different kind of heel than you need, Loretta. They make you look bowlegged."

"They dew?"

"Yeah, you oughta get a different kind of boot." Actually, that was also the truth.

"Wall, I'll tell you what," Loretta said. "If you go shopping with me today, I'll get some new boots, and then I'll let you have these."

So we went downtown. She had a mink car coat on, and she had her hair up in brush rollers. You women out there, do you remember those old rollers with the brushes in the middle of them? I still have a can of them lying around somewhere. They were great because they worked good for the hair, but boy did they hurt! Loretta would always wear them. She had no choice when she was on the road. She'd get on the bus, and she'd have to fix her hair. So in the back room of her bus, where she always had flowers, she also had all kinds of rollers, and her Adorn hairspray. Without them brush rollers and Adorn hairspray, Loretta Lynn couldn't have sung her songs. I don't think she could have gotten through *I was born a coal miner's daughter.*

We were supposed to do a show that night, so she had her hair up in those rollers. And all she had to go over them was one of those net-looking things that were like stiff chiffon scarves. It was pink and you could see the curlers through it because it was sheer. God, it was the ugliest dang thing. She had those boots on, a pair of jeans, the fur coat, her hair in curlers under that pink net, and no makeup.

So off we went to a department store that's by the town building that's shaped like two *U*'s together. The City Hall, I think it is. I remember learning that the man that made it died before he saw it finished.

A salesman came over to us.

"Can I help you ladies?" he asks, in this real "propa" voice.

"Oh, I wanna git some boots," says 'Retta.

"Well, come right this way." And we followed him to the bargain basement.

'Retta gazed at the displays.

"Oh, no, I don't want them boots. I want some pretty good boots," she said.

So he took us to the second floor, which was the second grade.

"Wall," she said, looking around, "I don't want them things either. They're fine, but they're not good for what I want."

The guy was getting irritated. Then we went up on the third floor—it was a real expensive area.

"I suppose *these* are the boots you had in mind!" he said.

Me and Loretta walked in there, and she didn't have any idea, and neither did I at the time (I figured it out later) that he was being sarcastic because of the way she looked. I'm sure he thought the coat was fake. Anyway, she picked out lots of boots, and she tried them all on, one after another. The salesman's getting more and more impatient.

Then she said, "I want that one, and this one, and that one, and this one." Twelve pairs.

His mouth was hanging open.

"Do you know how much they cost?"

"I know. I want 'em."

She paid him cash. We left him with his mouth still hanging open.

Then we went downstairs, to go out the store.

"Look, a miniskirt. I like that miniskirt," I said, pointing to one.

"You'd wyar a miniskirt? You mean to tell me you'd wyar something that short?"

"Yeah."

"Well, I'll tell you what, Roni. You try on that skirt, and I'll buy it for you, if you wyar it." She's always been real generous, Loretta.

So I tried it on, and she bought it and I wore it. And then I stepped into her lovely blue-gray boots. Feeling a little guilty—but not much. She really did look better in the other boots, and she had the money.

Away we went back to the hotel.

And there's Daddy, Donna, Jimmy, and Van, eating at the café. I walked in with them boots, and that short miniskirt. I had attractive legs, even if, as Faron joked, they were thin. Loretta was giggling. She'd go "Hee, hee, hee, hee." She was always cute that way—she'd get embarrassed easy. So we went in there and we sat down.

"We got her a miniskirt," Loretta said, and she giggled.

"I see you did," says Daddy.

"Oh, Roni, it's so short!" said Donna.

And Jimmy, well, if my brother Scott told a risqué joke on the stage, Jimmy would leave the stage and stand in the kitchen part of the honky-tonks. That was just his way. So Jimmy got a napkin and he put it on my legs, covering them up. And I sat there, real thin, with that skirt on, and the napkin, and Loretta giggling.

I kept the boots and I wore them all the time. I was ever so proud of them.

As I said, Loretta was in a sorry situation. She had a tough life. I'll never forget one time in Vegas. I was down there because Buck Trent was getting married for the second time, and a lot of the *Hee Haw* crew was there.

Loretta was playing one of the casinos, and she called me to come over. She had just came in from Hawaii on a tour. Now before she went to Hawaii, she had had an emotional breakdown. But they treated her with no mercy, her husband Mooney and her other managers. Right after she got out of the hospital, they sent her to Hawaii, and then out to Vegas. Though she's normally sharp as a tack onstage, at this time she was a wreck. She kept repeating things. She needed three doctors working on her to keep her going.

I went to her dressing room.

She lay down on her bed and started crying.

"Oh, Roni, my fifteen-year-old, one of the twins, got married," she said.

"Oh, Loretta."

"I didn't want her to be like me. And she married a boy I didn't want her to marry. Mooney called me and he was drunk, and was cussing me every kind of name."

"Oh, my God, Loretta! I know how you feel." And I got down by the bed, and I was crying with her.

"Roni, how do you get through it?"

"When it gets so bad, Loretta, all you can do is open the door and step across and keep going."

It was so sad.

Tanya Tucker

I really admired Tanya Tucker. Maybe Tanya's almost as famous for her relationship with Glen Campbell as she is for her singing. Now Tanya loved Glen very much and he loved Tanya I'm sure, but when I was out on the road with them, they fought constantly. About everything. I think they'd have fought over a French fry. One time we were playing somewhere, in Boston or someplace, some fancy city that we were proud to be in. I always liked to play for the city folks. They'd sit there and kind of not know what to expect. And then you thought, Okay, give them a little extra. C'mon, I'll drag you into our culture, and I'm going to make you like it. That was the exciting part of music to me, interacting with the people.

So, we were playing this fancy city, and we were eating dinner in a fancy restaurant. I was sitting right near to Tanya and Glen. A fight broke out and she punched him. Oh God, I don't know where that girl learned it, but she could fight. She didn't pull hair and scratch. She'd take a fist and haul off and punch. She socked him again, and they went down on the floor, and I mean it was just a scrapple there. My opinion: they were both talented people (she had her hit "Delta Dawn" when she was thirteen!), both taking things they shouldn't have been, and that made them touchy. Eventually, of course, they broke up and she went into rehab.

But there was another side to Tanya. One time we played a show together in California, and on the plane going back there were two little girls that were really raggedy looking. Tanya kept watching them. When we got off the plane in Nashville, she just took her hand and touched the little girls' faces. And then she gave their parents some money. She was really concerned about those two little girls. She said, "You know I wanted to adopt those children. I'm going to adopt me some children." Tanya later had her own child, Presley, and then another, and she's a great mother.

⌒

Sometimes it was not the particular famous people in unexpected circumstances but just the unexpected circumstances themselves that made being on the road interesting. You'd be stuck in situations where you'd have to improvise. Those times really called out the creativity in you.

Now improvisation can have its downside. I mentioned Johnny Cash and how kind he and June were to me, offering to help pay for my teeth. Johnny once said, "Roni Stoneman is great! She really missed her calling. She was another Judy Canova." John talked nothing but good things about me. No wonder. He hit me in the shin, and it liked to have killed me.

This was in Beaumont, Texas. He was singing *John Henry was a steel-driving man* . . . And he was supposed to bang two steel things together and make it sound like steel driving. But he didn't have the proper things, so he improvised. What he came up with was a Coke bottle and an iron railroad lantern cover. He sang *John Henry was a steel* . . . and he went CRASH, and the bottle broke and it shattered all over the floor. So he just took that iron lantern cover and threw it in the wings—like somebody's gonna catch it?—and it hit my shin. Blood ran chu, chu, chu, chu, all down my leg. I went "Ohhhhhh!!" And I was rolling around on the floor. He came dashing off the stage. "Did I hurt you? Did I hurt you?" "I'm okay. Go back out there, hon." He went running out from the wings, and, well, he slid on his knees right in that glass. And the blood was flying all over the stage. A disaster!

Mostly, though, the improvisation led to more positive experiences. I remember the Stonemans one time getting to a place where we were to play that night, but the stage was real tiny. Daddy went out and got some lumber and built a larger one that very afternoon. Playing on that new stage really made us feel great. And then another time . . . umm . . . well, did you ever iron a dress with a light bulb? Okay, once when I was on the road, I was in this awful rundown hotel room, and I was trying to get the wrinkles from my clothes. They didn't have an iron, so I got to looking around. And I said, Wait a minute, there's a big light over there. I can take that lampshade off and spread a little bit of water on the clothes and then hold them over the light bulb. Steam them. And that's what I did. Worked pretty good. I heartily recommend it to all you friends and neighbors out there, in case of an emergency. Now, when you figure out something like that, you don't get the best ironed clothes (take it from the Ironing Board Lady!), but it does give you a sense of power, gives you a real high.

The main high came of course from performances that turned out to be special. Often these were in hospitals and clinics. I got a lot of those jobs through Nat Winston, my dear friend, the psychiatrist. He treated a lot of country stars and was the one that helped Johnny Cash get off pills. He later ran for governor of Tennessee.

One time I did a show up in Murfreesboro, at a veterans' hospital.
Now this hospital also had an alcoholics ward. So a lady came up and
said the alcoholics would like to come too, was that okay? And I said,
"Sure." So in walk a bunch of people and I look up, and one of them is
my brother Jack! In the audience also of course are all these veterans in
wheelchairs, poor guys, hurt and with nobody to feed their brain and not
much entertainment. I'm thinking, I'm going to give them every bit of
any talent I have. They had been watching *Hee Haw* every week, so I had
worn one of my *Hee Haw* dresses, the red checkered gingham. I started
playing, and someone said, "Your brother wants to play with you." Now
Jack was a brother who wasn't so nice to me when I was growing up,
but I said, "Yeah, fine." And Jack found a bass. So we played *Don't make
me go to bed an' I'll be good / No, Papa, an' I'll be good / No, Papa, an' I'll be
good.* I had him play that because he shined on the bass in that. And that
let him show off to his friends.

So I was finishing up the show, and I'm up there singing and without thinking much, I said, "Now let's all sing a song called 'Mountain
Dew.'" And then I thought, Oh my God, there are all these alcoholics
in here, and I'm gonna sing "Mountain Dew"? I'm as bad as Van in the
unwed mother's home, hoping to see those pregnant girls again next
year. I quickly said, "This is one of Grandpa Jones's songs. And I want
everyone in here that can clap or wants to sing to go ahead, and we'll
have the best time because that's why Grandpa Jones recorded it, as a
fun thing." I was covering with everything I could think of to say!

So I started singing *Oh they call it that good old mountain dew, dew dew.*
And I took the mike around and held it to different people to sing. I
didn't pay too much attention to the alcoholics because they were really
getting into it on their own, waving their arms around and such! I was
focusing on the men that were in the wheelchairs. And they were that
way because of fighting for our country to be free and for me to be safe
enough to go out there and play my music. I'm thanking them for it by
taking the mike around. Then this one old guy got out of his wheelchair,
stood straight up and sang a whole verse. The psychiatrists, there were
about six of them lined up against the wall, gaped, and a couple of the
nurses started to lean forward. The guy was singing and I was singing
with him, and then he sat down. The doctors came up to me later and

said, "He's been here fourteen years and he's never stood up from that wheelchair. We try to get him to use his legs, but he doesn't." It was a magical moment for me.

And that's life on the road. There are some boring and exhausting times, but you end up with unforgettable experiences!

TWENTY-FIVE

Husbands 3, 4, and 5

Or, as I said to a country musician who made a snippety remark, "Well, at least I married them." And they were all totally different, so how was I supposed to know?

Anyway, getting back to my family life, it was real clear that George and I had no future together. The final straw was when I came in one day, exhausted from doing three shows in 103–degree heat, and he was laying on the bed so drunk he couldn't even talk. I got a divorce.

My third husband, Richard Adams, I met when I was playing a fair in Bucyrus, Ohio. I was with the Hager twins from *Hee Haw.* After the show we were taken by two girls to a radio station for interviewing and then to Mansfield, Ohio, to Westbrook Country Club for dinner. Now as *Hee Haw* fans might guess, Jim and Jon Hager are very hyper devilish little boys, so to speak. They kept saying loudly to everybody who came up to the table, "Here's Roni Stoneman. She's the one that plays the Ironing

Board Lady." "Oh yeah, nice meeting you," I'd say. I'm thinking, I want to go take a shower, turn on television—get out of here.

Then one of the girls brought a banker over to the table. Jim, or Jon, right away says, "This is Roni Stoneman. She's the Ironing Board Lady." And I say, "Yeah, nice meeting you." And Jim, or Jon, says, "Roni's not married at the present time, are you, Roni?" The banker says, "Oh, you're not married?" There was a little more chitchat, then next thing you know, Jim and Jon and the girls take off.

The banker, Richard Adams, drove me back to the hotel. I had to play two fair dates the next day, and he insisted on bringing me to the first one. I did my show and then we walked around the fairgrounds. He was in awe of everybody coming over to me. I wasn't paying much attention. He wasn't appealing to me, seemed too cold-acting. (I should've gone with my women's intuition right then. Any woman out there—honest to God, when you got the vibes, go by them!)

Well, then he kept coming down to Nashville to see me. And after a while I got to thinking maybe I oughta go and check this out. So I went up to Mansfield and it was a good visit. Okay, I thought, he has two children but they're grown, and I have Barbara and Georgia still at home, and I could use some help with them. (Becky and Gene were married. Bobby was in the army.) He's a banker, on solid ground. And he's a nice man—everybody in Mansfield likes him, and I like him. Although I don't like the way he kisses, those hard kisses. But maybe this is just my imagination, and anyway I can change that. (More advice: Don't ever marry somebody you don't like to kiss, okay, girls?) So I agreed to marry him.

Before we got married, in 1980, Richard had me bring all my tax things for several years up to Ohio. Then he had his CPA man go through all my contracts. I did not know anything about my financial life—I was just all caught up in trying to get work. But I *did* know enough to say to Richard when he looked at my contracts, "Now, I don't do this good every year. So don't be expecting that. This is the music business." That last year *had* been very good—besides *Hee Haw*, I'd been on the road a lot, played thirty-six dates in a three-month period. Well, he was seeing nothing but money.

It was a big church wedding. I rode there in a limousine. On the left-hand side of the church was a room, and on the right-hand side was a room. Richard was in the right-hand one with his lawyer and one of his stockbroker friends. He came and got me. Now I didn't want him to see me because I wanted to surprise him with this beautiful dress I had ordered out of New York. But he insisted that he wanted me to sign some papers. I shouldn't have, but I'm getting ready to go down the aisle, Chet Atkins is already playing, what the heck am I supposed to do? Say, "Wait a minute. Get my lawyers to read the papers"? He was pushing me: "You got to sign these, you got to sign these right now." I signed them.

Now, there was one really great thing that came out of the marriage—the education of Barbara at a wonderful place in Mansfield called New Hope School. That's where Barbara received excellent training and really got to feel like a human being. Richard went on the board of directors of New Hope School, and he was careful about making sure she got to the school when I was out on the road. When I came back to Tennessee and worked as honorary chairperson for the mental health committee, one of the things I wanted to do was to spread the message of New Hope School. I went to every workshop in the state, helping to teach people that special young adults can be trained, that they can have jobs doing things like setting tables in restaurants.

Back to Richard and me. I thought everything was going to be, like, we work together as a team. That's what you're supposed to do with your husband. I never talked to Richard about *his* money, or about *his* financial situation. It was not romantic, not loving, to talk about money. The girls at the country club in Mansfield, it was a group called the 9 Holers, took me aside and said, "Listen now, if it wasn't for you, Richard Adams wouldn't have anything." I was wondering what they meant by that. I didn't realize I was making that much more than he was, being that he was educated enough to be a banker and I was just a seventh-grade dropout. It was true that I didn't see him setting the world on fire, but he did buy a new house (with, I later found out, my money). I told him, "Honey, let's not try to keep up with the Joneses. Let's just keep a nice home that we'll be happy in." "What are you talking about?" he said. "We *are* the Joneses."

Now, I didn't want my job, my music, to interfere with the marriage.

We get to feeling guilty that way, girl singers and pickers. We think, "Oh, it's me, with my career, causing all the problems." Not only girl musicians, that's the way all the women growing up in the fifties were taught, that we were the ones responsible for any wrongdoing coming down in the marriage. The men knew that we felt that way. And they zeroed in on it, and they made you feel like you were nothing, not even cotton candy that just melts, that you were just, well, air. So to make sure Richard knew he was in charge, when he came in one evening, I said, "Honey, today I went out and I bought a calendar just for my jobs. And I want you to take this to your office, and when people ask me for bookings, I'm gonna say 'Call Richard.'"

Once in a while I'd get paid in cash. And I'd put it in my pantyhose, under my boots. That way I wouldn't have to worry about losing it. Then I would go home and call Richard into the room, pull off my pantyhose, and the money would fall out all over the floor. I'd say, "There, I brought some money home!" I was trying to make him proud of me. That's what I thought love is. I'm your buddy, I'm your helpmate. Turned out all I was doing was making him hate my guts!

Actually he would get mad even when I just handed him a check. One day I got a call from Brenda Dean, who worked at the bank with Richard. She was a dear friend.

"Well, I guess you brought in a lot of money over the weekend," she said.

"Yeah, I did pretty good. How'd you know?"

"Richard's a jerk today. Every time you come in with money, I know it because of the way he acts."

So I decided that the next time I would just put my check in the china closet and tell him it was there. I would just play it down. I tried that and things went a little bit better.

But there was another big problem with the marriage, aside from the money—me. I didn't fit in with Richard's life.

To give an example, one day at the country club they said, "We're having this wonderful event. Pierre from New York is a jewelry designer who's designed for Tiffany's, and he's going to be here with his show." Peggy Stanley, my friend from North Carolina, was visiting, and she and I decided to go. We fixed and we fixed. You had to wear everything you had to the jewelry show at the country club. That's what Richard told me. So I had my Halston shoes on ($250), a long black gown, beautiful rings, and a bracelet and a diamond watch. And Peggy's also wearing lots of jewelry, all genuine.

So we get to the jewelry show, and, after standing around awhile, we go over to the main table. "Pierre" looked down at my hand.

"Ohhhh, so you're the one that bought that ring," he said.

"Yes, I sure am. I sure am." And I guess just those few words with my accent gave me away.

"Oh," he said, in a small voice. "I designed that ring."

"Well, it's awful purty."

"Umm . . ." and he sounded real puzzled, "when they told me someone had bought that particular ring, I . . . I assumed that it was a very sophisticated woman."

He had this jewelry store in Ohio, and I had gone in, and out of all those rings I had picked that one because it was very unusually set. And he was surprised that a hillbilly would come along and pick it out.

I just looked at Peggy and grinned.

That accent business is a strange thing. I was once on the Oprah show. Now Oprah Winfrey started at Channel Five in Nashville, so I knew her a little bit. She's something else, sharp, attractive, and though she's got a lot of money, she still has sympathy for other folks, compassion. When I was on the show we were talking about how you get treated different by the accent you have. If you're up north and you have a southern accent, people have a tendency to believe you're not intelligent.

Richard made it really clear he was ashamed of me. "Roni, come here," he said one day. Then he took a pencil and he drew a diagram with several parallel lines. "This is the top environment," he said. "And you're from the low class. And you can't climb the social ladder because you can never get out of the low class."

Now I didn't know a lot about Richard's family when I married him. But later I found out that his father drank and his old homeplace in Missouri was as bad as Carmody Hills, real shambly looking. So I thought, Why are you after me? Why are you making me feel so bad?

Occasionally we would go on trips. One time we were at a bankers' convention in, I think, Chicago. It was connected with the Harris Bank.

And there was a lot of etiquette involved. The ladies could not go further than the foyer, and then they had to wait until the gentlemen came and escorted them to a room where there was a cocktail party. I was dressed up the best that I could. I had a beautiful Halston gown on, my Halston shoes, diamond earrings. And Richard said to me, "Now don't move over to the buffet table because it's not a proper thing to do. I'm to go over there and get the food and bring it to you. And don't talk to anyone. You're fine as long as you don't talk. Just don't say anything."

So Richard's gone. And I'm tired of him putting me down all the time. I looked around to see who's there, and there was this handsome hunk. He came over, and his badge said "Doctor of Law, Austria." I thought, Well, if I talk to him, then he won't know that I don't have good grammar, and that I'm a hillbilly. So we talked for awhile.

The next thing you know, they came to seat us at this round table. I was the only female, six bankers and me. Richard's sitting on the other side of the gentleman from Austria, and then across from me is another really nice-looking fellow. I remembered to put my left hand in my lap properly, and I'm sitting with my back just so straight. And the waiter came over with a rag on his arm, and said, "Madame, may I suggest a vichyssoise?" Well, I didn't know what the cat hair a vichyssoise was, but I said it would be fine. I thought, If it's an alligator, I'll eat some of it. I'll pretend I like it.

The soup was cold. It was milky with globs of white in it. And I thought, Well, this ain't much good . . . and I'm not even sure . . . this must be milk. But what's floating around in it? I was wanting to mash it, to see what it was. I put one in my mouth. I looked over to Richard, and he frowned. But by this time I'm getting peeved. I'm getting . . . like my momma would say, "I've had about enough!" And I looked at the man across from me. He smiled. Everybody was being real nice to me but Richard. I picked up the spoon, and I thought, I'll fix him. But on the other hand I had already put in all that effort. So I also thought, No, don't do it. And then I thought, Yes, go for it!

So I lifted the spoon up out of the bowl, and I just dripped the soup, let it drip. Then I put the spoon near my mouth, tasted it, and made a face like eeeoow gross, like a kid would do. And then I lifted my spoon up very high, and I dripped the soup back into my bowl—drip, drip,

drip, drip. And the guy across from me—I never seen anybody grin more like a possum in my whole life.

Then I looked at the maitre d' and I motioned for him to come over.

"Would you put this in the microwave? It's cold. It's not supposed to be cold, is it?" I said.

"Madame, it's vichyssoise."

"Well," I said, pointing to one of the lumps, "what is that?"

"That's a potato, a potato."

"Well, that don't look like a tater to me. Mommy used to make tater soup and it was warm and it had a thickening in it. This is nothing but old milky stuff, and it's cold. Might as well have brought me a bowl of milk to drink!"

Richard's trying to kick me under the table, and hitting the guy from Austria because he couldn't reach me. The other guys at the table were enjoying it. Richard was all red, and I thought he was going to have a stroke, but I also thought, Well if he does, that's his fault, not mine. Because I'd kinda had enough of boss, boss, boss.

After awhile, I excused myself and went to the ladies' room. And I ran across some ladies in there and started talking to them. I said, "Where are y'all from?" "Well, it's real nice meeting you," that kind of thing. Country talk. Hillbilly City. And with that space in my teeth and my crooked eye, I had a real "hot damn, where're y'all from" *Hee Haw* look. The ladies stayed in there and talked to me for the longest time. There was one lady who was really elegant, and it seemed like she was the one that was enjoying it the most.

Then a few months pass, and we're invited by the Harris Bank to go to San Francisco for a big conference. Richard was really excited that he was social climbing. There was a gala dinner, and before we went down to the dinner, I put on this beaded jacket that I had bought in Los Angeles a long time ago. The jacket had a big dragon on the back, a green Chinese dragon, was real beautiful. Richard says, "You're not going to wear that jacket! That's too loud. The wives do not wear that sort of clothing." "This is supposed to be a gala," I said. "Pretty things are supposed to be worn." We argued a little more, and I won. I got to wear the jacket.

It turned out that the theme of the dinner was the Chinese New Year. I didn't know what a Chinese New Year was. They had set the food up as the four food corners of the earth, and a good jazz band was playing on the stage. You didn't sit down. You'd just wander over to the tables and say, "Oh, I would like to have a bit of this," "Oh, just give me a little taste of that."

And then after awhile, I went to the ladies' room, and there was that same elegant lady from the last convention. We said hello and then she told me how she loved my jacket. I said "Well, thank you, I love your jacket." When I went back out on the floor, I stood next to Richard, and he said, "I told you not to wear that. You see the other women?" I said, "The lady liked it. The lady liked it." And then all of a sudden Chinese people came out in a big dragon costume and started parading around all over the place. So it turned out I was dressed just right.

The next morning, there's a knock at the door, a messenger with a note for us. We were invited to join Mr. and Mrs. Harris at the Blue Boar Inn in San Francisco for dinner. And we could invite a couple of our friends that came with us from Ohio. The limousine would be picking us up at such and such a time. Mrs. Harris would love to meet with us, spend some more time with the lady with the lovely jacket! And Richard was "Huh. Bluh," like a toad frog. But his president of the bank, in Mansfield, Ohio, got to go, and us, and practically no other people. We were taken in the limousine over to the restaurant. And when we got there, Mrs. Harris, the elegant lady, and me was talking, telling jokes, and having the best time. Most of the other people were afraid to move because *The Mr. Harris* was there. And next thing you know Mrs. Harris said, "Well, sing us a song." And I said, "Well, how 'bout one of them old Grandpa Jones songs—'Mountain Dew'"? She said, "Oh, that would be lovely." So I was singing *Oh, they call it that good old mountain dew . . .* Then Mr. Harris started to loosen his tie, and picked up a spoon, and was whacking it on the table. And Mrs. Harris said to me later, "I have rarely seen my husband loosen his tie at a dinner. I'm so delighted that you joined us."

Then on the way home, on the airplane, Richard, instead of saying, "Roni, it was great having you with me," or anything like that, was grumble, grumble, grumble.

When I went down to Nashville for the next *Hee Haw* taping, I was also playing at Faron Young's place. So I'm performing there and the divorce papers came to me. They served me the papers on the stage. It could have gone either way, but Richard got there first. He called it "mental cruelty." That didn't seem fair to me, but it certainly was true that we didn't get along.

I was married to him three and a half years, long enough for him to take what money I made and invest it in his name. I blame this on myself because I wasn't thinking enough about the financial side of things.

There were warning signs before the wedding, other than the first impression and his being a bad kisser. Peggy Stanley said, "I just don't like him. I just think he's not good for you." (She was the June Carter of my third marriage!) My body said the same thing. The day before the wedding, I broke out in hives as big as silver dollars. I should have paid attention.

I was back living in Nashville when I met Bill Zimmerman, my fourth husband. I had a girlfriend with me, and we stopped in this bar and grill after a long day of taping at *Hee Haw*. All the guys were throwing darts. I said, "Oh, can I try?" I took the darts. They felt funny—I had never held darts before. I threw them and they went blap, blap, blap, blap. Four bullseyes. I sat down and said, "I'll take a Coke."

There's a guy sitting on my left, at the bar, drinking a beer.

"Hi, you're not from around here, are you?" I said.

"No."

"I could tell from the way your face is."

"What way is that?"

"I don't know. Where you from? What part of the North are you from?"

"Iowa."

"Oh, welcome to Tennessee. What are you doing here?"

"Going to school, electronics school. I just got out of the army."

"Oh."

"I was a warrant officer."

"Oh."

"You throw darts real good."

"Thank you."

We continued talking and later he came down to see me. We went to the movies. Then we went out to the mall. Then we went to the movies again. And it was court, court, court. He had "Bill Zimmerman, Warrant Officer" on a nameplate. And I thought, Well, that's wonderful. He said, "Do you know what a warrant officer is?" "No." Then he explained a little about how it was a special kind of officer that it's hard to get to be, and he told me he was twice in Vietnam.

One day he said, "Well, let's go up to my apartment. I want to show you my apartment." So I went up there.

He had *Soldier of Fortune* magazines in a pile against the wall.

"What's this soldier of fortune thing?" I said.

"That's what I was thinking about getting into."

I looked through one of the magazines, and it was all these articles about going to war and pictures of guns.

"Well, there ain't no war going on," I said.

He looked at me like he was thinking, This is a real idiot, I need to marry her.

"There's lots of things going on," he said. "You know, out there in Colombia and Nicaragua. Like the Contras."

"Well," I said, "why don't you join 'em if that's what you want? What are they supposed to do, the soldiers of fortune? Do they help people?"

(I swear I said all this! I had been so busy trying to earn a living and raise the kids, I knew nothing about the world, zilch.)

"We go in the jungle and we do this and that."

"You get paid for it, don't you?"

"Yes."

"Well, you oughta get to going. You got enough magazines, you ought to know how to do the stuff! My opinion: Just join up with those contraries or contras."

I peered at one of the pictures.

"That's a bad-looking gun," I said.

"Jesus, it's not a gun! You don't call them guns. They're weapons."

"Okay."

He pursued me something bad. He kept begging me, "Marry me, marry me." Bill was very handsome, tall, about six-two, six-three. He wore cowboy boots and he drove a pickup truck and he was just, well, a good old boy. Very different from a banker that was trying to be king of the city and man about town. Bill was sensuous. And he thought I was. Which I was. I was loving, caring, romantic. So I thought maybe I'd marry again. (My thoughts are always getting me in trouble.)

We were married in the spring of 1985. Two or three days after the wedding, Bill started complaining about the electrical engineering. And I said, "Well, Bill, you can do something else. You're very very smart. Go back to college." He was younger than me, but he had seen things that I will never see and done things that I'd never done. So I figured he was a little bit older than me mentally. I didn't know about the other effects of being a vet. He kept on complaining. I said, "Well, just quit. And go on to something else." So he quit his electronics school.

Now one day I'm in the kitchen, fixing chicken or steak or whatever, and he comes in the back door, and he's carrying a big box. He puts it on the table. Blamp. Right in the middle of the table that I had set real nice. He opened the box up and inside there were hard plastic camouflaged packets of jungle survival food. The kind where you can eat the stuff right away.

"Here, taste this! Taste this!" he said. And he took his knife and cut the top off. "Here."

And his eyes are glaring, weird.

"Bill, for God's sake, I know I'm a bad cook but that's ridiculous! I'm not gonna eat jungle survival food. We're getting ready to eat dinner."

"I got four or five boxes out there in the truck. It's not bad. Here, taste 'em. We can live off of these!" And he started pushing it in my mouth.

Well, a little later that same evening, he proceeded to get his knife and show me how you kill people. The knife had a double edge on it, with the ridges on the top. He said, "We did it like this. We ripped this way and that way."

Then shortly after he did that, he started going into a depression. He'd just sit there in the chair and glare straight ahead and hate you. You didn't know what for.

I figured it was the memories of war, thinking about the jungle, showing me the survival food, and reliving the killing. He had talked about Vietnam before. He said, "The first time, I was in the navy. I rode the boats up and down the river, collecting bodies in body bags." First tour he might have had to go in, I don't know. But the second time, he signed up. So I have a hard time understanding all this. He *was* smart. He could learn anything he wanted to learn. He said the thing that was most hurtful to him was coming home from Vietnam and everybody spitting on him. The hippies spat on him as he was changing airplanes. That is so awful. I just know that I'm thankful for the boys who went to Vietnam. And at that time I didn't understand fully the problems that some of them came back with. A lot of folks didn't.

I told him to write about it. I said, "I can understand if you're sad. Well, honey, write your thoughts down. Maybe it will help you cope with it."

But sympathizing was one thing, living with him something else. Aside from the depression, he would have violent reactions to things. There was the time he got so mad about painting a little shed that he started cussing and just hurled the whole bucket of paint on it. Another time the lawn mower, it was a nice new big one, rolled over a coat hanger and just stopped. Bill got furious. He hoisted that lawn mower way up over his head and threw it. It bounced. He was strong. All the neighbors went "Aaahhh."

But although he could lose his temper real bad, like in those incidents, he was never violent against the kids or me. Even if he was provoked by the kids, or if he thought I was nagging at him, he never laid a hand on us. And he was really helpful with my Barbara.

He went back to school. He was going to take up photography. He's the one that took a lot of my best pictures. He was real talented. And he was doing writing and journalism. That was great, I thought, very promising for him to have a future. He didn't have to stick with me if he didn't want to. I just wanted him to be successful for himself.

I was trying to figure out the situation. I was trying to truly understand the Vietnam thing. And trying to understand the future of the marriage. So we had a discussion. When I asked him point blank whether he loved me, and he said he wasn't sure, I decided to call it quits.

It was honest, and it was the way to go, for both of us.

Then one day a few years later, we were playing a Stoneman reunion at the Station Inn in Nashville, and Van came in and said, "It's ex-husband night, ladies! Bobby's out there, Donna! Bill's out there, Roni!" Talk about a tough audience!

As I passed Bill, he said, "Roni, I found out what was wrong with me."

"You did?"

"Yes, I went to the veterans' hospital, and they said I had a chemical imbalance."

"Well, I'm glad, Bill. I'm really glad!"

"Don't get smart with me!"

And of course, I wasn't being smart with him, bless his heart. I was really thankful for him because I can imagine how awful it is being depressed all the time. And it was understandable after what he'd gone through. Sometimes I blame myself for not helping him more. But I don't know what I could have done. I never saw him again after that night. Patsy and Donna ran into him. And from what I gather, he got married again and he was writing for a newspaper in some small town. I would like to see him and say, "Hey, Bill, how ya' doin'?" And wish him and his wife well. I really would.

So that was my deal with Bill. He was not a mean sort. He was a fine man who was going through a really bad spell. But the marriage was not good for me. And it added another husband to my life, which is something I didn't need to add.

Because five husbands sounds really bad. And I was about to get a fifth.

His name isn't really Barry Denton, but I'm going to call him that because I don't want to give him any publicity. He's got so little sense he would think it was nice to have his name in a book, no matter how bad what I'm going to say is.

How I met him? That was my own fault, and I should've known better. Again I went to a bar and I met this guy and I started going out with him. Daddy used to write songs about tragedies, natural disasters like the mighty Mississippi Flood and the *Titanic*. My husbands are my natural disasters.

Barry was a very handsome man. He had pretty eyes, and he was clean-looking, dressed nice. But he was among other things, a liar. He lied about owning a house, and he lied about his job, which was house-painting, trying to make it sound as if he owned this big construction company. I didn't realize he was lying. Though later it made me furious—even though of course I didn't care that much about the house or the construction company. Later I also found out that he had been in the pen. He was a felon, counterfeit money and robbing a store. "When I was in Joliet . . ." he once said, but I didn't at first get what that meant. His uncle was "in Joliet" too.

Anyway, back when I started dating Barry, I was thinking, Well, this is an Indiana farm boy, a good guy. Barry was from Mt. Vernon. I'd gone there quite a few times with him and I saw the wooden covered bridges in Indiana, how beautiful they are. In the fall of the year we went coon hunting there with his buddy. I loved the coon hunt. Beautiful brisk Indiana weather and you're sitting on the back of a pickup truck and the moon is shining and you hear the dogs holler "Aooohhh," and you know which one has got which voice and you know they're going after the coons and how they've been trained for it.

So in 1987 I married him. Barry Denton was not a good guy. He turned out to be greedy, brutal, and unfaithful.

I let him handle my money, and that was a big mistake. I had this idea. I was going to have a yearly Stoneman family festival in honor of Scott. It would have a fiddling contest, banjo contest, guitar contest, and singing contest. Oh, my God, I worked so hard on it. Now, Barry found this piece of land up on a hill a few hours from Nashville. I said "Barry, we shouldn't go this big in the beginning." "Well, we gonna build a house up here and . . ." blah, blah, blah. So he talked to this lady and got the land. I gave her ten or twelve grand down on it. And I told her that after the next *Hee Haw* taping was over, I'd come up and give her the rest.

Well, we had the first contest. The signs said "Scotty Stoneman's Fiddling Contest, Stoneman Park." I put every penny I could into the festival. Besides *Hee Haw,* of course, I was doing shows. I'd run off and do a bluegrass festival, go home, and then bring the money up there. I was walking around in a daze, because I was so busy making the money and trying to arrange everything. I had an asphalt road built so RVs could go up there, I paid Jimmy Dickens thirty-five hundred dollars to perform, Charlie McCoy three thousand dollars. Then I paid out all the prize money right after the people won. The contest was a big success.

But next thing you know, my land was taken from me. The woman hid from me, would not let me pay her the rest of the money for the property. The sheriff and city officials laughed when I called them asking where she was. Something was clearly up. I had to declare bankruptcy and give up the festival. When I eventually found the woman, she said, "It's Barry. The city officials said he did some things I don't know anything about." So she had sided with the city officials and hidden from me.

Barry also took all the money I earned doing shows in Florida. We'd go to Florida and I worked those little RV resorts. We had gotten a used RV and I was traveling in it. The first time we went down, we didn't know where we were going. We were staying in this awful place. I had Barbara and Bobby with me, with Barry and myself, living in this little trailer, and it was really a horrible existence—roaches like you wouldn't believe!—but I had to start somewhere. I had to live there and find out what places I could go to play at. And I did it. I pulled it off. But it wasn't easy. Before I went down the second year, I would call and have posters made, and send them to be put around the coffee shops. This is what I'd say: "Hello, this is Molly Brown, representing Roni Stoneman. And she'll be down in Florida in your area and she would like to play the RV resort. She's the gal from *Hee Haw,* the Ironing Board Lady, and she plays the banjo, and would you be interested, etcetera, etcetera?" They were interested. So I'd send them the publicity. (The name Molly Brown meant something to me—as in The Unsinkable!)

I started to do pretty well. For the month of January one year, I only had one day off. There ain't an RV resort or campground in Florida that I don't know. Across Alligator Alley and up and down the coast.

But Barry took the money. And when I asked him for some, it was rough. One time I accidentally walked in the bathroom, and he had money piled up high on the commode lid. I said, "Oh, Barry, give me some money 'cause I got to pay the bills, gotta pay the car." He grabbed my wrist and squeezed it hard and said, "Leave that money alone, bitch, or your brains will be running off that bathtub there!" I turned around and looked toward the old-fashioned bathtub we had, and I could just see my brains running down the tub.

The violence was truly awful. Whenever you're married to somebody as viciously mean as he was . . . He was like Hitler. I never saw Barry drink a whole lot. He didn't need to. He was born mean. George was bad news, but he did have a softness about his soul, whenever he got sober, or wasn't on chemicals. Barry was totally different.

Sam Lovullo saw it. Sam barred him from all the grounds at Opryland. They put the word out front that the guard was not to let Roni Stoneman's husband come in.

Not only did he mess me up financially at that festival, he was also cheating on me with another woman there on the new land, and he about like to have killed me about that. I was doing this show up in Pennsylvania. And the family came to play with me. I get a call at the motel from a woman I'll call Mary. She said, "Roni, this is Mary. I want you to know that me and Barry's been having an affair." And she went on to tell me what all they'd been doing together. I was in shock. I shouldn't have been. I should have known. But I had ignored the telltale hairpins in the bed when I joined Barry after a weekend away. I went and knocked on Barry's door. "Barry, I need to talk to you." "What about?" "Mary called me. Would you come outside and talk to me about it?" I was speaking in a real calm tone of voice because I was going to give him the benefit of the doubt. He came outside and I said, "Barry, Mary told me some things that I feel awful bad about." And then I repeated what she had said.

He got angry. You know how some men will be when they get caught? He grabbed me by the throat and he fractured my neck. They always put their thumb hard aginst my throat when they choke me, but Barry choked me so hard and jerked me so viciously that it cracked my neck. I didn't know that at the time, but I knew I was in severe pain and I got away from him. There were some thorn bushes with real long thorns. And he said, "I'll throw you right in the middle of that," and he called me every name, just as if Satan himself had come alive and was truly after me. So I ran, and it was, I guess it was about 1:30 in the morning. It was real dark in the parking lot, and those bushes were all around. There was a big rock, big as a table. And he said, "Your brains'll be running off of that." Just like with the bathtub. He was dangerous. He's not to be reckoned with in any way, shape, or form because he's very very evil.

I rode all the way back from Pennsylvania to Nashville with a scarf around my neck so my family wouldn't see the bruises. I never had such pain in my life, but I had to be really quiet. I had to play it his way until the family got paid. I was so scared, driving all that way. I can't . . . there's no way to describe how frightened you get. You're walking on eggshells to please them. When I got home, I went to a chiropractor and he took an x-ray. He said, "You have a fractured neck, Roni. If you ever have a car accident, you're going to be dead immediately." I had trouble with it for a long time, bad pain and my neck would swell up. But God over time healed it.

It was not only the violence that was awful, it was also the other women. I should've seen trouble from the beginning. Okay, here we were married four days, and a package comes, a wedding gift, I thought. It was a foot-long rubber dildo. With a bunch of dirty books and an obscene note from one of Barry's former girlfriends. I went into the bathroom and vomited. Later there was another Mary-like phone call. I pick up the phone and a woman says, "Is this Roni Stoneman?" "Yes, it is." And right off she says how she'd been having sex with Barry, "down here at the parking lot of Piggly Wiggly. He'll be home in a little while. We do it a lot."

His ex-girlfriends seemed to have some kind of compulsion to talk to me.

The last such phone call came soon after Barry left me—because strange as it may seem, Barry's the one left me. Anyway, the phone rang.

"Hello," I said.

"I want you to know that I have special bras made for me," a voice said.

"Okay, who is this?"

"This is Francine." (Again, I'm disguising her name.)

"Oh, yeah, yeah, how're you doing?"

"Oh, I just came back from my bra maker."

"Bra maker? Like brassieres?"

"Yeah, I just came back. I wear a size K cup."

"A K what?"

"Cup. A size K cup."

"A K?"

"Yeah, like A B C D E F G H I J K."

"Oh!"

"There's a woman in Madison who makes them special for me."

"Oh."

"Barry's with me now."

And I said, grinning into the phone, "Well, honey, you're fighting with weapons I don't own."

I mean, a K cup!!!! I couldn't comprehend, me with my 32 triple A! I don't think Dolly's that big—not a K cup. That sounds like the slingshot that David killed Goliath with.

Well, as I said, Barry left me. We had been in Florida, and I had worked hard that whole winter, earned a lot of money. We came home, and as usual, he had the money. He said he'd be back in an hour, said he was going to service the RV. But he left for good, took the RV and all my money. I had real financial problems. Big time. I didn't have a cent, nothing, zero, zilch.

But I was so happy when he left. Now at least I got to keep what money I could earn.

I really wanted to be divorced from him. I went to a lawyer. But I could not find Barry to sign the papers.

Finally, seven years after he left, I did manage to get ahold of him. It sure wasn't easy though. Here's how I did it. Now, I have a good friend, name of Ronnie Buff. He's an old country boy, works in construction, but he also writes good songs, sings good, and plays good guitar. He calls me one day.

"Ronnae, how're ya doin' Ronnae?"

"I'm doin' fine, Buff, how're ya doin'?"

"Walll, I gotta find out how my best girl is."

You know, one of them kind of boys. Great big fellow with a beard and his hair's all black, and all the girls say in a high voice, "Can I feel your muscles?"

"Guess who I saw the other day?"

"I can't imagine, Buff. Who'd you see?"

"Well I was in this little ol' convenience store and this guy came up to me and we was talking, and he said 'I write songs and I was married to Roni Stoneman. I made a star out of her. Yeah, and then she leaves me, abandons me.' I says, 'Oh, is that right? Well, I play guitar with Roni every now and then.' And he got real quiet and he said, 'Well, good God, don't tell her where I'm at.' And I'm thinking, Well, why in the world did he say that? So I thought I'd tell ya!"

And apparently Barry told Ronnie Buff that he was living with the girl working behind the counter at this convenience store. I said, "Is that right?" And then I said, "Buff, you gotta help me. I want to get this divorce over with and done. I gotta think of a plan. Can you call me back in the morning?"

Next morning when he calls, I said, "I want you to help me, Buff."

"Anything you want me to do, Ronnae, I'll do it. You want me to whup his ass?"

"No, no, no, I don't want you to whup his ass."

"I would, you know, and I can."

"Yeah, I know you can, Buff, but I don't want you to whup his ass. That ain't gonna do any good. I'll tell you what I want you to do."

My plan was for Buff to get Barry's phone number by saying he needed him to judge a coon dog contest. Buff did, and I called the number. I got an answering machine. I said, "Hello, this is Roni Stoneman, would you please tell Barry to give me a call, that I would like to meet him to get him to sign these divorce papers? I have them all ready. And I'm sure that you would like for him to get this out of the way. I know I would."

Well, the plan worked. Barry called back. Just like I guessed, he had not married this girl because he kept telling her that he wasn't divorced yet—that I was so awful that I wouldn't give him a divorce. But my message on the machine ended that lie.

After the divorce, it was like I was walking around in a daze, I was so happy and relieved.

But what I said to that snippety country musician about at least I married them wasn't strictly true. There were a number of men I dated but didn't marry, as I mentioned earlier. Dating to me is really interesting. To round out this account of my love life and my history with men, here's a story from shortly after the Barry disaster.

I was dating this surgeon. He was a handsome hunk, and he knew nothing about country music or about my history. That was wonderful to me because I could dress up prissy and be Veronica. Not Roni Stoneman, Picker. But Veronica Stoneman, Woman!

Now, the best place to eat in Nashville was the Stockyard, good steak, tablecloths, enough silverware for an army, and really atmospheric. Buddy Killen owned it. He was just a picker from the old days and he ended up with his own publishing company, which he sold to Sony Music. We were always proud of Buddy Killen. So when this surgeon came to town, and he was so nice and looked so good with his cashmere coat, I said, "Well, let's go to the Stockyard."

I was dressed up real proper. A black dress to make me look chic and stockings with lines up the back, makeup on just right.

So we're sitting there, eating dinner and talking.

Then he said, "I hear music downstairs, and they have informed me that it's rather good country music. Perhaps we should go down."

Oh God no, I thought to myself. I knew the band—it was Tommy Riggs and the Bullpen Lounge Band, some of the best pickers in Nashville. I was sure if I went down there, they would call on me to play, and then, well, goodbye, sophisticated Veronica.

"No, no, let's not go downstairs now," I said. "It's so pleasant here."

"You don't like country music?" he said.

"Well, no, it's not that exactly."

"I think some of it is really okay. Of course you have to get used to it."

"Well . . ." I'm fiddling with the salt and pepper shakers, wondering how I'm gonna get out of this.

"And someone told me this band is good."

I picked the pepper shaker up, tilted it and watched the little sprinkles fall into my palm.

"Well now," I finally said, "let me tell you, honey, if you really really want to go down, well . . . you should know that I occasionally play music myself . . ."

"You do?"

"So the band members might know me . . . And sometimes I get up and play a little, just a little."

"What do you play?"

"Oh I play guitar . . . and a wee bit of a banjo."

I'm still fooling around with the salt and pepper shakers as if I've never seen such critters before. "So if the musicians know me, don't think anything. You know, they'll always be friendly to me."

"Sure, no problem."

"And if anybody happens to recognize me in the audience . . . Well, most of my fans, actually I have some fans . . . And a few of them have hardly any teeth. So because of my space and my smile, they always kind of think like . . . like I'm one of them."

"Oh, well, that's all right," he said, leaning back. "I wouldn't mind that at all."

"You're sure?"

"Of course not."

So we go downstairs. The band is superb. They're going, "Hi, Ron, Hi Ron." And I waved a little delicate wave.

"See, I told you the band might know me," I said.

And I'm sitting there and I'm really still trying to act nice and re-fined, and about this time somebody grabbed me by the shoulder, and he stooped down, and it was Hillbilly City. I mean bigtime, a real mountain man. Something like I'd marry.

"Hot damn!" he says. "I sure do like you! You're my fa-vo-rite!"

"Well thank you."

"And there's my Maw over there. She's never been to Nashville, al-ways wanted to come to the Grand Ole Opry. She's gettin' up in years, so we brought her."

He waved to another table: "Hey, Maw, c'mere!" And here she comes, with some brothers of his. My friend's sitting there like the gentleman he was, and his eyes so big around.

"Will you take a picture with my Maw?"

"Yeah, sure," I said. "C'mere, Mom, I love you, honey." I stood up, and of course I realized that I really mean it, I love them, I really love these people. She grabbed my arm, and then hit me on the back. Knocked the breath out of me. I went, "Aahhh." Her son got me around the neck. It was like a wrassling hold, an armlock. And my head was sticking out, and again I go "Aahhh." And he said, "Wilbur, look! By golly she's just like us!" And he dragged me over to their table, where there were some more brothers, to take a picture with the whole family.

My friend's sitting back there. And I thought, How am I gonna be able to get him back on the track? But there was no way. That was the end of him. And he was a fine dude. But I asked myself, What is more important, my fans or my love life? And I thought, From the looks of things, my love life has let me down. My fans have not. Ever. The answer was clear. My fans were more important.

TWENTY-SIX

Losing *Hee Haw*

At the same time Barry left me for the last time, took my RV and all my money, I lost *Hee Haw,* which was why his taking the money was such a disaster. According to the newspapers, *Hee Haw* was ranked number four or five in the country. But the higher-ups had been thinking for several years they had to "update" it. They started doing things like putting blue jeans on Grandpa Jones. They also fired Buck Owens. I was stunned. Buck Owens was one of the stars. Sam's face was blood red when he told me the head office had ordered the move.

Well, about four years go by, and then there was a real curious incident. We were all in the studio taping, and we broke for lunch. As we were coming out of the studio past the makeup room, we looked in and saw a bunch of new young girls. The *Hee Haw* girls were worried. "I wonder why they're in there for?" they kept saying.

Later, when we came back to the studio, Sam Lovullo told us that these girls had won contests, Miss County Fair or State Fair, and part of their prize was to get to be on *Hee Haw* for a season, clapping their hands to the music.

So we taped several segments, and the directors said, "All right, take ten." They had a place where you could get coffee. We always used honey in our coffee for energy. Because it was a high-energy show, and you really had to put the energy out. Why honey not sugar? Some people said it was better for you. All the girls from California said, "No, it makes us faaatter!" But the ones for honey were louder. "High energy and better for you—natural honey!"

Anyway, they gave us a break, we got our coffee with honey, and we all went into the dressing room. Everyone's still saying, "I wonder why they're here." Then Sam came up and said, "Let me tell you something. We shot each and every one of the young girls. They said none of them was as pretty on camera as our girls."

So we figured it was okay. We trusted Sam. Here's an incident about Sam and the girls that shows how we got along with him. Lisa Todd was the tall girl that had, well, she was loaded down with chest, really well built. And had these, what do you call them?—vampy eyes, and that long black hair. She was the weather girl, with Gailard Sartain, for awhile. And she'd say in a real high cute voice, "Now, ladies, and oh yeah, you fellers too, we gonna have rain storms today." And she would breathe real heavy.

When you'd go into the studio, down the hallway, they had a little area where you could just duck in and change fast behind a screen. Well, one day Sam came behind the girls and saw that Lisa wasn't with them, and he knew that she had stepped behind the screen. Sam says, "All right, Lisa, c'mon, let's get in the studio. Bring them boobs down." She was hiking them up because she knew the camera was going to be on her. But they had got some letters from the friends and neighbors saying there was just a little bit much of the boobs being shown by Lisa. So he said, "All right, Lisa, drop them boobs." Just like it was his daughters or something. Everybody giggled. We really trusted Sam.

But then the *Hee Haw* Honeys were fired. It was a mistake. I mean when you've got a bunch of women like the *Hee Haw* girls, you can't just replace them with these little girls that are just brand spanking new and don't, well they didn't know what *Hee Haw* was all about. They were just sweet young girls. Our girls knew how to put a line over or giggle over something hillbilly-ish. And most of them weren't hillbilly at all. There was Linda Thompson, there was Lisa from California. They were professional actresses.

My opinion? The head office didn't realize what all went into that show, how much talent there was. They just saw the girls with the boobs and thought that's all they needed. But the fans out there in TV land, they realized the difference. The new "improved" program only lasted one year.

The first I heard of the firings was on August 12, 1991. I get a call from Sam: "Roni, they're letting some of the people from *Hee Haw* go. But they're keeping you." I'm relieved, but I'm also upset, thinking, Oh my gosh, there goes my friends. He says, "Now, we're gonna start October 6 instead of October 15 and we're gonna tape twenty-six shows, not thirteen, like we usually do. I don't want you doing any fair dates. We're gonna even be in the studio on weekends." Well, of course *Hee Haw* came first to me, so I didn't book any new fair dates, and I called the jobs I had and managed to cancel them.

I thought, I'm sure it's going to be the last season or why would they change the schedule, but at least this taping will give me a chance to take care of my finances really good.

On September 28—my mother's birthday, that's how I remember so well—Sam called me and said, "Roni, don't come to the taping. We're not going to be using you. We've got to let you go. I tried to hang on to you, but there was no way." Well I went into . . . I just stood there. I almost dropped the phone I was so stunned. Aaagh I had no job and I was putting everything on this last taping. Putting all my eggs in that basket. Because I had canceled a lot of dates.

I think I almost had an emotional breakdown. I would sit and stare. And I'd smoke one cigarette after another. Just sit out on the swing under a tree and smoke and stare straight ahead.

I knew I had to get a grip on myself. I tried to get work, but I couldn't. And I didn't have any money coming in from nowhere, none. I really tried. My buddy Noka had a little talent agency called From the Heart, and she also tried to get me working. I told her, I said, "You can't do it. I know, Noka, I've been trying." She thought I was just feeling depressed. So she called around, and . . . well, sometimes I would come in and she would have tears in her eyes. I'd say, "What are you crying for?" "Nothing." And then I'd find out she'd been getting rejections. Later I found out why. I was told by an insider. Now I'm not saying how true this is, but it matches the truth more than anything that I can think of. What this person said was there was some problem with the legal rights to the *Hee Haw* characters, and that meant it was risky to hire those of us who were closely identified with the show.

Well, that stopped me from getting work performing as Roni Stoneman. I didn't know what to do. So I went over to Mom and Dad's grave. I sat down right beside the graves, in fact touching Mom's tombstone. I said, "What in the world am I gonna do?" And there was a sound, like a magnified voice in my head. It said, "Go to work. I did." And I thought, But what kind of work? Then I thought, Well, better get to finding out. Better get to going.

So I drove to a store where I bought a newspaper. I went home, sat down on the floor, and spread out the classified ads. But everything seemed like it was computer, or electronic, and they wanted you to have a high school diploma and a good résumé. I didn't have those things.

First thing I saw that looked possible was "Hotel Maids Needed." All over the page, hotel maids wanted desperately. I thought, I'm good at that. I can do things like housecleaning real fast. And I took pride in it. So I called. I said, "This is Veronica Stoneman, and I'm looking for . . . I hear that y'all need some hotel maids." "Oh, yes, we're really low. We need all the maids that we can get." I called five different hotels and got the same answer. I said to myself, Well, I'll make my rounds and whoever offers me first, I'll go to them.

So I went on down to a hotel and walked into the manager's office.

"My God, you're Roni Stoneman!" he said.

"Yes, now, I never worked hotel work before but I'm awfully good. I raised seven children. And I'm healthy, and I'm thin, and I can get around the beds real quick, and I can do the job real good."

The guy looked straight at me. "But we can't hire you as a maid!"

"Why?"

"Because you're too recognizable. We can't have the tourists and the fans of country music come in here and see our stars cleaning toilets!"

I went to all five hotels. They all told me the same thing—"But you're Roni Stoneman! We can't give you a job."

I went home and I cried for about an hour and a half. Then I prayed some more. And cried some more. And then I thought, Now what do I do?

What I did was I went down to this place that said Boutique Academy or something of that nature. It was a home care thing for little children. I went in and talked to the lady, and, well I don't know, I don't understand it to this day because I'm excellent with children. I can read to them and I can play with them and teach them while they're playing. But the woman acted so hostile to me—"I hope you realize that after you pay for your playground insurance, you'll be earning less than four dollars an hour," she said coldly.

I went around to two other places. They acted the same way.

So I thought and thought, and, again, like that time years ago, decided that it had to be music. I decided that if I could get a band together with some young girls, it would be so different from my *Hee Haw* characters that maybe people would feel they could hire me. So I met this young lady by the name of Beverly Nolan. Well, Beverly's an excellent drummer and she sings great. She said she had some friends, one named Terry Lee, one named Melissa Smith. And then I said, "Well, we'll call ourselves the Daisy Maes." It was kinda corny (terrible pun, sorry), but they went along with it. When we rehearsed, I liked the sound we were getting. These girls had been playing with country bands in Nashville, so they were seasoned. But they were also young and fresh. That's a combination that's hard to find.

Terry Lee was pretty as a picture and one fine musician. She would hold a fiddle under her chin while playing the keyboard and then take a terrific fiddle break. Melissa played the bass and sang. And we had Beverly on the drums and singing.

Ralph Emery let me come on his show with my all-girl band. It was at 5:00—in the morning. We had to get up at four. To give you a hint of how bad my financial situation was, after arranging the booking I had gotten back to the crummy place I lived in and thought, Well, it's awful early but at least they'll probably give us a free breakfast. So we got down to the studio, and we played a romantic country song, and then we did "Wabash Cannonball." I had rearranged it where we go "*Whoooooo*," and everybody was singing really good: "*Whoooooo. From the great Atlantic Ocean . . .*"

We did so well I was able to use the video of the show to get a gig at a Holiday Inn in town.

Right before we started that, we went to Huntsville, Alabama, to be on a show. Somebody Walker, a really good guy, can't remember his full name. He said, "We want you to come down. Bring your girl band." He was trying to be nice to me.

Now, the girls had been saying that we needed a lead guitar player. "Well, find one," I said. It's hard to find a good girl lead guitar picker. But it was true, we needed another lead. Terry was working herself to death on the keyboard and fiddle. So they picked up this girl named Doris (not her real name). Anyway this girl was wilder than a can of kraut—like Grandpa Jones used to say. She played two nights with us down in Printer's Alley, and I knew she was trouble.

So I took the girls aside.

"Y'all better think on this. My opinion? Sometimes it's best to get a musician that's not so good as y'all say she is."

"But she's our friend and she can really sing great."

So we took her to Alabama. We drove down, five women in this van, all picking and singing. Now, this girl Doris used to sing in church. She was from the old tradition of church gospel singing, had been singing for years with her family. She had really great harmony. I was impressed.

We get to the studio. By now she's high. I don't know what she took or when, but she sure was high on something. When we were getting ready to do the soundcheck, I looked over and Doris was cussing.

"Son of a bitch! That son of a bitch!"

"Honey, what is it?"

She had her hair slung over, and it was thick and pretty. She was brushing it and pulling it up. "That son of a bitch made fun of my guitar!"

"What son of a bitch made fun of your guitar?"

"That man out there. He laughed at my guitar, that damn son of a bitch!"

So I went out and I said, "Beverly, who made fun of her guitar?"

"Nobody."

I go back, and this girl's still cussing. She did have a guitar that was shaped like a V. It was electric, looked like a rocket, shot to the moon. She was a rock 'n roll picker. I could handle that because she also really knew our kind of music.

Well, we do the soundcheck. Doris is clearly in Never Never Land.

The next thing you know, the men were gathered around. They had drinks with whiskey, where you put whipped cream on top of it, and you stick your tongue way down to the bottom. And Doris was drinking one.

Whipped cream was all over her face, and then she had another drink and then another. She had five of them, downed them. All the men were going, "Yes! Yes!" cheering her on. This was the little gal that had grown up singing in church, that did such great harmony on the gospel songs! Then Beverly had one of them.

"Beverly . . ." I said.

"Hey, it's okay, Roni. I can do them. I done it before. This is okay, this is okay."

Maybe I'm in the wrong league here, I thought. I'm too old or something. And these girls are grownups. Two of them have children. Then Melissa started laughing so hard. When Melissa gets nervous, she'll laugh and laugh, and she's got the most beautiful laugh. I'm thinking, desperately, Well, if she does that on camera, it'll look cute, add to the effect, a little like *Hee Haw*.

"Did you see how many drinks she . . . ?" she asked, laughing.

Unbelievably, the performance was great.

We went down to Alabama again. But we didn't take Doris with us. That's because she was working with us a couple of more nights, down in Printer's Alley, and on the second night it was over. She just took off early, disappeared.

We got a replacement, but soon Beverly had to go back home to care for her sick grandmother, and Melissa's father died and she left to be with her mother. So the band just, well, disbanded. It's not easy holding a band together, especially when you're not making much money.

When I got down, real despairing, and needed some money, Bill Deaton wrote for me to see if he could get me some money from the musicians' fund. They wouldn't give me any. Now when *Hee Haw* was on, they had us do shows for the Opry Trust Fund. We would go in there after we'd been filming all day. I was happy to do it. I thought it was for a good cause and that everybody should help each other. But when it came down to helping me, they didn't.

And what was told to me was that a pretty famous singer I'm gonna call X was on the board, and he's the one said no. Now I don't know how true that is. But it might be, because I didn't make out with X. The incident happened back when we Stonemans had not been in Nashville too long. We were playing at the Black Poodle and we had our television show, but we had been working so hard that I hadn't had any chance to get out and visit with the country music people. I was too busy taking care of the children, trying to find a place for them to live.

One night X was in the audience. After the last show he came up.

"Roni, would you like to go have breakfast with me? We could go to the Downtowner."

The musicians would go there after playing all night. Good pancakes and eggs and ham and stuff. So I agreed and said, "I'm just gonna tell Daddy." Daddy usually drove me home.

I didn't realize the reputation that X had because of how he was with his lady friends. But I remember leaving—and Daddy watching me get in the car with X. He looked real funny. This was during the time I was separated from Gene.

X's car was nice. A good thing because we ended up spending a lot of time in it. We drove around the block and then went around to Union Street. There was a red light there, and we stopped. And he started kissing on me. The light turned green. I said, "X, it's time to go." And he kept kissing and kissing. Then he started trying to talk me into going to his condominium with him.

"No. I don't know . . ."

"C'mon." Then he started kissing on me some more, and the light turned red, then it turned green again.

"X, we better go! Somebody is going to smack into the back of us!"

"No, no, everything's okay. Let's go to the condo."

"No, I don't think now . . ."

Well, finally he drove to the Downtowner and we went inside to eat. About four booths up sat my daddy. He always stopped there for food anyway, but also he knew I was going there. Daddy had his crutch leaning straight up in the booth. By this time his hip had disintegrated from his arthritis and he needed the crutch real bad. It was aluminum and made a racket when he used it.

So I ate my breakfast, and X ate his breakfast. I looked over to Daddy and I saw him reach for his crutch with his check in his hand. I said, "Excuse me, X." I got up and went over to Daddy. "Daddy, can I ride home with you?" "You sure can." Then I went back to X and said, "X, I'm going home with Daddy."

I never have been looked at or talked to much by X ever again, until that thing came up about the money. And then I didn't get it. Now I don't know for sure if he remembers, but a man like X is likely to remember something like that. Because he don't get turned down every day of the week, in front of his buddies, especially from somebody that looked scrawny like I did. My girlfriend said, "Oh, you oughta see X's place. He's got mirrors on the ceiling." And I was even gladder that I didn't go. I was young, and I was worked to death. You know how a dog looks after it had a litter of puppies? That's what I looked like. I was wore out. The mirrors would have shown a grasshopper making out. It would have been an awful picture.

If I could get any work at all in those first few years when I lost *Hee Haw*, it was often in honky-tonks. And that was so hard, after being in all those big auditoriums. To give you an idea, one time I was down in a place on Broadway, in Nashville, and I had to play with just my recording machine as a backup band. I had to play my banjo over my banjo. And I had to sing my songs over my songs, word for word.

TWENTY-SEVEN

My Religion

Throughout all the bad times, and the good times, and the middling times, there was one steady thing in my life—my religion. When I was little, I went to the Baptist Church on Sundays. During the summer I went to Vacation Bible School every day for six weeks. I really loved Vacation Bible School. I remember how we would make a tray out of a big oak leaf. You lay the clay out flat and then you can make an imprint of the leaf. You paint it and you have it fired and it comes out glazed. Funny, that has never left my mind. I'm not so sure what that has to do with religion, except if they meant us to learn that all of nature, the flowers, the leaves, and the trees are God's work. But of course there was also other stuff, stories like Jonah and the whale and David and Goliath. And religious ideas about being good to other people and such.

But when I grew up, I began to have my doubts about some of the religious leaders, and also some of the religious teachings. (Not the one about being good to other people—no question about that one.) Southern mountain women let the men take the lead, and the religious leaders say that's the way it is in the Bible, you're supposed to submit to your husband. When you get older, you might find yourself thinking, I don't have to put up with that. And you're almost shocked at yourself for having such a thought.

Like when I was married to George and he was beating up on me. I was just trying my best to do the right Christian thing. So I had the preacher come to the house to talk it over. I said, "I'm having severe trouble in this home. And I think the demons are here—when George is so mad and so hateful." The preacher said, "Well, we can go into each room where he drinks, and pray." So we did that. And this went on for five straight weeks of praying (the preacher would bring his wife so it was totally on the up and up).

This was about in the middle part of the marriage. I was living in that big fine house that I bought. I was fed up, but I thought, I've been married before and I can't just hop from one man to the other. The minister said, "Well, you gotta keep trying to heal the marriage. That's what a woman is supposed to do." And I assumed that the praying would get the devil out.

But you can't pray it out. The man's gotta do something too. It does help the woman if she prays a lot, though, because it will give her strength, and her mind will get clearer and clearer.

And so finally I told the preacher I'd had enough. I told him I knew God wouldn't want me to abuse my mind anymore. I said to him, "Here's a song I wrote for you." I picked up the guitar, and I sang: *The preacher stopped by awhile today to pray / To pray awhile with me / If you really want to know what hell's about / I'll give my man to you / Then you can figure it out for yourself / I ain't livin' it anymore.* His wife was sitting there. She just looked at him and blinked.

That preacher was not a bad man, but some of those so-called ministers . . . Well, a few years ago, I had a run-in with somebody of the other sort. Remember Jimmie Davis, who wrote "You Are My Sunshine," and was the governor of Louisiana? Well we were playing the Lewis Family Festival, and Jimmie Davis came. I went up to his bus. "Jimmie Davis, it's so good to see you," I said. And he looked fabulous. He was very handsome, an older, distinguished gentleman. And his wife was gorgeous—used to be a famous gospel singer, Anna Carter Gordon Davis.

And from the back of the bus, here comes out this squirrel of the world, with a silver-looking Pentecostal hairdo. For those of you who don't have too much experience with the expression "Pentecostal hair," it's hair that looks like a piece of plastic, like it's drawn on. It's thick and every hair is in place, with hairspray that's enough to start your own company. I call it Pentecostal hair because most of the gospel preachers that you see on television have it. If anybody's real . . . well, you don't see Billy Graham with it. It's just on the phonies. They are the people that give us Christian people down in the South a bad name. Now if you make a statement like "Oh, Roni, guess what? I got all my work coming in and I'm really doing wonderful," I'd say, "Well, praise the Lord! That's great. Thank God for that!" That's the way we do it in Nashville. That's our Christianity. We don't need some squirrel with a hairdo that smells like Aqua Net.

Anyway, back to Jimmie Davis's bus. This guy came from the back, this deacon or whatever, and he had gold rings, and diamonds, and he had that Pentecostal hairdo.

"It's real nice to have you here," I said.

"What religion are you?"

It's the first thing he said to me. And I looked up at the man, and I despised him immediately.

"I'm not!"

All three of them gasped.

"You're not?"

"No, I'm a Christian."

And Jimmie Davis's wife says, "Oh I love that! I love that!"

"Uhhhh uhhh," blabbered the squirrel.

"Thank you," I said to Jimmie Davis's wife, and I didn't go any further with it.

When we were growing up, Daddy used to say, "Any religion is good if it'll make you do good for one day, even one day." In our family there was a Catholic, there was an Episcopalian, there was a Presbyterian, there was a Pentecostal, there was a Baptist—there was a variety of all religions. I just say, pray to God.

Now in the mountains there's also another strong kind of spirituality. Daddy would say that my mother's people were very "talented" people, "unusual." My mother's Aunt Phinney was, people said, like a witch, able to foretell the future. Just about everybody in the mountains in the early 1900s, they always felt that this is a talent some people are born with, being able to foretell the future, or to see light at night upon the mountains. It's where tales about seeing ghosts got started. Like "Bringing Mary Home," the song about a driver stopping his car and picking up a little girl and then she disappears and it turned out she died thirteen years ago and every year her ghost comes back and gets picked up by some driver who brings her home. That's a true story, they say. When you live in the mountains and all you go by is the moonlight and the sun, and when the sun goes down, it's pitch black, and then the moon comes up—when people live that life, and that was the era that Momma was raised in, they would get these kinds of ideas about the other world.

Aunt Phinney only had one child, Dowe Leonard, Dowey. He was somehow connected to "Grandaddy" Green Leonard, one of the master fiddlers of Galax. That was the worst haint story that ever was for children, that Grandaddy Green Leonard's fiddle was haunted. Somehow we got it, and it was under our bed, in the old case that had been made for it, and every once in a while you really could hear a sound coming from it.

To me the fiddle was like the monster—the Waron. Back in World War II, when I was a little kid, they'd say, "Now behave yourself! Don't you know there's a war on?" And, honest to goodness, I thought the "Waron" was a monster. And you just knew it was going to get you. Between the fiddle that was playing all by itself and the "Waron," you was up a creek!

"Ma," I'd say, "there's a Waron under my bed!" To me that was the name of the most Godawful monster in the world. I guess it really is, but not under the bed.

Aunt Phinney's in a picture in the book about the Stonemans, playing a big autoharp. She was known as a very "handsome" woman. People didn't say beautiful, gorgeous, glamorous, sexy. They said "handsome" and that was it. Her son Dowey got to be drinking very heavy, and he'd go from one house to the other and fall asleep on somebody's porch. So one time he went down to an old buddy's house about 2:00 in the morning and fell on the porch and lay there. And a man came out there, didn't recognize him, thought he was an intruder, and shot him. Dowey was a very dashing, debonair type of gentleman, always dressed nice, in his thirties. And there he was, deader than a mackerel.

But Aunt Phinney, at the same time, was lying dying from a heart condition, heart dropsy. Everybody all gathered around her bed and she looked up, and her eyes half closed, and she said, "Dowey's dead, isn't he?" They all stared at each other—they had been trying to keep it from her. And then she died. Momma was standing there beside Aunt Phinney's bed when it happened.

Momma would tell me these things when I was a little girl. They would scare me and make me have nightmares and then I'd pull the covers over my head, and not want to get out until I heard the rooster crow. If I heard the rooster crow, then I knew that I was okay, I had gone through the night without getting caught by a bogeyman—or the Waron. I don't think anybody else in the family remembers that sort of thing, but it stuck in my mind. It's as if the older people were saying, "How can we carry this from our generation to yours? Well, you're the one, Roni We'll latch it onto you." I guess that's the way these things get passed on. And, in spite of my daughter saying, "Mom, don't tell Virginia those tall tales," I tell them to my granddaughter.

So Aunt Phinney had that special power, and then it came over onto Momma. In the twenties, when my momma was dressed the prissy way she was and always playing music for Daddy, you didn't see it. It was when she got older and times got harder that she relied on her superstition to help her.

During the Depression my sister Nita was ailing. She had pneumonia and mastoiditis—where they had to cut into the ear and lance it every day or so. She would be screaming. As Momma told it, before Nita died, she knew. Five years old, and she said, "Momma, I'm gonna die soon. And I want you not to cry." Anita was so smart and beautiful, and she'd just sit there. One time they had the window open—it was a pretty summer day—and a bird came in and flew onto Nita's hand. Then after a minute the bird flew out. Momma said, to humor Nita , "Just a minute, I'll go get it for you." The bird was way out there in that woods, but Momma was trying to get Nita to think of something else besides her sickness. She went into the woods and held out her hand and the bird flew on it! Then Momma walked back in the house and handed it to her sweet little girl. And she sang "You Pretty Bird." The next day Nita died. From that time on, if a bird got into the house, Momma would start crying because she thought it was a sign of death.

She always said that she was like Aunt Phinney—she was born with a veil over her face, which meant she could foretell the future.

Now sometimes I can tell little things. One night I was down at the Nashville Palace, and there were some guys that came in from a convention. I was just sitting there waiting to go on.

"Hi, how are you doing?" they said. Blah, blah.

"I know you're a captain," I said to one of them. "I know you fly planes."

"How'd you know?'

"I don't know. I just knew."

"What the hell is this? A psych person? Are you targeting me?"

"No, I just could tell."

"Come and listen to this," the captain says to his buddies, "you won't believe this girl."

"Well, you were easy to figure out. And this other guy is too," I said, turning to his friend. "You are too careful sometimes. Just recently you lost a lot of money because you were too careful. You're too afraid to take chances."

It turned out he was a stockbroker and had recently missed making a lot of money because he hadn't taken a certain risk.

"My God, how'd you know that?" he asked.

I really don't know how I know. It may be partly from reading audiences. I don't like to think about it much—the whole thing's pretty weird.

When I was a little girl and I was psychic a little bit, I said, "Mommy, what do I do?" She said, "Pray it away, it's not fittin'." So she was definitely bothered by it.

Well, to make matters short, I believe in God and the Bible, and I believe that there's things we don't know. I also really believe that everything I've accomplished in this world that was good was His work. Not me. I owe it all to Him.

In California we played at the folk festival in Monterey. What a beautiful place. Almost scary. You know how strong God is. Whooo. Those big redwoods and the roaring surf.

Now, one day when I was going to do a show, I was sitting in my hotel room watching television and had on the Learning Channel, and there was a professor of Duke University. He was talking about how you could get strength from things. He said, "Hug a tree. If you ever need strength or get bluesy, go find a forest and hug a tree. Put your arms as tight as you can around it." And I thought, Hot dang, that's pretty cool. So when I was at Grandfather Mountain in North Carolina with my friend Peggy Stanley and we took a walk, I told her about it. I said, "Well, you know, as mountaineers we never paid much attention to such things as hugging a tree. But we respected nature. My father'd go in the forest and could tell every tree and so could my granddaddy. I guess I could too. Everybody could."

Anyway, right then and there on Grandfather Mountain I hugged a tree. I did it. And it works. This sounds far out, like left field, but any time you get bluesy, or sad, or feel "poor old me"—or if you're happy, even if you're happy—hug a tree. And thank it for being there. And let Him give you some blessings.

TWENTY-EIGHT

Now

Well, it's about fifteen years since the end of *Hee Haw,* and eight years since I got my last divorce. So what's going on now in my life? Where am I now? Well, things are good.

On the personal side, in spite of my horrendous track record with marriage, I'm still dating. Optimistic, huh? Why do I date so much? Well, I'm friendly. And with my personality, and the comedy that I naturally can't help . . .

Well, dating's only fun and games, but the really important part of my personal life has turned out terrific. My kids and grandkids are wonderful, and I spend a lot of time just enjoying them. They're intelligent and talented and thoughtful and compassionate. Eugene has his important job, and a marvelous wife, Angela, and the kids, Dustin, Lucas, and Matthew, all in college. Bobby's got a day job and he plays music at night. And Becky's all set doing so great in her career, and having a steady boyfriend, and providing a home lots of the time for Barbara as well as her own wonderful kids, Michael and Stephen. Barbara's very involved with training her dog—and still can sing to beat the band. And Georgia's going to school to become a drama teacher and trying to stay one step ahead of her daughter, my precious Virginia.

On the professional side, I've been working a lot. That lull time after *Hee Haw* ended is over, and I'm back to playing bluegrass festivals, college auditoriums, and nightclubs. I feel very fortunate that I still am healthy and I can still do my comedy and make people laugh. And I can still play the banjo really fast—I just found a new kind of glue that helps me keep my finger picks from flying off!

So, I guess we're at the conclusion of all this. But there doesn't seem to be a conclusion, a neat way to wrap this book up. At least I can't think of some one sentence that I could point to and say "Yep, that's it! That's my life in a nutshell!"

I was trying to think of something to compare my life to. Maybe a roller coaster, with all those ups and downs? But it wasn't that organized. Or maybe those little skits from *Hee Haw*, just little scenes. Except that those segments on the show always ended on a happy funny note. And my life wasn't always all that funny. Though you could say that even a lot of the really sad unfortunate things did lead to good results. For instance, the family was pooristic. But that meant that we had to learn how to be creative, like when Momma painted the linoleum and taught us to make things out of the red clay. And because I had no toys, I had to learn to compete with my brothers, obsess over the banjo, get good enough to play with Scott.

Another sad thing was my feeling insecure when I was growing up, what people now say is "low self-esteem." I never felt attractive or intelligent, and in many ways this was because I was growing up like a typical southern mountain girl. I did heavy work around the house, and I got picked on by my brothers. It seemed my religion taught me that the men were the bosses and that I should always turn the other cheek. I think that all set me up for not getting enough love in my marriages, and for staying in those marriages even when the men were abusive.

But that lack of love also led to good things. I poured my love into my kids, who turned out so good. And into my entertaining. I really think all that insecurity and lack of love was necessary to my performing. Because if you're happy, you're totally self-confident, you're not going to be a very good entertainer out there. You gotta have a special relationship with your audience. You gotta need them, need their love. I know I usually felt beneath everybody in the audience. And I did need that love flowing back to me.

When George was beating on me so much, and I felt like I was drowning and gasping for air, the comedy, well, it was like therapy, me laughing and trying to make the audiences laugh.

I'd spend a lot of time thinking about making the audiences happy. I'd really work at it, wondering what people'd want me to wear, what they'd want me to do. I'd say to myself, What do the people want to see me doing on stage? Jumping around? In high heels? Think that's what they'd want?

And people would come up—"Hi, sure liked you," "You were terrific!" "Wow, you play good banjo!"

My love for all my audiences and their love for me really saved me. I'm so lucky that I love people and that I can express my love for people, both onstage and offstage. Even if it is because of not getting enough affection from my family or my husbands. So maybe my life was like those skits in *Hee Haw*, because even the sad unhappy parts seem to have had some good come out of them. Or, here's another comparison—that kaleidoscope of colors, all shining at once, that I saw when I looked up at the light bulb in that one-room shack. Maybe that's what most people's lives are like—all mixed. Not really straight like in novels or a roller coaster with clear ups and downs, or even clumped into segments like on *Hee Haw*. Because the good and the bad happen at the same time. There I was at the same time of my life, creating Ida Lee and other comic characters, getting punched by George, earning enough money to buy a fancy house, freezing in Alaska, and having those precious moments when I hugged and sang to my children.

As I said, I wrote this book to put down on paper what it was like to grow up as a poor uneducated mountain girl, to be a woman musician in a world of men, to get in a bunch of lousy marriages and have to support your kids by yourself—but also to be part of a hit TV show and get to know some amazing people. I wrote it partly because I was guessing that my life was interesting historically because lots of it had to do with famous people, or with experiences that were typical but hadn't been written about much—sort of like those *Foxfire* books. Of course another reason I wrote this book was just to talk with you all who have shared my life—either because you've had some similar experiences, or because you've been giving me support all these years by watching me perform. And when you come up after a show and we're wanting to talk, there's never enough time. So now we'll have a head start.

There was a third reason I really wanted to write this book—for those of you who are feeling downtrodden. And I want to stop here and talk just to you specially. We Americans are real lucky because we live in our land of opportunity where if you're in poverty or in a bad relationship, there are ways for you to get out. I could divorce George because I had my performing, but for most people it's gonna be education that works best. You may not be expected to graduate from high school, or even go to high school, but do it anyway. If you never finished school, find a continuing education program. My opinion: people can do you wrong—my family was cheated right and left, and I was treated bad by my husbands—but they can't take your soul unless you let them. You got to guard it, and you got to know that you can use it to turn your life around. Press on. It's hard, but you can do it.

We Americans are lucky not just because of our great land of opportunity. We're also lucky because we share with people all over the world our beautiful Earth. I remember one night when I was in Ohio, and there were big snowflakes falling, I mean they were doorknob size, falling down from the sky. I was walking down the street with Georgia and Barbara. And I said, "Just hold your face up and look at the sky, and the snow." The streetlights were illuminating the snow. And the beautiful snow was falling, making a ch, ch, ch sound as it fell.

I don't have too many materialistic things, but, as I said, I feel very very very fortunate. I'm so thankful to God for the life I've led and all the joy I've had.

I just want to say one final thing to my "fans," you "friends and neigh-bors" out there: "It's the other way around. I'm really your fan. You've been wonderful to me. Thank you so much. I'm really looking forward to talking with you down the road. Oh, and by the way, I've had my eye and teeth fixed real good, so I'll be staring straight at you and flashing a gorgeous smile of thanks when we meet. See ya soon. I love ya."

AFTERWORD

Ellen Wright

I met Roni Stoneman on a February evening in 2001, in Evanston, Illinois, when a musician friend, Gus Friedlander, invited my husband and me to one of his gigs at a local bar. Roni was to be the guest star. My husband, John Wright, had written a highly acclaimed book on Ralph Stanley, and Gus hoped to interest him in writing the story of Roni's life. During a break between sets, Roni and I started talking. We immediately clicked. It was clear that I should be the one taking on the project.

But at first I was leery. Although I had been playing traditional mountain music for a few years, and had written on the subject, this collaboration of northern urban scholar and southern mountain musician seemed bound to present problems. My husband had managed it, of course, but his was a different kind of book. The book with Roni would focus far more on her personal life and demand a much more intimate relationship. And I knew that clicking was one thing, a sustained common effort something else. But I decided to give it a try, and I started taping Roni talking about her life. Then I got even more leery. Some of her stories seemed totally improbable—that she had talked with the victim of the latest sensational celebrity murder, that she was a good friend of the characters in a bestselling novel. But one by one Roni's stories were corroborated—details she gave about the murder victim came out in later newspaper accounts, I heard her telephone one of the "fictional" characters. A guitar store owner in Nashville once said to me, "She'll stand here telling some story that's obviously wild and unbelievable, and then—never fails—some guy walks in and starts talking about the

same thing!" I soon had great trust in Roni and in her motives for writing this book, one of which was to document for history the kind of life
she had led. I am quite sure that if there's anything nonfactual here, it's
completely unintentional, a failure of memory.

The collaboration, which I started calling Culture Clash at Cripple
Creek, worked surprisingly smoothly. Roni gamely bought sneakers and
shed her Nashville stiletto heels when we taped in the Chicago Botanic
Garden. (The sneakers now live in my closet.) I gamely tackled Southern
food. (Though I had traveled in Europe and in Asia, no food ever baffled
me as much as those mysterious fried lumps and sticks that appear on
the plates in Nashville restaurants.) I put up with her occasional abrupt-
ness-verging-on-rudeness (her friends chalk it up to "impulsiveness";
she says she's "hyper"). She put up with my definite rudeness (cutting
her off when she started repeating an anecdote; I couldn't afford any
needless transcription costs). I diligently did research to fill in the gaps
in my knowledge of country music. She resolutely relived, in painful
detail, times when her life had been truly agonizing.

We ended up with about seventy-five hours of tape. It had become obvious to me that this story had to be told in Roni's words. I had developed
an enormous respect for her sense of humor, her intelligence, her compassion, her philosophical turn of mind, and her verbal facility. If those
qualities were to be filtered through my sentences, the reader would, I
thought, be losing something essential. The difficulty was that in doing
the taping, I had made a strategic decision—to give Roni her head, and
let her go wherever her mind wandered. The result was a wonderfully
detailed account, but nothing approaching a linear narrative. So I had to
do a fair amount of what all oral historians end up doing—eliminating
repetition, supplying transitions, rearranging segments.

In my editing I was most concerned about capturing two things:
Roni's humor and her warmth. The humor is an essential part of Roni's
psyche. For me the problem was in making sure that the written word
accurately reflected the subtleties of the oral word—finding a phrase,
say, that would convey an inflection in her voice or a facial expression.

As for the warmth, well, Roni really loves people, loves talking to
them and loves comforting them. She is successful as an entertainer
because people sense this and respond. Just two examples. The first

occurred when she was giving a banjo workshop at the University of Chicago Folk Festival. During the workshop, a woman in a wheelchair was uttering little cries and clapping her hands at inappropriate times. She was obviously handicapped mentally as well as physically. After the workshop Roni spotted the woman in the hallway. She left me abruptly (rudely?), went over to the woman, put her arm around her, and said, "Well, how are you, my dear friend?" She talked to her for about five minutes. When I complimented Roni later, mentioning the amount of time she had devoted to the woman, she said, "I guess it was because I felt so bad. You know, in the middle of the workshop I had wanted so much to go to her and hug her, but of course I couldn't."

Another example: I spent three days interviewing the four of Roni's children who lived in Nashville. Roni was clearly agitated at the prospect. When the children were young, she had had to be away from home a lot, and she had always felt guilty about that, felt that they had reason to resent it. Still, because she was determined that this book be an honest account, she left us alone during the interviewing so they could speak freely to me. (She would go for long tense walks.) The children did speak freely. But, interestingly, they dwelt very little on that early hard time. They mentioned it and they mentioned other things that were trouble-some to them growing up, Roni's impulsiveness and her sometimes embarrassing extrovertish nature, but they minimized all that. What they focused on, over and over, was her constant loving and caring. The morning after I had completed the interviews, Roni's phone kept ringing. Her children were solicitously checking in to ask how she was feeling after going through three days which obviously had been very stressful for her.

This book took many more months to complete than I would have imagined that February evening. Looking back, I think what kept me working enthusiastically through all those months was that I so admired Roni's warmth and humanity, and that I so wanted to describe how those qualities were called upon in a life that I found both historically reveal-ing and just downright fascinating.

INDEX

RONI STONEMAN is perhaps best known for her years as a musician and comedian on *Hee Haw*. A renowned performer, Stoneman—the First Lady of the Banjo—continues to tour and perform.

ELLEN WRIGHT teaches in the Writing Program at Northwestern University. She is author of numerous articles on literature, and plays guitar in a bluegrass band with her husband.

Music in American Life

The University of Illinois Press
is a founding member of the
Association of American University Presses.

———————————————————————

Composed in 10/14 Palatino
with Cheltenham and Bureau Eagle display
by Jim Proefrock
at the University of Illinois Press
Designed by Paula Newcomb
Manufactured by Sheridan Books, Inc.

University of Illinois Press
1325 South Oak Street
Champaign, IL 61820-6903
www.press.uillinois.edu